STRATEGIC WINERY TOURISM AND MANAGEMENT

Building Competitive Winery Tourism
and Winery Management Strategy

ADVANCES IN HOSPITALITY AND TOURISM BOOK SERIES

Editor-in-Chief:
Mahmood A. Khan, PhD
Professor, Department of Hospitality and Tourism Management,
Pamplin College of Business, Virginia Polytechnic Institute and State University,
Falls Church, Virginia, USA
email: mahmood@vt.edu

BOOKS IN THE SERIES:

Food Safety: Researching the Hazard in Hazardous Foods
Editors: Barbara Almanza, PhD, RD, and Richard Ghiselli, PhD

Strategic Winery Tourism and Management: Building Competitive Winery Tourism and Winery Management Strategy
Editor: Kyuho Lee, PhD

Sustainability, Social Responsibility and Innovations in the Hospitality Industry
Editor: H. G. Parsa, PhD
Consulting Editor: Vivaja "Vi" Narapareddy, PhD
Associate Editors: SooCheong (Shawn) Jang, PhD, Marival Segarra-Oña, PhD, and Rachel J. C. Chen, PhD, CHE

Managing Sustainability in the Hospitality and Tourism Industry: Paradigms and Directions for the Future
Editor: Vinnie Jauhari, PhD

Management Science in Hospitality and Tourism: Theory, Practice, and Applications
Editors: Muzaffer Uysal, PhD, Zvi Schwartz, PhD, and Ercan Sirakaya-Turk, PhD

Tourism in Central Asia: Issues and Challenges
Editors: Kemal Kantarci, PhD, Muzaffer Uysal, PhD, and Vincent Magnini, PhD

Poverty Alleviation through Tourism Development: A Comprehensive and Integrated Approach
Robertico Croes, PhD, and Manuel Rivera, PhD

Chinese Outbound Tourism 2.0
Editor: Xiang (Robert) Li, PhD

Advances in Hospitality and Tourism

STRATEGIC WINERY TOURISM AND MANAGEMENT

Building Competitive Winery Tourism and Winery Management Strategy

Edited by
Kyuho Lee, PhD

Apple Academic Press Inc.	Apple Academic Press Inc.
3333 Mistwell Crescent	9 Spinnaker Way
Oakville, ON L6L 0A2	Waretown, NJ 08758
Canada	USA

©2016 by Apple Academic Press, Inc.

Exclusive worldwide distribution by CRC Press, a member of Taylor & Francis Group

No claim to original U.S. Government works

Printed in the United States of America on acid-free paper

International Standard Book Number-13: 978-1-926895-68-0 (Hardcover)

International Standard Book Number-13: 978-1-4822-2341-5 (eBook)

Typeset by Accent Premedia Services (www.accentpremedia.com)

All rights reserved. No part of this work may be reprinted or reproduced or utilized in any form or by any electric, mechanical or other means, now known or hereafter invented, including photocopying and recording, or in any information storage or retrieval system, without permission in writing from the publisher or its distributor, except in the case of brief excerpts or quotations for use in reviews or critical articles.

This book contains information obtained from authentic and highly regarded sources. Reprinted material is quoted with permission and sources are indicated. Copyright for individual articles remains with the authors as indicated. A wide variety of references are listed. Reasonable efforts have been made to publish reliable data and information, but the authors, editors, and the publisher cannot assume responsibility for the validity of all materials or the consequences of their use. The authors, editors, and the publisher have attempted to trace the copyright holders of all material reproduced in this publication and apologize to copyright holders if permission to publish in this form has not been obtained. If any copyright material has not been acknowledged, please write and let us know so we may rectify in any future reprint.

Trademark Notice: Registered trademark of products or corporate names are used only for explanation and identification without intent to infringe.

Library and Archives Canada Cataloguing in Publication

Strategic winery tourism and management : building competitive winery tourism and winery management strategy / edited by Kyuho Lee, Ph.D.

Includes bibliographical references and index.
Issued in print and electronic formats.
ISBN 978-1-926895-68-0 (hardcover).--ISBN 978-1-4822-2341-5 (ebook)
1. Wine tourism. 2. Wineries--Management. 3. Wineries--Marketing.
I. Lee, Kyuho, author, editor

TP548.5.T68S73 2015	641.2'2	C2015-905366-8	C2015-905367-6

Library of Congress Cataloging-in-Publication Data

Strategic winery tourism and management : building competitive winery tourism and winery management strategy / [edited by] Kyuho Lee, Ph.D.

pages cm
Includes bibliographical references and index.
ISBN 978-1-926895-68-0 (alk. paper)
1. Wine tourism. 2. Wineries. I. Lee, Kyuho.

TP548.5.T68S77 2015	663'.2--dc23	2015028655

Apple Academic Press also publishes its books in a variety of electronic formats. Some content that appears in print may not be available in electronic format. For information about Apple Academic Press products, visit our website at **www.appleacademicpress.com** and the CRC Press website at **www.crcpress.com**

ABOUT THE SERIES EDITOR

Mahmood A. Khan, PhD, is a Professor in the Department of Hospitality and Tourism Management, Pamplin College of Business at Virginia Tech's National Capital Region campus. He has served in teaching, research, and administrative positions for the past 35 years, working at major U.S. universities. Dr. Khan is the author of seven books and has traveled extensively for teaching and consulting on management issues and franchising. He has been invited by national and international corporations to serve as a speaker, keynote speaker, and seminar presenter on different topics related to franchising and services management.

Dr. Khan has received the Steven Fletcher Award for his outstanding contribution to hospitality education and research. He is also a recipient of the John Wiley & Sons Award for lifetime contribution to outstanding research and scholarship; the Donald K. Tressler Award for scholarship; and the Cesar Ritz Award for scholarly contribution. He also received the Outstanding Doctoral Faculty Award from Pamplin College of Business.

He has served on the Board of Governors of the Educational Foundation of the International Franchise Association, on the Board of Directors of the Virginia Hospitality and Tourism Association, as a Trustee of the International College of Hospitality Management, and as a Trustee on the Foundation of the Hospitality Sales and Marketing Association's International Association. He is also a member of several professional associations.

CONTENTS

About the Editor .... *ix*

List of Contributors .... *xi*

List of Abbreviations .... *xiii*

Preface .... *xv*

1. **The Business of Wine** 1
   Anisya Thomas Fritz

2. **Wine Tourism Strategy Making: A Model for Planning
   and Implementation** 9
   Robert J. Harrington and Michael C. Ottenbacher

3. **Strategic Winery Management and Tourism: Value-Added
   Offerings and Strategies Beyond Product Centrism** 31
   Dr. Marc Dreßler

4. **Wine Versus Weddings: Wine Tourism in the Emerging
   North Carolina Wine Industry** 69
   Ian M. Taplin and Minh-Trang Thi Nguyen

5. **Wine Tourism in Bordeaux** 89
   Tatiana Bouzdine-Chameeva, Christophe Faugère, and Pierre Mora

6. **Emerging Issues in Wine Tourism** 115
   Liz Thach

7. **Winery Tourism in China** 127
   Jinlin Zhao

8. **Analyzing the Effects of Short- and Long-Term Customer
   Relationship on the Wine Customer Lifetime Value** 143
   Michael R. Santos and Vincent Richman

9. **Designing for Sales: Winery Design and the Visitor Experience** 157
   Douglas Thornley

10. **Using ANNs to Determine Place Evoked Affective Consumer Reactions in Wine Tourism**.. 167

Albert Stöckl, Wolfram Rinke, and Andreas Eisingerich

11. **Effective Winery Tasting Room Management**...................................... 187

Stephanie Friedman

12. **Service Quality, Brand Loyalty, and Wine Tourism** 205

Melissa A. Van Hyfte

13. **Exploring an Effective Winery Revenue Management Strategy**....... 237

Kyuho Lee

14. **Financial Ratio and Valuation Analyses of Constellation Brands Inc.: A Case Study** 247

Michael R. Santos and Vincent Richman

15. **The Rise of Wine Education in Mainland China: A First-Hand Account and Analysis** 269

Edward Ragg

Index... *291*

ABOUT THE EDITOR

Kyuho Lee, PhD
Kyuho Lee is an Assistant Professor of Wine Business and Marketing at Sonoma State University, California, USA. Dr. Lee received his PhD in Hospitality and Tourism Management at Virginia Tech. Also, Dr. Lee received an AACSB Post-Doctoral Bridge to Business Program Certificate (Marketing) at Virginia Tech in 2009 and an Executive Brand Management Certificate from the Kellogg School of Management at Northwestern University in May 2014. He specializes in the study of wine brand management, wine consumer behavior, and services marketing.

Dr. Lee has published his works in leading academic journals such as *Journal of Retailing, Service Industries*, and *Journal of Hospitality & Tourism Research*. Dr. Lee has also presented his academic work at a number of top-tier academic conferences such as the Strategic Management Society and the Annual Meeting of the Academy of Management.

LIST OF CONTRIBUTORS

Tatiana Bouzdine-Chameeva
Kedge Business School, Bordeaux, France, E-mail: tatiana.chameeva@kedgebs.com

Marc Dressler
University of Ludwigshafen, Germany

Christophe Faugère
Kedge Business School, Bordeaux, France, E-mail: christophe.faugere@kedgebs.com

Stephanie Friedman
Direct Sales Manager, Gary Farrell Vineyards and Winery, 10701 Westside Rd, Healdsburg, CA 95448, United States

Anisya Thomas Fritz
Proprietor, Lynmar Estate, 3909 Frei Rd, Sebastopol, CA 95472, United States

Robert J. Harrington
University of Arkansas, Fayetteville, AR 72701, United States

Melissa A. Van Hyfte
Program Director, Assistant Professor, Hospitality and Event Management, Lasell College, 1844 Commonwealth Avenue, Auburndale, MA 02466, United States

Kyuho Lee
Assistant Professor of Marketing, Sonoma State University, Rohnert Park, CA, USA

Pierre Mora
Kedge Business School, Bordeaux, France, E-mail: pierre.mora@kedgebs.com

Minh-Trang Thi Nguyen
Wake Forest University, Winston-Salem, NC 27109, USA

Michael C. Ottenbacher
Heilbronn University, Max-Planck-Straße 39, 74081 Heilbronn, Germany

Edward Ragg
Co-founder, Dragon Phoenix Wine Consulting, Associate Professor, Department of Foreign Languages and Literatures, Tsinghua University, Beijing 100084, China

Vincent Richman
School of Business and Economics, Sonoma State University, California, USA

Wolfram Rinke
Andreas Eisingerich, Imperial College London, Great Britain

Michael R. Santos
School of Business and Economics, Sonoma State University, California, USA

Albert Stöckl
University of Applied Sciences Burgenland, Austria, E-mail: albert.stoeckl@fh-burgenland.at

Ian M. Taplin
Department of Sociology and International Studies, Wake Forest University, Winston-Salem, NC 27109, USA; Bordeaux Ecole de Management, Bordeaux, France

Liz Thach
Department of Business Administration, Sonoma State University, California, USA

Douglas Thornley
AIA Principal, Gould Evans, San Francisco, CA, USA

Jinlin Zhao
Professor, Director of Graduate Programs, Director of Asia and Pacific Development, Chaplin School of Hospitality and Tourism Management, Florida International University, 3000 NE 151 Street, North Miami, FL 33181, USA, Tel.: 305-919-4540; Fax: 305-919-4555; E-mail: zhaoj@fiu.edu

LIST OF ABBREVIATIONS

ANNs	artificial neural networks
BF-B	Brown-Forman Corporation
BPS	book value per share
BW	Baden Württemberg
CAPM	capital asset pricing model
CE	customer equity
CLV	customer lifetime value
COFOC	china oils and foodstuffs corp.
CQI	continuous quality improvement
CRM	customer relationship management
CV	continuing value
DEO	Diageo
DGM	dividend growth model
DMOs	destination-marketing organizations
DTC	direct-to-consumer
EM	earnings model
EPS	earnings per share
FBI	future behavioral intentions
FCF	free cash flow
GDP	gross domestic product
GWC	great wine capitals
NCS	net capital spending
OCF	operating cash flow
OTTI	office of travel and tourism industries
ROA	return on assets
ROE	return on equity
SKU	stock keeping units
SPS	sales per share
STZ	Constellation Stock
SVB	Silicon Valley Bank

TIE	times interest earned
WACC	weighted average cost of capital
WTO	World Tourism Organization
WTTC	World Travel and Tourism Council
YTM	yield to maturity
ΔNWC	changes in NWC

PREFACE

Wine has emerged as a lifestyle product among a growing number of consumers. Visiting wineries has become a leisure and tourism activity among winery tourists. For example, winery tourists visit wineries not only to taste wines but also to experience the winery's scenery, traditions, and heritage. Winery management can also involve consumers in their wineries proactively through winery tourism and cellar door sales. They can demonstrate the wine production process and present their vineyards and gardens to winery visitors. Specifically, winery tourism can be effective in increasing brand awareness and loyalty among winery tourists, which can help a winery increase its revenue.

Given that there are over 100,000 wine brands globally, attaining high brand loyalty and awareness has become a daunting task. Furthermore, 98 percent of US wineries produce less than 12,000 cases of wine a year (Insel, B., in *Wine Tourism: An Overview of the Economics*, Wine Tourism Conference November 2011). Thus, winery tourism is crucial to these small wineries that do not have the marketing and distribution resources of major wineries. Nonetheless, developing a competitive winery tourism and management entails considering several issues from managing winery service quality to creating an attractive winery architecture design. Therefore, winery operators need to look at winery tourism holistically rather than focusing on just one aspect of tourism or cellar door sales to make winery tourism sustainable.

Despite the growing importance of winery tourism, there has been little research published in the area of winery tourism and winery management. This book encompasses crucial components of strategic winery tourism and management. Specifically, it provides readers with critical theoretical foundations underpinning strategic winery tourism and management by addressing a variety of topics related to strategic winery tourism and management. Importantly, this book illuminates a global perspective on winery tourism since researchers from France to China have contributed chapters. In addition, the book echoes a practical perspective on winery tourism and management since a number of chapters are written by wine industry practitioners—from a proprietor to an architect specializing in winery designs.

In sum, I would like to thank all the authors who contributed to the book. Without their efforts and contributions, I would not have been able to develop this book.

Kyuho Lee, PhD
Editor

CHAPTER 1

THE BUSINESS OF WINE

ANISYA THOMAS FRITZ

Proprietor, Lynmar Estate, 3909 Frei Rd, Sebastopol, CA 95472, United States

CONTENTS

1.1 Introduction 1

1.2 Typical Trajectory of Wine Business Entrepreneurs 2

Keywords 7

1.1 INTRODUCTION

1.1.1 THE EXPLOSIVE GROWTH OF THE WINE INDUSTRY

The allure of wine has endured the test of time. It has transcended culture and geography, and taken its place in the stories of generations across much of the world. It fascinates because it captures the imagination, a living thing that includes within a combination of terrain and climate, science and craft. It has been credited with sparking creativity, inspiring poetry and cementing ties.

In the United States, which has a relatively new wine making tradition, the wine industry has seen explosive growth in the last decade. Since 2004, the total retail value has increased over \$12 billion from \$24 billion in 2004 to \$36.3 billion in 2013[1]. California produces 90% of the wine

---

[1]Source: Gomberg-Fredrikson & Associates and Wine Institute.

made in the US United States, and is the 4th largest wine producer after France, Italy and Spain. The wine industry in California alone 121.8 billion impact on the national economy, supplied 820,000 jobs nationwide, and brought in 20.7 million tourists in 2012[2]. Wine has become a significant, global business with the attendant competitive factors.

In 2012, there were 8,805 bonded wineries in the United States[3], up from 2904 in the year 2000, and 1610 in 1990 an x and y percent growth, respectively. It is interesting to note however the vast majority and an overwhelming 77% are very small or limited production with less than 5000 cases produced. In other words most US wineries are entrepreneurial startups that are also small family businesses.

Nonetheless, they operate in an extremely competitive environment. In 2013 alone, the US tax and trade bureau approved nearly 99,000 wine label registrations, mostly from wineries producing abroad. In addition, the Wine Institute reports that over the past five years, permits for alcohol production have increased 47% if wineries, craft breweries and distilleries are included[4]. To be successful, even these small producers now need to be strategic about wine, understanding that like companies in other industries, wineries are *systems* that must create value, manage costs and develop talent to survive. With limited access to resources, including financial and professional, these organizations are the ones that most require good management of people and resources. It is precisely because of these pressures that Wine Business Education is critical to the stabilization, professionalization and development of the industry.

1.2 TYPICAL TRAJECTORY OF WINE BUSINESS ENTREPRENEURS

1.2.1 PHASE 1: WINE AS PRODUCT

An entrepreneur is someone who perceives a market opportunity and organizes resources to pursue it. In the wine industry, the passion for wine draws new entrants into the wine business. These entrepreneurs range

---

[2](http://www.discovercaliforniawines.com/media-trade/statistics/
[3]Wine Institute.
[4]Wine Institute California Wine Sales grow.

The Business of Wine

from winemakers who want to start their own brand to executives who have been successful in other fields of endeavor and enter the world of wine to fulfill a lifestyle aspiration, and everything in-between.

Bobby and Shannon Donnell are wine business entrepreneurs who had a dream of starting their own label. Bobby is a winemaker, and Shannon, his wife, managed vineyard relations for a large winery operation. With a friend, they created artwork for their label and named their company to be Screen Door Cellars. Hailing from Texas, Bobby associated screen doors with family and friends. During his childhood, the screen door to the kitchen, led in to the heart of the home where people gathered and out to the yard for freedom and play.

To make their dream a reality, Shannon leveraged her long-term relationships with growers to acquire excess fruit. Bobby negotiated with his employer, an established winery with the required licenses, to allow him to crush a limited quantity of grapes at their facility for favorable rates and the first vintage of 200 cases of Screen Door Cellars came to be. Since it was clear that these first cases could not support their family, even when it was sold in 12–18 months, both Bobby and Shannon decided to keep their current jobs. This meant that they had to work at nights and on weekends to make their wine, establish contacts with distributors. Shannon's mother became the accountant for the label, and friends and family in Texas and Arkansas, their first direct to consumer market.

During this early stage of the business, they are entirely consumed by the creation of the product and making sure that the decisions they make during harvest, crush, fermentation, aging, blending, finishing and bottling are consistent with their vision of an high quality Pinot Noir that bears their dream on its label. They understand that even with a $40 per bottle retail price, it will be several years before they will have the opportunity to focus full-time on building the distribution network for the wine.

However, as they look to the future with their label, they are aware of the fact that despite the relatively low start-up and overhead costs they have managed, because of the virtual nature of their winery, they are vulnerable to fluctuations in grape prices. Additionally, their production model will have to change if they want to expand the number of cases they want to sell. This will require capital beyond what is available from the sale of their wine.

1.2.2 PHASE 2: WINERY AS A SYSTEM

After wine entrepreneurs work through their early production and distribution issues, they see the need to ensure the sustainability of their enterprise. It is at this stage, they begin to think about the winery as a system made up of multiple elements that each contribute to the revenue or the expenses. To truly manage the enterprise, the entrepreneur must be able to calculate true wine cost (cost of goods) over time for each blend in each vintage, the operating costs for the fiscal period and manage cash flow to pay expenses. Equally important, he or she must understand the sources of revenue and the timing of the revenue.

The wine business has unique complexities that often obscure the financial situation in an organization. Grapes and barrels are purchased and paid for two to five years before the wine is released. Once released, it may take another year before the entire inventory is sold and paid for. Thus, the cost of a vintage, and the profit or loss it generates is onerous and difficult to calculate. Yet, without an accurate understanding of costs, the owner or manager can easily put the entire business at risk. Further, since grape purchased in the current year are being paid for by the sales of wine made two years previously, a poor crop could result in the need to borrow capital to keep the business going.

Nicole Abiounous graduated from college in Virginia with a passion for food and wine. She moved to Napa to pursue this interest, taking every course she could on wine. Wanting more, she began to work in the cellar of Swanson vineyards and decided that her future lay in winemaking. Following a stint in Australia's Barossa Valley, she worked for two years in France and honed her skill in making Burgundian varietals. When she returned, she began her own label, working closely with growers to obtain grapes that met her quality standards.

Her passion and talent, soon brought recognition, and she established relationships with brokers in California and Virginia. Although she managed to support herself nicely, a decade later, this dynamic one-woman show did not know if in fact she was profitable. So with the help of her partner John Herrguth, they began to take apart and analyze the business as a system, tracking and allocating costs with the help of an accountant. Now, they have set goals for direct distribution, as their analysis made it clear that she either had to increase her volume

The Business of Wine 5

of wine produced and sold, or sell directly to the customer to support the couple and the baby they were about to have.

It is almost impossible to manage a wine business without metrics that indicate whether the business model is on track or not. The balanced scorecard methodology is one often used in business and can also be applied to wine businesses. It includes measuring financial performance such as return on investment, customer satisfaction and retention, internal performance with measures of profitability and an assessment of the learning and growth of employees.

1.2.3 WINE AS AN EXPERIENCE: DIRECT TO CUSTOMER SALES

Even after a business model has been established and metrics created and monitored, internal or external pressures can upset the balance. In the wine industry profitability is largely dependent on maintaining a reasonable cost of goods and cost of sales. Thus if there is a year where the cost of grapes goes up, organizations will have to adjust their cost of sales or increase prices to maintain the same profit margins. Alternatively, when there is a recession and distribution and sales of wine are affected, inventory can pile up and cash flow slow to a trickle, putting companies at risk. Within this context, most small producers, with limited bargaining power in the marketplace of distributors and retailers have realized that the only leverage they have is to sell wine directly to the customer, cutting out the middleman, increasing margins and retaining the relationship through a mailing list and regular email and phone communication, a wine club, a tasting room, social media or all of these. However, finding, converting and retaining customers to a wine club require a mindset and discipline all of its own.

Lynmar Estate is a small producer of ultra-premium pinot noir and chardonnay in the Russian River Valley that released its first small vintage 1994. Situated on an iconic vineyard, Quail Hill, its early vintages were all sold through a network of distributors.

Realizing that the margins from distribution would never be adequate for the quality of wine we wished to produce, we knew we needed another approach. Working on the premise that the experience of wine was just as important as the quality of the wine, we commissioned the building of a

Tasting Room with expansive views of the vineyard. Inspired by the delight we witnessed at beautiful public gardens around the world, we planted an organic garden comprised of heirloom, ornamental and native varietals of vegetables and flowers. Local staffs with a passion for Sonoma County Pinot Noir and Chardonnay were hired to tell the story of the land and its stewardship. The goal was to provide the customer with a multisensory experience of terroir and wine. Slowly, we began to build a base of customers who loved the wine and the story.

In 2008, after the recession dried up orders in the distribution market, the company was at crossroads. Although it had a reputation for excellent wine, it was barely profitable. Being a small brand in the national marketplace, it did not have any bargaining power with distributors who increasingly were pressuring for lower prices and sales incentives.

Faced with few alternatives, the proprietors decided that rather than compromising on the quality of the vineyards, which were expensive to farm or the winemaking, which was meticulous, it was time to reexamine the business model. To maintain excellence and cover costs, the company would need to sell the same amount of wine at the same prices or a smaller quantity at higher prices. They decided to change its strategic focus from primarily distribution in national markets to selling directly to the consumer.

There was little infrastructure in the company to support such a strategy, but once made, the whole organization was aligned to it. The company went from making 4 appellation and Estate wines to making more than 20 different stock keeping units (SKU's), each with small production and distinguished by flavor profile, vineyard source and winemaking style. Production was scaled down, and a new point of sales and customer tacking system was incorporated. The labels were redesigned and a wine club started. The goal was to grow aggressively by getting each customer that came to Lynmar to refer their friends.

Before the shift in strategy, Lynmar did not count the number of customers that came in the door, only the number of people that purchased wine. Thus, they had no way of knowing what proportions of guests were being converted to purchase and to the wine club. The point of sale system did not allow tracking sales by employee, so proper incentives were hard to implement. There was no record of customer preferences, and so no real understanding the buying behavior of the people who walked in the door.

The Business of Wine 7

Six years later, all this has changed. Now we track the number of people that come in the door. We implemented a tasting fee, so we could track what proportion of all our guests actually tasted wine, and of these how many bought wine. We track the conversion rate to the wine club, the sales per taster and sales per employee, per hour. We are able to measure our inventory turns when we have a promotion and also track this metric by week by month, year over year. We have a goal for average price per case, and watch sales very carefully to make sure the flights have the appropriate product mix to make this goal. When our numbers do not make projections we ask why and take appropriate action. In addition to this data, once a year we conduct a survey of our customers to determine that we are also meeting and exceeding their expectations. Their feedback then becomes a training tool for our front-line staff.

Despite our success with the direct to consumer model, we have to vigilant about costs as the nature of farming is such that a poor harvest can wipe out the reserves built in the company. Competition has escalated and many more wineries are pursuing the same customer. We review our business model and metrics each year as well as that path of the customer from the time they drive into the property through the end of their experience. We have now begun to look at other luxury and service industries such as hotels and restaurants to develop more rigorous metrics.

The journey into wine, although fueled by passion needs to be seen as a process that can be managed. To achieve this, the entrepreneurs need to expand their lens to include the business of wine, and the experience of wine as components that are as important as the production of wine.

KEYWORDS

- **Lynmar Estate**
- **wine industry**
- **wine making tradition**
- **winery product**
- **winery system**

CHAPTER 2

WINE TOURISM STRATEGY MAKING: A MODEL FOR PLANNING AND IMPLEMENTATION

ROBERT J. HARRINGTON, PhD, MBA, CEC[1] and
MICHAEL C. OTTENBACHER[2]

[1]*Professor of Hospitality Management, University of Arkansas, Fayetteville, AR 72701, USA*

[2]*Professor, Heilbronn University, Max-Planck-Straße 39, 74081 Heilbronn, Germany*

CONTENTS

2.1 Introduction 9
2.2 Literature Review 10
2.3 Earlier Research on Wine Tourism Strategies 11
2.4 Deliberate vs. Emergent Strategy-Making Processes 13
2.5 Discussion 14
2.6 Conclusions 24
Keywords 27
References 27

2.1 INTRODUCTION

Tourism organizations are recognizing the potential of culinary and wine tourism as a powerful tool to promote destinations or regions (Alonso et al.,

2013). Despite the growing interest in wine tourism as a field of study and as a way to promote a destination, the process knowledge about how to successfully develop and implement a wine tourism strategy is limited. For example, Charters and Ali-Knight (2002) argue that wine tourism research should be more strategic rather than descriptive. Therefore, the objective of this chapter is to explore the key issues in the strategy-making process and successful implementation in wine tourism campaigns. Specifically, the authors synthesize earlier case studies and literature to identify key elements for wine tourism initiative success in a conceptual framework derived from the learning school of strategic management. Key initiative elements are discussed in the context of the strategic process and strategy-making framework adapted to wine tourism strategy. In other words, following the model of the strategic process described by Mintzberg et al. (1998), the authors present a revised version adapted to a wine tourism strategy scenario.

A longstanding concept of the strategic process has been tied to deliberate and emergent concepts of how strategy is created. While the deliberate vs. emergent concept has in most cases been viewed as two dichotomous approaches (Boyd, 1991), Mintzberg and colleagues described the two terms as ends of a continuum with multiple elements. By adapting this conceptualization, the conceptual framework components include intended strategy, unrealized strategy, deliberate strategy, emergent strategy, and realized strategy.

The chapter points out key elements in the wine tourism strategic process that are applicable for each component in the framework as well as point to key challenges derived from a synthesis of previous studies. A key implication of this conceptual model is its use as a framework for future wine tourism research, wine tourism development, and wine tourism strategic planning.

2.2 LITERATURE REVIEW

Numerous studies have portrayed the importance of food, wine and dining as a key contributor to the tourist experience (e.g., Correia et al., 2007; Gross et al., 2008; Hall and Sharples, 2003; Kivela and Crotts, 2006).

A travel study in the US found that while traveling in the past three years, 17% of leisure travelers engaged in culinary or wine-related activities; it is predicted that this figure will increase significantly in the future (Leahy, 2007). Further, food and beverage dining experiences are frequently described as the most frequent leisure activity of travelers and represents the second largest daily expenditure (Hall and Sharples, 2003). As a result many state and regional offices have put together wine tourism initiatives to enhance and promote food and wine tourism as part of a tourism strategy (e.g., Canadian Tourism Commission, 2003; Hall and Macionis, 1998). Based on perceived opportunities of wine tourism, there appears to be a growing interest in the promotion of wine tourism in many areas of the world that are not traditionally known as a wine producing region nor for its cuisine or as having a clear identity (e.g., Canada, the US, Argentina, South Africa, etc.) (Faugère, et al., 2013; Harrington, 2008).

2.3 EARLIER RESEARCH ON WINE TOURISM STRATEGIES

Earlier research on wine tourism strategy has generally focused on factors related to the supply of wine tourism services and explanatory dimensions of wine tourism performance. For the most part the factors related to the supply of wine tourism have focused on external factors, activities offered, promotional tools, and investments. External factors include regional capital and branding; Alant and Bower (2004) provided evidence of the importance of an identified wine region as a key pull factor for wine tourists. Mitchell et al. (2012) recognized the importance of the role of the wider context a region's physical and cultural landscape as a key driver of wine tourism. This broader concept is what Hall and Mitchell (2002) describe as 'touristic terroir.'

Famularo et al. (2010) provided evidence of the important role a regional brand or place of origin in the context of wine tourism visitation decisions. This regional brand connection was shown to be impacted by wine knowledge and wine tourism involvement to ultimately impact wine purchase decisions during and after the visitation. Meanwhile, Telfer (2001) and Ottenbacher et al. (2012) provided evidence of the need to develop strategic alliances with cooperation among multiple stakeholders: wineries, food service, lodging, local crafts industry, tour operators and regional government.

Earlier studies have also looked at the role of activities offered as part of a wine tourism strategy. The role of local food and place of origin wine has been described as a fundamental tactic to differentiate a region or location. The services desired for consumers of wine tourism include visitor friendly wineries (Getz and Brown, 2006), stories tied to local food and culture, and a variety of wine and food related activities (Harrington, 2008).

However, still only limited research has been done in this field (Getz et al., 2006) and a subject of wine tourism research that has received little attention is the consideration of the strategic process used for the implementation of wine tourism products. A key reason for this is that this area of research is not as easily assessed in any meaningful way using survey or secondary data methods (e.g., Patten and Appelbaum, 2003). As with other process type research, more qualitative methods have generally been applied (e.g., Eisenhardt, 1989; Ottenbacher and Harrington, 2007). Earlier authors have provided several suggestions to increase the likelihood of successful implementation of a wine tourism program or strategy (Cambourne and Macionis, 2003). While many of these are typical issues stressed in the general strategic management literature, other issues are more specific to wine tourism products.

Following the standards of a general strategic process, a higher likelihood of success is determined by: (i) clearly defining the strategy and goals (tangible and intangible outputs), (ii) doing sufficient research into market potential, (iii) clearly identifying marketing and product development priorities, (iv) communicating strategy to all stakeholders, and (v) engaging a variety stakeholders early on (Bryson and Bromiley, 1993; Canadian Tourism Commission, 2003). Additional strategic process issues that are specific to tourism in general and wine tourism in particular include: (i) focusing on geographic areas with the greatest potential for growth, (ii) creating strong partnerships between government, agencies, and the private sector, (iii) creating longer-term management of the initiative, (iv) supporting training and development programs, and (v) defining and maintaining quality assurance requirements (e.g., criteria for participant businesses, locally-based quality or training-related programs, etc.) (Boyne, Hall and Williams, 2003; Ontario, 2008).

2.4 DELIBERATE VS. EMERGENT STRATEGY-MAKING PROCESSES

A longstanding concept of the strategy-making process has been tied to deliberate and emergent concepts of how strategy is created. While (in the majority of studies) the deliberate vs. emergent concept has been viewed as two dichotomous approaches (Boyd, 1991), Mintzberg and colleagues (e.g., Mintzberg et al., 1998; Mintzberg and McHugh, 1985; Mintzberg and Waters, 1985) described the two terms as ends of a continuum with multiple elements.

Deliberate strategies are defined as "intentions realized" and develop out of strategies that are formulated in advance (Mintzberg and McHugh, 1985: 161). Specifically, deliberate strategy is defined as "a pattern in a stream of decisions or actions" (Mintzberg and McHugh, 1985: 161). In contrast, the emergent approach can be defined as less comprehensive with emerging strategic patterns "despite or in the absence of intentions" (Mintzberg and McHugh, 1985: 161). This approach can be defined as a process that may develop a specific or generic overall strategy that allows for or adapts to changes as information becomes available. In other words, patterns in a strategy will form outside of intentions in response to a variety of stakeholders and forces in the environment.

Thus, our conceptualization of the deliberate versus emergent debate follows the work of Mintzberg et al. (1998). This model has several important and interesting components that define a strategic process' placement on the deliberate/emergent continuum. The implications of this concept to the strategy-making process for wine tourism campaigns are important for the development and execution of regional tourism strategy success. Because regional tourism policy and strategy should theoretically integrate the ideas and needs of a variety of regional stakeholders, a question remains as to whether actual regional tourism strategy making demands a predominately deliberate approach or a predominately emergent one. Further, it begs the question if the levels of deliberate or emergent strategy-making process varies by strategic ends and strategic means. A deliberate strategy-making process would have very specific ends (many, precisely quantified, formally documented, time-limited ends) and very specific means (reflected in plans that set out exact plans and/or programs for implementation, describing in detail the actions and steps required for implementing ends) (Brews and Hunt, 1999: 893). In contrast, an emergent strategy-making process approach would be typified as having a "few broad ends that change and evolve as conditions dictate ... [and] unspecific means would be broad and unstructured, evolving as circumstances warrant..." (Brews and Hunt, 1999: 893).

Other research in hospitality and tourism indicates the deliberate or emergent nature depends on the level of volatility in the environment. Environments with less volatility are theoretically able to achieve greater success using more deliberate strategy approaches and those operating in environments with more volatility require a more emergent strategic process to enable adaptation to emergent changes in the competitive field (Harrington, 2005). Although several studies have portrayed the importance of wine, cultural and culinary aspects as a key contributor to the tourist experience, there is a lack of research focusing on strategy-making process issues related to wine tourism. Therefore, the objective of this chapter is to explore the key issues in the strategy-making process in the context of wine tourism strategy.

2.5 DISCUSSION

Following the earlier model of the strategic process described by Mintzberg et al. (1998), we propose a revised conceptual model adapted to a wine tourism strategy scenario. Therefore, conceptually the key implications for successful strategy-making and implementation of a wine tourism product can be divided into five main strategic concepts based on planned strategic approaches (intended, unrealized and deliberate strategies), emergent strategic approaches, and what gets realized (realized strategies). A fundamental part of this process that receives less attention is the concept and importance of middle-up-down approaches to strategy making and implementation (e.g., Harrington and Kendall, 2006). This concept is particularly relevant when applied to regional wine tourism level of development and unit of analysis. These elements are discussed in the following sections.

2.5.1 PLANNING APPROACHES TO STRATEGY

In Fig. 2.1, two areas of the model relate to a 'planning school' or strategic approach: intended strategies and deliberate strategies. For a regional strategic plan, this step occurs after an initial assessment of wine tourism-related assets have emerged, how tourists perceive the bundle of activities

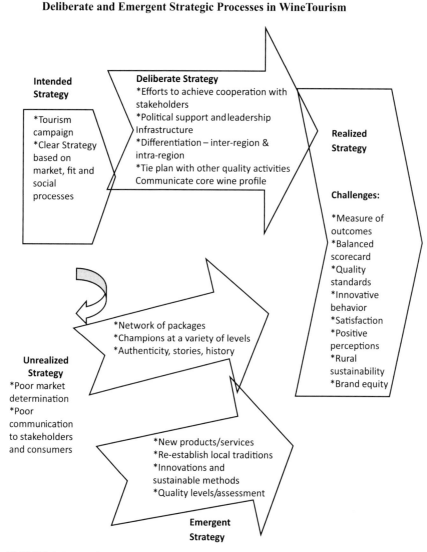

FIGURE 2.1 Deliberate and emergent strategic processes in wine tourism.

2.5.1.1 Intended Strategy

The intended strategy is viewed as an analytical approach to strategy-making driven by formal structure and planning systems (Hart and Banbury, 1994). Proponents of the planning school suggest this approach applies to all situations. The proposed framework indicates the approach appropriate for regional wine tourism strategy requires elements of both the planning and learning schools (e.g., Mintzberg et al., 1998). Creating intended strategies in advance is dependent on relatively stable competitive environments that allow for the anticipation of competitive threats and opportunities (Harrington, 2005; McWilliams and Smart, 1993). The intended strategy concept of the strategy-making process appears to apply to two key elements of the wine tourism initiative: the general wine tourism campaign and defining a clear strategy based on market assessment, fit and social process issues.

In the case of wine tourism strategy, defining intended strategy in advance appears to also be useful in communicating areas for growth and differentiation for firms across a region as well as for creating demand for wine tourism services in a region. Thus, as part of the tourism campaign strategy, regional planners need to address the strategic planning challenge of: What wine tourism brand should we promote? Branding is a powerful tool by which tourism regions can effectively communicate a strategy to firms in the area as well as can set themselves apart from other destinations (Famularo et al., 2010; Foley and Fahy, 2004).

A further condition for a successful branding strategy is creating a brand that is easy to identify (Kotler et al., 2006). Therefore, the tourism brand name should be characterized by what is distinctive in the region, the benefits and qualities of the destination, and the resulting wine-related product and services profile. For instance, in the interviews regarding wine-related tourism in a recent study by the authors, participants pointed out that tourism should not just be related to haute cuisine, high-end wines and other exclusively luxury elements but especially to traditional, casual authentic culinary and wine products or services. Furthermore, more local products should be used and the stakeholders need to develop pride in local culinary, crafts and wine products. However, this appears only possible (or a good fit) when the regional products provide high quality (Ottenbacher and Harrington, 2013).

Thus, a second key element of the process of defining intended strategy is the determination of a clear strategy that is based on market, fit and social processes. This process and definition is the same as the traditional SWOT market analysis but integrates the fit with regional strengths and weaknesses with reputation, products, perceived authenticity and uniqueness of the region. Of course, wine products alone are not sufficient for a successful wine tourism brand or strategy. Instead, the key is to combine wine and culinary experiences in creative packages with other tourism offer such as wellness, sports, cultural events and landscape (Harrington and Ottenbacher, 2010). In short when planning a wine tourism strategy, wine tourism destinations should not copy other tourism campaigns but should differentiate the destination from the competition on its unique cultural, geographical, natural, and culinary resources and characteristics.

In general, strategic planning (i.e., intended strategy) is effectively managing the environmental threats and opportunities in the light of a region's strengths and weaknesses. Marketing research is often used to identify such opportunities and threats. However, for a regional tourism initiative, reaching a consensus on a region's strengths and weaknesses as well as possible environmental opportunities and threats can be a challenge. In our experience with tourism endeavors in Germany and France, little research exists intra-region in wine tourism. While the tourism agencies we interviewed would like to undertake more research, (generally) time pressure and financial restrictions do not permit sufficient market research. Earlier research has provided support for the value of empirical analysis in strategic decision-making to reduce risk, diffuse objections by organizational members or other stakeholders, and sell the solution to a variety of stakeholders (Harrington and Ottenbacher, 2009). Thus, as shown in Fig. 2.1, key challenges in market determination and effective communication to stakeholders and consumers provide important barriers to overcome in any regional wine tourism initiative. The lack of empirical research to support strategic initiatives does little to minimize "naysayers" across a diverse region.

2.5.1.2 Unrealized Strategy

One of the elements of the learning school model of the strategic process put forward by Mintzberg et al. (1998) is the realization that even if strategic intentions are provided in advance some of these intentions will not become realized for a variety of reasons. Implicit in this model is the idea that intentions will get replaced by emergent strategies that develop as more information becomes available and as an outcome of the learning that takes place from planning through implementation. In other words, even if strategic objectives are specified in advance, these may become unrealized due to a lack of knowledge that later materializes or if there is a dynamic shift in the competitive environment that no longer makes a strategy viable. In the case of wine tourism strategy, intended strategies may become unrealized due to market determination challenges and challenges in communication to stakeholders and consumers (Fig. 2.1) about – what the strategy is, how it will become implemented, and how the strategy can create a positive perception in the eyes of the consumer? These challenges are discussed further in the realized strategy section.

2.5.1.3 Deliberate Strategy

A key implication of the findings from the authors' study and shown in the conceptual framework is the importance of regional tourism leadership to consider and deliberately deal with several issues that appear essential for a wine tourism initiative: (i) Efforts to achieve cooperation with stakeholders, (ii) Political support and leadership, (iii) Infrastructure, (iv) Differentiation – inter-region and intra-region, (v) Tie plan with other quality activities, and (vi) Communicate core wine region profile.

A challenge that demands deliberate efforts from central leadership in a regional wine tourism initiative is continuous efforts to achieve cooperation or alliances with the diverse body of stakeholders in the region. Most regional wine tourism and other related activities are dispersed across a variety of relatively small businesses or at least geographically dispersed units of chain operations. Both of these groups create challenges in achieving cooperation and promotion.

Internally, regional initiatives must have political support and leadership that signals there are "champions" for on-going efforts to assist and promote the current initiative as well as future strategies to continue driving the tourism effort forward. This political support includes deliberate strategies to deal with infrastructure issues including education components, quality strategies and transportation infrastructure needs. This process also needs champions to serve as lobbyists to ensure appropriate investments are made by regional organizations and governments (e.g., Correia et al., 2004).

Another key deliberate strategy is the efforts for a wine tourism differentiation strategy. Of course, the core idea of wine-related tourism is to create a regional identity based on local culture and place of origin that differentiates one region from another. In our case study of the federal state of Baden Württemberg (BW), the study of the region pointed out the need to deliberately think about differentiation from both an inter-region perspective (e.g., the Mosel vs. BW, etc.) and intra-region perspective (e.g., Baden vs. Württemberg, etc.). This deliberate strategy includes the need to communicate core 'touristic terroir' profiles inter-region and intra-region for both consumers and the regions stakeholders

Finally, a deliberate strategy that goes along with a successful wine tourism initiative is to tie the plan with other quality activities such as sports, nature, health, other cultural activities, etc. This need has been shown in many wine tourism destinations and appears to be an important strategic concept for deliberate approaches in both new world and old world wine tourism areas (Harrington and Ottenbacher, 2010).

2.5.1.4 Emergent Strategic Approaches

A number of schools of thought have been developed in the area of strategy with two prominent and divergent schools described as learning or emergent concepts of strategy versus a planning concept (Mintzberg et al., 1998). In conceptualizing an appropriate and effective process for regional wine tourism strategy, it seems that both concepts of strategy development are important.

Emergent strategy is based in the belief that strategies do not always develop in a holistic predetermined plan but instead may be realized counter to the predetermined (deliberate) strategy, in lieu of having a clear strategic plan, or in a more incremental process (Mintzberg et al., 1998). An emergent conceptualization of the strategic process has been shown to be more effective in environments with greater dynamism and when combined with a more participative leadership approach needed for more complex situations (Harrington, 2005). These issues appear particularly relevant for a regional wine tourism strategy given the volatility of tourism demand, dynamic nature of political support and the complex nature of a stakeholder network integrating a variety of related and unrelated industries. These issues were shown to be important characteristics in earlier studies for both traditionally branded wine regions and emerging ones (Beer et al., 2012; Ottenbacher and Harrington, 2013).

Many wine-related products and services are established at the grassroots level. Identifying touristic assets of a region requires information from a variety of industry and academic sources to create an understanding of quality experiences available and assuring their authenticity. This identification requires a bottom-up approach to not only identify a unique selling proposition for a region based on the bundle of quality products and services available but also to identify potential champions in a variety areas of industry who are likely to provide leadership at the local or specific industry level to increase the likelihood of implementation success. The emergent concept of strategy also applies due to continual efforts for emerging changes as new products/services emerge over time, local traditions are re-established, or innovations of varying types emerge (new wine products, sustainable practices, traditional or newly adapted varietal, etc.). As these new items become part of the touristic terroir, they should be integrated into the communication strategy to enhance a destinations brand and create motivation for visitors to return for "seconds."

Additionally, this emergent approach to strategy should include research to determine tourists' perceptions of the region and specific locales within a broader region to ensure new promotional ventures will be able to build on previously held perceptions. Or, as suggested in earlier research, it is important for tourism managers to ask the question – what does the brand stand for in the mind of the consumer (Kotler et al., 2006)? Further, this emergent process will create a determination of an initial fit between tourist perceptions and the bundle of touristic products and services in the wine tourism destination. This determination will provide information on communication needs for altering perceptions (if possible) and/or building on these perceptions.

Several questions surfaced from our earlier studies of Rhone-Alps and Baden Wuerttemberg (BW) that are shown in our framework's heading of emergent strategy: Network of packages or activities and quality levels/assessment. A network of packages is tied to the notion of creating a unique bundle of activities that create a tourism experience (Harrington and Ottenbacher, 2010). The network of service providers in a region (e.g., lodging, dining, leisure, theater, etc.) are the best sources of creating these emerging bundles of activities based on a growing level of trust over a period of time and partner interactions. The perception of quality can be enhanced through an emergent policy of quality designation level for a region. A good example for wine-related tourism is tying the rating the use of local products or wine quality indicators such as VQA (Vintners Quality Assurance) in Canada.

2.5.1.5   Realized Strategy

The final element shown in Fig. 2.1 is realized strategy. A conceptual definition of realized strategy is based on some combination of deliberate (planned) strategy and emergent strategy. This is the strategy or strategies that actually become realized (Mintzberg et al., 1998). To assess the realized strategy, business researchers would determine whether or not the strategy is derived from strategic ends (i.e. missions, goals, and objectives) or strategic means (i.e. strategies, policies, and action plans), an overall deliberate proportion, an overall emergent proportion and a (potentially) realized strategy ratio (Harrington et al., 2004). As demonstrated in the discussion in this chapter, deliberate and emergent elements of the wine tourism realized strategy appear to include both ends and means as well as at regional, local and firm levels.

Part of the definition of realized strategy for an implementation standpoint is the assessment of whether or not objectives (strategies) were achieved. This presents a challenge for most wine tourism initiatives. For instance, how does a region determine the impact of a wine tourism strategy given a variety of variables that complicate this assessment (variations in the economy, other tourism promotions, promotions by competing regions, etc.)? Further, just defining what and how this should be measured is a key challenge and one that demands further research.

Figure 9.1 includes a variety of key elements that could conceivably be part of any wine tourism initiative and were explicit in our study of BW and Rhone-Alps. Coming up with adequate measurement outcomes appears to be a challenge based on conversations the authors had with regional leaders. As researchers in this area, future research into measurement methods used in related tourism studies could prove useful as a contribution to the literature as well as to regional leaders embarking on a wine tourism effort. Related studies that could prove useful are leisure studies, cultural tourism, agricultural tourism, rural tourism, etc.

Other measurement issues that should be considered in this process include using a balanced scorecard approach (including quantitative and qualitative elements), defining and implementing quality standards for a region, assessing the impact of initiatives on innovative behavior and the economic impact that assists in promoting rural sustainability. From the customer perspective, measurement should include visitor satisfaction and retention (do they return for 'seconds'?), positive perceptions of the wine products/services, and brand equity perceptions for the region or sub-region.

2.5.2 STRATEGY IMPLEMENTATION: MIDDLE-UP-DOWN IMPLICATIONS

Any discussion on the strategy-making process or strategy implementation would not be complete without consideration of leadership aspects or who is involved (Harrington, 2005). The notion of top-down and bottom-up management styles is pervasive in management research and the popular press. Implicit in the idea of a top-down or bottom-up approach to leadership is the concept of both the type and level of involvement across the organization in the management process. In addition to these two generic approaches, authors have indicated the value of involvement by middle management, franchisees or multi-unit managers in the strategy implementation process. This management approach has been coined "middle-up-down." Basically, the middle-up-down concept is linked to an improved ability to process information and speed the ability to adapt to environmental change. In this approach, the vital role of middle management as a synthesizer of information up, down and across the organization is theorized (Harrington and Kendall, 2006; Nonaka, 1998).

While the concepts of top-down, bottom-up and middle-up-down strategy implementation approaches are implicit in the network and tourism literature, this chapter supports the importance of the middle-up-down communication process for successful implementation of a destination initiative, particularly, when the initiatives involve local and culturally derived activities (as is the case for wine tourism initiatives).

For instance in the BW and Rhone-Alps examples, the role of middle-up-down communication efforts during implementation of the wine tourism initiative is crucial at local and regional levels. The middle-up-down approach can be useful in communicating up the communication chain to tourism ministries to express concerns for infrastructure limitations (e.g., public transportation, education initiatives, needed supporting materials, etc.) as well as to provide on-going communication of additional products or services that create promotional opportunities in specific locations (e.g., itineraries, packages, new activities, etc.). While middle management takes on this role in organizations, the key middle role in the implementation of regional tourism initiatives may include the role of academic members in this field, industry members, association leaders and governmental leaders at more local levels. Many times this middle level becomes a "champion" of the initiative and can assist in communicating the value of the promotion up, down and across the network of stakeholders as well. Because of the diversity in types of businesses that provide the bundle of services and activities that motivate wine tourism (e.g., wine, food, lodging, leisure, attractions, sports and retail), these middle level champions are critical for creating on-going cooperative networks. As earlier studies have indicated, tourism destinations are complex to manage and control due to the numerous components, stakeholders, organizations, governmental agencies and suppliers that come together to deliver the destination product (Fyall and

Leask, 2007; Fyall et al., 2006); thus, effective leadership at multiple levels is very critical. This need is implicit in our model as a key element to successfully manage the strategy-making process of regional wine tourism initiatives.

In the BW example, most interviewed tourism experts agreed on the importance of effective leadership in tourism but at the same time indicated a lack of strong leadership and cooperation among politicians, tourism people, wineries, agricultural producers, chefs, restaurants, hotels and investors in BW tourism. Successfully managing tourism destinations also includes the openness and willingness to enter into strategic relationships with industry partners or even competitors who can together offer a flawless and outstanding experience for the guest (Fyall et al., 2006). As a result, stakeholders in wine tourism have to look for opportunities for stronger collaboration.

2.6 CONCLUSIONS

The objective of this chapter was to utilize recent destination initiatives that highlight wine-related tourism to determine important and successful elements of implementation, how the conceptual notions of deliberate or emergent strategy process applies to wine tourism, and challenges in wine tourism execution.

Based on recent qualitative studies in Germany and France, six key strategic process elements emerged that were closely associated with wine tourism strategy success: (i) the strategy itself, (ii) cooperation among stakeholders, (iii) leadership issues, (iv) region promotion, (v) regional products/services, (vi) and quality standards. A challenge in assessing success is the lack of measurement tools available to the tourism leadership and the researchers. It is difficult to objectively measure the success of the tourism initiative as a whole (Ottenbacher and Harrington, 2013).

These cases provide some interesting findings tied to the notion of a deliberate vs. emergent strategic process and how these theoretical concepts are applied to a wine tourism situation. As shown in Fig. 2.1, the development and implementation of this regionally driven process provides support for both deliberate and intended strategy as well as for a use of emergent strategic approaches. Following the earlier model of the strategic process described by Mintzberg et al. (1998), we have created a revised version adapted to a wine tourism strategy scenario.

Deliberate and intended strategy seems critical in (i) formulating the wine tourism campaign, (ii) defining a clear strategy based on market, fit and social processes, (iii) facilitating efforts to achieve cooperation with stakeholders, (iv) expressing political support and leadership, (v) developing infrastructure, (vi) communicating what differentiates the region (inter-region and intra-region), (vii) tying the initiative with other quality activities, and (viii) communicating a core profile or identity.

The emergent strategy concepts seem to develop from the organizational level, resulting in the emergent of new wine products and services as well as cooperative efforts from local stakeholders. The resultant strategy appears more tactical in nature and includes: (i) activity packages from local networks, (ii) emerging champions at a variety of levels across the region, (iii) greater authenticity (emerging stories, history, etc.), (iv) new products or services, (v) re-establishment of local traditions as they become more economically viable, (vi) incremental and new-to-the-world innovations, (vii) sustainable methods (green practices, rural sustainability, cultural sustainability, etc.), and (viii) local establishment of quality levels.

An element that emerged from this chapter that is conspicuously absent from many concepts of the strategic process (e.g., Mintzberg et al., 1998) is consideration of a middle-up-down approach and the important role of middle level champions for regional promotion. This middle-up-down strategy tactic appears to create a positive flow of ideas and communication up, down and across a network of regional stakeholders.

A key challenge acknowledged in this chapter is the issue of measuring outcomes associated with a wine tourism initiative. This presents an important challenge for regional tourism entities but provides an important area for future research and potential contribution to the wine tourism literature. An effective measure of outcomes should use a balanced scorecard-type approach to assess economic impacts as well as other more qualitative impacts (visitor satisfaction, intent to return, cultural sustainability, innovative behaviors, etc.).

2.6.1 FUTURE RESEARCH

Future research should address in greater detail the relationship between deliberate and emergent approaches to strategy making in a wine tourism context. This research area is important to determine the "best" approach for successful wine tourism strategy-making and how or whether strategic leaders predominately use a design approach to strategic initiatives or learn-by-doing process that is more grassroots-oriented?

For a researcher to assess this concept, a measure of the deliberate aspects or emergent aspects alone does not determine whether or not the realized strategies are predominately deliberate or emergent. The model (Fig. 2.1) and arguments by Mintzberg et al. (1998) suggest that the amount of realized strategy is a ratio between deliberate strategy and emergent strategy. Deliberate strategies represent intentions in advance and emergent strategies represent alterations or additions to previous intentions. For a clearer sense of this process in a wine tourism context, this relationship can be portrayed in a number of ways. First, some sort of difference score could be calculated between the deliberate elements and the emergent elements in the strategic process (Deliberate value – Emergent value). This provides a clear indication whether the strategy-making process is predominately deliberate or emergent based on the mathematical sign. The difference score's main weakness is that it does not indicate the magnitude in their difference. For example, if region A has a deliberate value of 2 and an emergent value of 1, the difference is a positive $1(2-1 = +1)$. If region B has a deliberate score of 4 and an emergent score of 3, the difference is again positive $1 (4-3 = +1)$. While conceptually, the realized values are significantly different in terms of the extent of deliberate or emergent impacts in this example – mathematically the values are exactly equivalent.

Therefore, a ratio representing the realized value would provide researchers with a better representation of whether a strategic process is predominately deliberate or emergent. A ratio calculation method could be utilized to account for differences in the deliberate/emergent nature of the strategic process, the extent of these impacts, and to address mathematical inconsistencies. A specific conceptualization of the realized ratio could be devised as:

$$D{-}E/D{+}E = R$$

where, D is the notation for deliberate strategies, E is the notation for emergent strategies, and R is the notation for realized strategies in ratio form.

Therefore, the value for realized strategy can range from $+1$ to -1 with positive one representing a purely deliberate process and negative one representing a purely emergent process. No study to date has satisfactorily assessed both sides of the deliberate/emergent equation. This equation is grounded in the deliberate and emergent approach following existing theory and definition of the construct by Mintzberg and colleagues (Mintzberg et al., 1998; Mintzberg and McHugh, 1985; Mintzberg and Waters, 1985). The majority of studies on strategic management in general have focused on measuring deliberate strategies exclusively; this may be a necessary but not sufficient requirement in this area of study. Future research is also required to fully extract a more exact relationship between deliberate and emergent values used by regions in wine tourism initiatives.

KEYWORDS

- **deliberate strategies**
- **planning school**
- **touristic terroir**
- **wine tourism**

REFERENCES

1. Alant, K., Bower, J. (2004). Wine tourism behavior in the context of a motivational framework for wine regions and cellar doors. *Journal of Wine Research*, 15(1), 27–37.
2. Alonso, A. D., Bressan, A., O'Shea, M., Krajsic, V. (2013). Perceived benefits and challenges to wine tourism involvement: An international perspective. *International Journal of Tourism Research*, DOI: 10.1002/jtr.1967.
3. Beer, C., Ottenbacher, M. C., Harrington, R. J. (2012). Food tourism implementation in the Black Forest destination. *Journal of Culinary Science & Technology*, 10(2), 106–108.

4. Boyd, B. K. (1991). Strategic planning and financial performance: A meta-analytic review. *Journal of Management Studies*, 28(4), 353–374.
5. Boyne, S., Hall, D., Williams, F. (2003). Policy, support and promotion for food-related tourism initiatives: A marketing approach to regional development. *Journal of Travel & Tourism Marketing,* 14(3), 131–154.
6. Brews, P. J., Hunt, M. R. (1999). Learning to plan and planning to learn: Resolving the planning school/learning school debate. *Strategic Management Journal*, 20(10), 889–913.
7. Bryson, J. M., Bromiley, P. (1993). Critical factors affecting the planning and implementation of major products. *Strategic Management Journal*, 14, 319–337.
8. Cambourne, B., Macionis, N. (2003). Linking food, wine and tourism: The case of the Australian capital region. In C. M. Hall, L. Sharples, R. Mitchell, N. Macionis and B. Cambourne (Eds.), *Food tourism around the world* (pp. 268–284). Oxford, UK: Elsevier Butterworth-Heinemann.
9. Canadian Tourism Commission. (2003). *How-to guide: Develop a culinary tourism product.* URL (consulted, February 14, 2008): http://www.canadatourism.com/ctx/files/publication/data/en_ca/product_development/culinary_tourism_product_development_guide/howtoguide-cuisine.pdf.
10. Charters, S., Ali-Knight, J. (2002), "Who is the Wine Tourist? *Tourism Management*, 23(3), 311–319.
11. Correia, A., Oom do Valle, P., Moço, C. (2007). Why people travel to exotic places. *International Journal of Culture, Tourism and Hospitality Research*, 1(1), 45–61.
12. Correia, L., Passos, A. M. J., Charters, S. (2004). Wine routes in Portugal: A case study of the Bairrada wine route. *Journal of Wine Research*, 15(1), 15–25.
13. Eisenhardt, K. M. (1989). Making fast strategic decisions in high-velocity environments. *Academy of Management Journal*, 32, 543–576.
14. Famularo, B., Bruwer, J., Li, E. (2010). Region of origin as choice factor: Wine knowledge and wine tourism involvement influence. *International Journal of Wine Business Research*, 22(40), 362–385.
15. Faugère, C., Bouzdine-Chameeva, T., Pesme, J-O, and Durrieu, F. (2013). The Impact of tourism strategies and regional factors on wine tourism performance: Bordeaux vs. Mendoza, Mainz, Florence, Porto, and Cape Town (January 16, 2013). Available at http://ssrn.com/abstract=2201563
16. Foley, A., Fahy, J. (2004). Incongruity between expression and experience: The role of imagery in supporting the positioning of a tourism destination brand. *Journal of Brand Management*, 11(3), 89–100.
17. Fyall, A., Garrod, B., Tosun, C. (2006). Destination marketing: A framework for future research. In M. Kozak and L. Andreu (Eds.), *Advances in tourism research: Progress in tourism marketing* (pp. 75–86). Oxford: Elsevier.
18. Fyall, A., Leak, A. (2007). Destination marketing: Future issues – strategic challenges. *Tourism and Hospitality Research*, 7(1), 50–63.
19. Getz, D., Brown, G. (2006). Critical success factors for wine tourism regions: A demand analysis. *Tourism Management*, 27(1), 146–158.
20. Gross, M. J., Brien, C., Brown, G. (2008). Examining the dimensions of a lifestyle tourism destination. *International Journal of Culture, Tourism and Hospitality Research*, 2(1), 44–66.

Wine Tourism Strategy Making: A Model for Planning and Implementation   29

21. Hall, C. M., Macionis, N. (1998). Wine tourism in Australia and New Zealand. In R. W. Butlerl, C. M. Hall, and J. Jenkins (Eds.), *Tourism and recreation in rural areas* (pp. 197–224). New York: John Wiley & Sons.
22. Hall, C. M., Sharples, L. (2003). The consumption of experiences or the experience of consumption? An introduction to the tourism of taste. In C. M. Hall, L. Sharples, R. Mitchell, N. Macionis and B. Cambourne (Eds.), *Food tourism around the world* (pp. 1–25). Oxford: Elsevier Butterworth-Heinemann.
23. Hall, C. M., Mitchell, R. (2002). The touristic teiror of New Zealand wine: The importance of region in the wine tourism experience. In Montanari, A. (Ed.), *Food and environment: Geographies of taste* (pp. 69–91). Rome: Societa Geografica Italiana.
24. Hall, C. M., Mitchell, R. (2005). Gastronomic tourism: Comparing food and wine tourism experiences. In M. Novelli (Ed.), *Niche tourism: Contemporary issues, trends and cases* (pp. 73–88). Oxford: Butterworth.
25. Harrington, R. J. (2005). The how and who of strategy-making: Models and appropriateness for firms in hospitality and tourism industries. *Journal of Hospitality & Tourism Research*, 29(3), 372–395.
26. Harrington, R. J. (2008). *Food and wine pairing: A sensory experience.* John Wiley & Sons.
27. Harrington, R. J., Kendall, K. W. (2006). Middle-up-down and top-down approaches: Strategy implementation, uncertainty, structure, and foodservice segment. *Tourism: The International Interdisciplinary Journal*, 54(4), 385–395.
28. Harrington, R. J., Ottenbacher, M. C. (2009). Decision-making tactics and contextual features: Strategic, tactical and operational implications. *International Journal of Hospitality and Tourism Administration*, 10(1), 25–43.
29. Harrington, R. J., Ottenbacher, M. C. (2010). Culinary Tourism – A Case Study of the Gastronomic Capital. *Journal of Culinary Science and Technology,* 8(1), 14–32.
30. Harrington, R. J., Lemak, D., Reed, R., Kendall, K. W. (2004). A question of fit: The links among environment, strategy formulation and performance. *Journal of Business and Management,* 10(1), 15–38.
31. Hart, S. L., Banbury C. (1994). How strategy-making processes can make a difference. *Strategic Management Journal*, 15(4), 251–269.
32. Hitt, M., Ireland, D. (1985). Corporate distinctive competence, strategy, industry and performance. *Strategic Management Journal*, 6 (3), 273–293.
33. Kivela, J., Crotts, J. (2006). Tourism and gastronomy: Gastronomy's influence in how tourists experience a destination. *Journal of Hospitality & Tourism Research*, 30(3), 354–377.
34. Kotler, P., Bowen, J., Makens, J. (2006). *Marketing for hospitality and tourism* (4th ed). Upper Saddle River: Pearson Education.
35. Leahy, K. (2007). Tapping the culinary-tourism trend. *Restaurants & Institutions*, URL (consulted November 5, 2008): www.rimag.com/article/CA6521601.html. Long, L. M. (2004). *Culinary tourism.* Lexington, Kentucky: University of Kentucky Press.
36. McWilliams, A., Smart, D. (1993). Efficiency v. structure-conduct-performance: Implications for strategy research and practice. *Journal of Management*, 19(1), 63–78.
37. Mintzberg, H., Ahlstrand, B., and Lampel, J. (1998). *Strategic safari.* New York: The Free Press.

38. Mintzberg, H., McHugh, A. (1985). Strategy formulation in an adhocracy. *Administrative Science Quarterly*, 30,160–197.
39. Mintzberg, H., Waters J. A. (1985). Of strategies, deliberate and emergent. *Strategic Management Journal*, 6, 257–272.
40. Mitchell, R., Charters, S., Albrecht, J. N. (2012). Cultrual systems and the wine tourism product. *Annals of Tourism Research*, 39(1), 311–335.
41. Nonaka, I. (1988). Toward middle-up-down management: Accelerating information creation. *Sloan Management Review*, 29, 9–18.
42. Ontario. (2008). Wine and culinary tourism in Ontario. URL (consulted December 13, 2008): http://winesofontario.org/PDFs/ExecutiveSummary.pdf
43. Ottenbacher, M. C., Harrington, R. J. (2013). A case study of culinary tourism campaign in Germany: Implications for strategy-making and implementation. *Journal of Hospitality & Tourism Research*, 37(1), 3–28.
44. Ottenbacher, M., Harrington, R. J. (2007). The innovation development process of Michelin-starred chefs. *International Journal of Contemporary Hospitality Management*, 19(6), 444–460.

CHAPTER 3

STRATEGIC WINERY MANAGEMENT AND TOURISM: VALUE-ADDED OFFERINGS AND STRATEGIES BEYOND PRODUCT CENTRISM

DR. MARC DREßLER

Professor, Hochschule Ludwigshafen, BWL und Entrepreneurship, Studiengang Weinbau and Oenologie Breitenweg 71, Germany

CONTENTS

Abstract 31
3.1   Introduction 32
3.2   The German Wine Market Context 34
3.3   Literature Review on the Value of Wine and Tourism 40
3.4   Strategic Positioning of German Wineries 48
3.5   Strategic Tourism Clusters of German Wineries 56
3.6   Summary and Outlook 60
Keywords 62
References 62

ABSTRACT

This chapter explores wine and tourism from a managerial and strategic perspective of the wineries. Despite a lot of recent literature there is a lack of empirical data of the wineries' strategic behavior and the role of tourism in their strategic grouping. Wineries' active engagement in tourism should be strategically motivated and not only rest upon free-ridership. Hence, the questions of the impact of tourism for the wineries, whether they should all engage more intensively, whether tourism represents a strategic lever, and which tourism activities and with what intensity fit which strategic orientation still need to be addressed. A panel on German wineries' strategic grouping and innovation measures provides empirical insights of winery management and value-added offerings in the context of wine and tourism.

3.1 INTRODUCTION

Wine and tourism experiences high attention in academia and literature. Practical development and exploitation of according synergetic potentials in Europe is stated to be mainly driven by authorities or wine producers seizing opportunities when sales are lagging (Menival and Han, 2013). Although wine region profiling and marketing efforts for regional wine and tourism are declared to be key success factor for the wineries only recently research on "value of wine tourism" explores the strategic perspectives of the wineries (Charters and Menival, 2011). Activities to market regional and destination values are strongly increasing. Cluster theory supports such approaches and explains the value-creation potential for the involved organizations (Hira et al., 2013, Charters et al., 2011, Porter, 2000). Meanwhile efficiency and effectiveness of cooperative efforts is not to be put into question the individual strategic motivation of participants might differ and the unanimously expressed claim that wine producers should support or even drive such activities might not reflect their individual benefit or wineries' rewards such as increased profitability. This chapter evaluates wine and tourism from a strategic perspective of the wine suppliers exploiting empirical data. So far, empirical approaches were restricted on best practice examples of wineries realizing new winery design, touristic attractions, integrated regional tourism efforts of wine and tourism. The success or financial reward of such entrepreneurial initiatives is less analyzed or challenged (Charters and Menival, 2011). Work on strategic profiling or strategic grouping of wineries with a touristic focus is still scarce (Faugère et al., 2013).

Empirical evidence needs to back or even substitute general recommendations (Capitello et al., 2013). Therefore, this article exploits a strategy and innovation panel that explored the value-propositions, strategies, and offers of German wineries also considering the impact and outcome of the pursued business strategies. Tourism was not in the focus of the panel but the data allows to derive insights into their strategic tourism behavior.

Indeed, more business knowledge is needed. Creative approaches or offers on the basis of tourism of one winery might not work for others, some examples of wine tourism highly praised by the community might not even be profitable. Causal relationships and strategic measures need to be evaluated in more depth and arguments for more cooperation as well as activity of the wineries to develop wine tourism might foster the success of regional concerted efforts (Menival and Han, 2013). Wineries actively offering touristic attraction should be strategically motivated to increase destination attractiveness (Dreyer et al., 2011a).

Germany as market of analysis apparently fits nicely for the analytical purpose. The German wine market appears to be highly attractive for wine suppliers due to a stable consumption on a high level meanwhile other wine drinking western European countries are characterized by diminishing wine consumption. In fact, although wine substitutes other alcoholic beverages in Germany and being the world championship in sparkling wine consumption, it is a very demanding market for the producers and suppliers (Hoffman, 2010, DWI, 2013, DWI, 2012). Fierce internal competition, dominating competitive imports, changing consumers with a transition from traditional to modern values impacting consumption and buying behavior, and a dynamic market environment push a lot of players to market exit (Schallenberger, 2009). Meanwhile the remaining ones increase in professionalism they still struggle to gain sustainable competitiveness and profitability (Oberhofer, 2011, Mend, 2009b, Mend, 2009a).

Independent vintners, cooperatives, and large wineries serve the customers and their needs with a rich world of products and offers with a great mix of tradition and creativity providing convenience or experience. To tackle that market with a vivid and complex environment requires strategic positioning of the producers and distributors. Strategic offer design seems to be of paramount importance to avoid being forced out of the market as a lot of players are resulting in massive structural changes (Dressler, 2013d). A grip on the customer, direct sales, and brand creation are important levers for the wineries to succeed (Dressler, 2012b). Service extension and especially the exploitation of tourism based market opportunities allow to intensify customer contact, to realize additional sources of income, and to increase direct sales and hence represent strategic levers to outperform competition (Faugère et al., 2013). Today's winning business models might profit of innovation, stronger integration of clients in the world of production, and enrichment of the clients. Transparency on wineries' strategies to exploit tourism opportunities and results impact of such activities might motivate the wineries to increase activity level and therefore render cooperative and cluster initiatives of wine and tourism more efficient and successful.

In the context of this book we assess environmental perception of the paneled wineries, strategic positioning, strategic measures, and innovative offer design of German wineries. Can value-added services and a symbiotic approach to wine and tourism provide competitive advantage and which wineries should approach what strategies with what profit impact? To answer the question empirical research on value-added strategies and leveraging tourism and hospitality opportunities for wineries is exploited.

In the following, an overview of the German wine market to explain market dynamics and resulting challenges and business model impact on wineries will be provided. We then explore the themes of wine, tourism, and innovation to lay the foundation for the following strategic analysis. The core of this article consists of an assessment of strategies of German wineries in regards to value-added services or offerings with focus on wine and tourism. We draw a map of strategic interest in wine and tourism of the wineries that allows to explain a potential lack of success of regional efforts and that might motivate wineries to exploit strategic profiling opportunities and market niches to enhance their competitive positioning and results delivery by adding tourism based offer components.

3.2 THE GERMAN WINE MARKET CONTEXT

Germans drink more than 20 million hectoliters of wine (DWI, 2013). Germany ranks number 4 among the countries in total wine consumption in the world but to satisfy the wine thirst it is world leader in wine imports.

Strategic Winery Management and Tourism: Value-Added Offerings 35

More than half of the wine consumed in Germany is imported (Hoffmann, 2010; Pilz, 2012). There is a great diversity of wine consumption patterns and occasions in Germany, from home consumption to private events to restaurant wining to public events with wine being served and consumed (Schipperges, 2013). To understand the synergies and interrelations of wine and tourism as well as actual or potential offerings of the wineries the supply and demand sides of the German market and the wine tourism market in Germany are described in more detail.

3.2.1 CHARACTERISTICS OF GERMAN WINE PRODUCTION AND SUPPLY

With a constant grapevine area of about 100.000 hectares Germany yields 8 to 11 million hectoliters of wine annually. Hence, Germany ranks at the end of the 15 leading grapevine countries and number ten in volume of wine produced. Thirteen regions in Germany are not only producing wine with regional vine portfolios, wine styles, and consumption patterns, they are also characterized by strong regional pride and assertiveness (Hoffman and Szolnoki, 2011). Wine production has a positive impact on landscape and touristic offers (Bruwer and Alant, 2009).

Production of wine shows high fragmentation with three different clusters of suppliers. There is a strong population of small viticulturists that either produce and market individually or join forces in cooperatives. Additionally, few large wineries produce wine out of home grown or imported bulk ware. The market supply is roughly split into tiers – one-third by individual viticulturists, one via cooperatives and one by the large wineries. In the last 30 years, the number of wine growers generating their income with wine halved (BMELV, 2011). As planted vineyards remain stable and the number of producers decreases the average size of the producers increases. Today, almost 50.000 wine growers are active with about 40% of them stating wine to be their main source of income (DWI, 2013). Despite a continuing small average size of the wineries they are generally highly integrated – from growing to harvesting to producing to sales and marketing. The average profitability of the producers in the German market is low (Oberhofer, 2011; Mend, 2009a; Oberhofer, 2012).

Indirect sales channels such as supermarkets or discounters are efficiently building bridges from producers to the customers. Although wine represents a minor segment of their revenues, making up for only 2–3% of their sales (Nielsen, 2012), the category is frequently used for positioning as well as to attract customers (Engelhard, 2011b; Markgraf, 2012). Offer variety and scope is impressive, one channel partner reporting a wine portfolio of more than 1.000 different wines. Those channels jointly with imported products are declared to be the main reason for overall low prices for wines in Germany since discounters in average sell wine for about 2.50 € per liter. An international comparison supports the notion of low wine price levels in Germany reporting an average grocery retail bottle sales price in Germany of 3.32 € compared to 6.36 $ in the US and 4.02 GBP in the UK (Rabobank, 2012). About 56% of German consumers react on price increases by substituting either the product or the supplier whereas the global average is less than 40% with such a reaction. For the United Kingdom or USA only 35% of the consumers pronounce such a switching reaction (OC&C, 2012). Consumers' price sensitivity as well as fierce competition characterize the German wine market and allow the discount markets to grow their market share.

When segmenting wine sales by price levels the "mass buy" segment with buying-decision dominated by price and therefore low prices makes up for $3/4^{th}$ of the market in volume. Supermarkets and discount chains dominate that market. Indeed, one discount market chain owns a market share of more than 27% (Engelhard, 2011b; Engelhard, 2011c; Engelhard, 2011a). Still, $1/4^{th}$ of the German wine market belongs to the "value buy" segment characterized by wine centric shopping with customers searching for an emotional buying experience. The sales channels for the value buy segment are primarily direct sales of the wineries and specialized wine stores. Jointly they combine almost 50% of the wine sales by value (DWI, 2012). Direct sales have a strong tradition and are important for the independent German wineries, allowing for higher prices and direct contact to the customers (Schallenberger, 2009). But this sales channel is characterized by decreasing loyalty of German customers and lowering of the average sales volume. Not only direct sales but also a mix of sales and on-premises consumption characterizes the offers of a lot of German producers. Offering wine and food, historically often restricted for a limited period of time, have become a regional gastronomic component of wine regions (depending on the region they are called Besenwirtschaft, Straußwirtschaft, Heckenwirtschaft etc.) (Dreyer et al., 2011a). Additionally, wine festivals and local events provide the opportunity for producers to interact with the customers to increase loyalty and retention and to acquire new customers. All these activities and offerings relate to synergetic worlds of wine and tourism (Mason and Piaggiaro, 2012).

Indeed, on premises consumption is highly relevant for the German wine market. Wine leverages gastronomic revenues, allows to win new customers, increase loyalty and margin for on-premise locations. Price calculation depends on the restaurant type and the underlying market positioning and strategy. Frequently, wine subsidizes food sales. A multiple of 3.8 to 4.5 on purchase prices is applied for wine compared to 3.3 to 3.7 for food (Ernest-Hahn, 2005). For on-premise channels imported wine is important. More than 50% of the on-premise wine sales originate from foreign countries. Surely, in case of specialization on food of other countries such as Italian, French or Austrian restaurants an according wine offer is expected. High-end restaurants are expected to serve nationally and internationally recognized wines, especially icon wines from French regions Bordeaux or Burgundy or from Italy. The more restaurants offer regional food and are located in wine regions the more their wine portfolio consists of German and local products.

German wineries hence experience increased competition from different suppliers and channels resulting in decreasing customer loyalty. Service offerings and winning new customer access by profiling as well as fostering direct sales is the key to win in the value segment, targeted by the wineries. Tourism certainly can provide possible customer inflow.

3.2.2 WINE CONSUMPTION IN GERMANY

German households spend about 14% of their income on food and beverages (DBV, 2012). Alcoholic drinks' "share of mouth" in beverages is about 20% (Nielsen, 2012; DWI, 2012 Although generally characterized as a beer drinking society, wine substitutes beer given a stable wine consumption but a decrease in alcoholic beverages and beer (Aizenman and

Brooks, 2008; DWI, 2013). While wine makes up for only 17% of the alcoholic consumption in volume, it exceeds 40% in value (DWI, 2011; Freter, 2008). Germans hence consume more than 8% of the global wine production. In many western societies, wine is declared as more cultural and stylish alcohol consumption (Haupt, 2010). The average annual per capita consumption in Germany equals 24 liters of wine, only half of per capita consumption of France, the global leader in per capita wine consumption. But meanwhile wine consumption in France decreases, in Germany it grows. In 1970, the German average consumption was only 17 liters of wine (Frank, 2010; OIV, 2012). Furthermore, Germany has the pole position in the market segment of sparkling wine as more than 20% of the global production is consumed in Germany. (Markgraf, 2012)

Personal preferences in a heterogeneous and prosperous society with a liberalized market and personal freedom in regards to choices, consumption, and lifestyle result in varying demand. Furthermore, as described for the supply perspective, consumption shows regional characteristics. Wine drinkers in the south or west of Germany are characterized by above average interest in wine, in North-Rhine Westphalia and Bavaria consumers rely more on specialized wine stores and in the south consumers are aiming for more variety (Hoffman and Szolnoki, 2011). Meanwhile the wine drinking population in Baden as well as Württemberg consumes by far more than average they also prefer German wines. Eastern parts of Germany and Berlin drink less wine with a interest for foreign products (DWI, 2012). German wine consumers show interest in the country or region of origin, in according wine landscapes, and in people and cultures that are behind the product in the bottle or the glass.

Emotions and gained impressions of wineries, winemakers, or regional characteristics influence the consumers in the buying decision and allow to ask for higher prices (Schipperges, 2013). Looking at customer segments to explore wine tourism there are numerous possibilities to cluster the consumers and their wine buying and consumption behavior. Income, education, styles and preferences, region, age, consumption intensity, behavior, involvement etc. are used to determine clusters (Riviezzo et al., 2011; Arnold and Fleuchaus, 2010). Demographical factors as basic segmentation criteria proof high explanatory power also for the wine business (Brunner, 2011). For wine, situational segmentation proofs to be valuable, since drinking occasions influence the buying decision and behavior. Buying wine as a present or ordering it in a restaurant are characterized by different decision making compared to solitary home consumption (Olsen and Newton, 2011; Corsi et al., 2011). An empirical study results in six German wine consumers segments that also allow to evaluate wine tourism segments and characteristics. Meanwhile, three segments "discount customers," "food retailer customers," and "supermarket customers" belong to an aggregated group with preference for basic wines, the three segments "direct customers," "wine store customers," and "variety seekers" prefer premium wines and search for experience not only convenience. The cluster criteria are sales channels, competence in and curiosity about wine, price sensitivity and price levels, wine style, product origin, and age. Premium wine oriented segments show a more sophisticated approach to wine and spend more on wine (Hoffman and Szolnoki, 2012; Hoffman and Szolnoki, 2011). Indeed, producers highly appreciate the segment "direct customers" since they pay higher prices with lower costs of distribution (Thach, 2007). This segment seems to currently be the prime target for wine tourism offers of German wineries. But there is a risk of a dying population since the average age for the segment "direct customers" is almost 60 years with conservative values. Suppliers with strong penetration of that segment in their customer portfolio need to take strategic measures to secure future market success.

Furthermore, the societal change matters. The segments characterized by modern norms and values are growing (DWI, 2003). Wineries will profit of an overall growing interest in wine but need to accept and prepare for the changing environment, although it is difficult to forecast (Brunner, 2011) as, for example, wine consumers increase channel diversity and interest in imported wines. Overall, quality products with attractive offerings and entrepreneurial and brand efforts are imperative and tourism will feed new and very attractive customers to the wineries. A change in offers, access, and in paradigm – more active involvement of the clients and sales orientation – allows to further penetrate the existing customer base, to win new customers, and to profit of the trend that consumers want to be integrated and active (Dressler, 2012b; Brunner, 2011; Kotler, 1986; Grün and Brunner, 2002; Holbrook and

Hirschman, 1982; Bloemer and Ruyter, 1999). For direct sales, the buying decision is impacted by the taste of the products and brand orientation, mostly created by the winery owner and his storylining around the product and the offer (Dressler, 2013a). Buying experience is therefore important and tourism activities are pivotal (Schipperges, 2013). Indeed, the willingness to pay a premium also positively influences the satisfaction since consumers connote higher quality in case of more expensive wines (Szolnoki et al., 2009) but the wineries need to create brand value by positioning in the competitive market with an attractive offer design and delivery.

Ecological and sustainable behavior also impacts the wine market (Römmelt, 2012). Organic and ecologically produced wine gains in market share, although penetration is less than in food. Even more important is the trend to buy regional products (Nestlé, 2011). It reduces logistical efforts and has a positive impact on sustainability. As in other countries sustainability, ecological or biodynamic production serves in communication and profiling of the producers.

Overall, Germany is one of the most liberal markets with global supply, intense internal rivalry, changes of consumer behaviors and preferences (Gilinsky et al., 2008; Hoffmann, 2005). A challenging yet rewarding market for suppliers. Direct consumer access remains a key success factor for the independent wineries and cooperatives serving that segment and therefore tourism should be regarded as crucial, even if only parts of the producing and supplying population are strongly relying on that market approach today and in the future.

3.3 LITERATURE REVIEW ON THE VALUE OF WINE AND TOURISM

The following literature review on the value of wine and tourism firstly extracts the research approaches and results from a global perspective. A part focusing on the German market wine and tourism activities supports that such activities are declared to create value for the economy as well. Additionally, the question of symbiotic value creation of wine and tourism in the context of innovation is explored.

3.3.1 RESEARCH APPROACHES AND ASSESSMENT OF VALUE CREATION POTENTIAL

When analyzing the published research on wine and tourism three distinct research approaches can be identified. The subject matter has been analyzed either in the context of destination management and therefore guiding marketing of regions and their touristic offerings, or with a research focus on consumer behavior, or from a management perspective of the wine producers and sellers – hereby called the "strategic winery management perspective" not restricting on any supplier organization type (see Fig. 3.1). Each perspective and the derived insights deliver additional insights for the efficient and effective exploitation of wine and tourism opportunities as will be described in the following.

Wine and tourism has strongly been researched from a travel and tourism perspective creating enormous value for destination management (Dreyer et al., 2011a). Indeed, regional attractiveness on the basis of a wine industry and its economic value creation of and for regions – the core of that field of research – experiences increasing attention. The gained knowledge results in constantly increasing and more professional marketing activities to position geographic regions and tourist destinations. Wine and tourism is identified to be a great opportunity to differentiate and to win an attractive touristic customer

FIGURE 3.1 Identified research approaches for wine and tourism.

base for a region. The increased tourism creates significant positive economic results for the region and its organizations (Getz and Brown, 2006). Destination management has initially been the driver for research on wine and tourism and attracted most research interest in the subject matter (Getz et al., 1999; Thach, 2007; Skinner, 2000; Nohl, 2001; Getz and Brown, 2006; Fäßler, 2008; Bruwer and Alant, 2009; Charters et al., 2011; Dreyer et al., 2011b; Kagermeier, 2011; Bruwer et al., 2013). Additionally, research guided by the cluster theory contributes to that body of knowledge as will be explained when approaching wine and tourism from an innovation perspective (see Section 3.3.3). The new world and especially Australia explain their global wine market success by the concerted efforts and integrated activities to exploit wine and tourism (Anderson, 2010; Aylward, 2004; Aylward, 2006; Cusmano et al., 2010; Dana and Winstone, 2008; Getz and Brown, 2006).

To better understand the motivation and decisions of the specific potential customer base that is targeted by destination management, research focused then on consumers, customer behavior, and decision making. The resulting work has added great value to the wine and tourism literature providing insights to the complex decision making processes and providing more transparency on customer behavior (Brunner, 2011; Charters and Menival, 2011; Orth et al., 2011; Getz and Brown, 2006; Mason and Piaggiaro, 2012; Menival and Han, 2013; Charters and Ali-Knight, 2002; Capitello et al., 2013). Understanding the wine tourist, the decision making process for destinations, interest for attractions, buying behavior in regards to wine, underlying preferences, buys and satisfaction, helps to form the offers from a regional but also from a winery perspective.

The third approach assesses wine and tourism from a strategic winery management perspective. This research approach has apparently experienced by far less attention in the literature (O'Neill et al., 2002; Charters and Menival, 2011; Hall and Mitchell, 2010). Despite the economic value created of synergetic wine and tourism activities as stated by the body of destination management literature and gained transparency in regards to the client the research identifies that wineries might not fully exploit the market potentials. Explicitly for European wineries a skepticism to whether they individually profit of tourism activities is stated. A more tactic approach towards tourism only engaging actively when local sales or export are lagging is observed (Charters and Menival, 2011). Meanwhile regional authorities push wine and tourism activities the wineries might be reluctant and only engaged or motivated to push tourism based activities in case of sales crisis (Menival and Han, 2013). Premium wineries are reported to even fear that active engagement in regional tourism might damage their premium and brand strategy (Choisy, 1996; Menival and Han, 2013; Charters and Menival, 2011).

The stated reluctance of European wineries to strongly commit or even position on tourism activities despite regional efforts or authorities engaging and asking for joint efforts finds further support when analyzing joint marketing efforts – not only in the context of wine and tourism. Although empirical studies provide evidence of increased efficiency and effectiveness in case of joint marketing (Hanagriff et al., 2009; Anderson, 2010; Hanagriff and Lau, 2009; Blisard, 1997; Shamsuddoha and Ali, 2006; Alston and Freebairn, 2001; Brester and Schroeder, 1995; Kaiser et al., 1992; Kaiser Harry M. et al., 2003; Kaiser Harry M. and Yuqing, 2009; Jordan et al., 2006; Govindasamy et al., 1998; Govindasamy et al., 1999), the profiting organizations often deny to support it. Free-ridership explains such an observed behavior. Why investing if one earns equal profit without it? For the wine industry, where consumers' often have only a limited ability to judge on product quality, "collective reputation" of a wine region matters and therefore the free-ridership is highly relevant. Individual wineries profit in case of a regional efforts to increase quality or gain in regional attractiveness. Potential customer inflow or higher prices are possible, even if the winery has not individually supported in such activities or changed their offer (Castriota and Delmastro, 2008; Kaiser, 2008; Visser and Langen, 2006; Frick and Simmons, 2013; Cardebat and Figuet, 2013).

An explorative study comparing wineries of different regions provides empirical evidence that wineries' tourism approaches can be either focused on cultural or educational effects or by a more holistic approach – from tasting to hosting to long term client relationship – depending on the regions' fame or historical capital. But for both approaches strategic intention, a fitting offer design with invest and resource dedication is needed to fully exploit tourism opportunities (Faugère et al., 2013).

3.3.2 WINE AND TOURISM IN GERMANY

Tourism is an important industry for Germany. More than 7% of the German employees depend on tourism. International tourists spend about 28 billion Euros when visiting Germany and therefore contribute 1.4% to the GDP. Germans spend more than double that amount when traveling internationally. Additionally, the German in-country tourism spending reaches more than seven times the spending of foreign tourist in Germany (Dapd, 2012). About 60% of that budget is spent on daytrips. As a result, wine tourism in Germany strongly depends on short trips as well as in-country tourists. The stated increase in accommodation and in short term trips supports that it is a growing market (Fäßler, 2008).

German wineries show a history of synergetic market exploitation of wine and tourism. Direct sales to customers as well as on premise consumption of clients are and have been strong backbone for wineries' sales. Especially independent wineries of smaller size sell the majority of their wine directly to the consumers with a high pick-up rate of customers, as do some cooperatives. For example for the wine region of Franken direct sales make up for 72% of sales for independent wineries and 25% for the cooperatives. To foster and expand direct sales, wineries open new sales facilities (Göbel, 2012), add a wine bar to the winery, offer B&B rooms, or offer wine in local wine counters as well as in wine festivals (Mason and Piaggiaro, 2012; Dreyer et al., 2011a). Germany is not only famous for its beer festivals such as the Oktoberfest in Munich but also for a great variety of regional or local wine festivals. More than 270 events a year are declared as pure wine festivals with longstanding historic roots and tradition (Cohen et al., 2008). In order to render such business opportunities financially successful active travel and tourism is needed. Attractive touristic regions increase the number of visitors and therefore enhance the possibility for stops at the wineries providing an opportunity for direct sales and additional revenues. Regional tourism is rewarding for wineries as the example of the region Franken illustrates (Miller, 2007; Kolesch, 2013; Kolesch, 2009; Kolesch, 2010):

- about 2/3 of visitors planned to buy wine before departing;
- additionally 17% of the visitors spontaneously bought wine;

- one-third of the visitors spend more than 200 € on wine;
- on average hospitality customers of wineries buy 18 bottles of wine;
- touristic offers of wineries feed new customers.

The interrelation of wine and tourism is bidirectional. Not only do wineries profit of tourism but also have wine and its production a positive impact on the touristic value of the region. Steep hills planted with vine or vineyards with charming ancient buildings originally providing shelter and today representing unique attractions (Dreyer et al., 2011a) are examples that wine production enriches the nature related factors of tourism. As Bruwer states, nature related factors are the most significant determinant for destination choices (Bruwer et al., 2013). Besides attractive winery landscape regional gastronomic offers with regional food and wine add value to attract tourists. Hence, wine became a strong component and often differentiator for regional touristic offers. All German wine regions have developed campaigns to market the specifics of their region communicating regional culture, nature, attractions, and wine. Branded marketing approaches (Charters et al., 2011) with claims were created and guide the regional measures. The wine region Franken in Germany, the prospector of German wine region destination management, based their measures and activities explicitly on the cluster theory (Kolesch, 2010; Kagermeier, 2011) with success: For 1 € of wine sales 9 € of regional value is created by wine tourism (Miller 2007) .Despite regional emphasis the approaches seem to target on identical customer segments, mainly the direct customers as well-off clients with conservative values. Looking at the claims illustrates the uniformity of the activities: e.g., WeinKulturLand Mosel, Kulturland Rheingau, Weinreich Rheinland-Pfalz, Franken Wein. Schöner.Land.

Despite the economic value creation of wine and tourism (Kagermeier, 2011), wine suppliers might still resist touristic engagement. Their prime interest is selling their wine. For some strategies it might be counterproductive and even for the independent wineries targeting the value market segment and an intention to foster direct sales or to gain additional income besides wine sales strategic evaluation might result in reluctance. Those wineries want to escape local and regional competition characterized by a variety of offers but uniform sales approaches and therefore participating in centrally organized tourism raises doubts in regards to differentiation. In order to increase their activity level for tourism and to overcome freeridership of central and authority driven tourism activities their intrinsic motivation has to be increased. Wineries need to recognize the opportunities of niche strategies. Joint activities need to be highly efficient, cost-return equations have to be addressed, and the potential of individual business models within the local competition to fully exploit cooperative yet competitive behavior needs to be addressed. Furthermore, wineries are stretched by constant push for innovation resulting in financial and personal time investments without clear indication of effectiveness. The resources of wineries as SME enterprises are restricted (Barney, 1991; Barney, 2001) and yet they are asked to professionally engage on all aspects of production and marketing. An organizational resistance to change has to be overcome (Abrahamson, 2000).

Besides winning the wineries, which from an external point of view should profit of tourism a realistic assessment of the impact and opportunities of wine tourism has to take into consideration the supplier groups without strategic interest to foster tourism since it does not add value to their business models. As explained in the above market analysis there are for example suppliers relying primarily on indirect channel partners. To gain more insights into potentials and realistic ambitions of wine tourism, the strategic positioning of wineries and their measures and activities are in the core of the following analysis.

3.3.3 WINE AND TOURISM IN THE CONTEXT OF INNOVATION MANAGEMENT

Innovation is commonly declared to be the key for companies to develop, grow, position, and sustainably secure profitability in competitive business environments, especially in case of changing customer needs (Johannessen et al., 1999; D'Aveni, 1994; Denton, 1999; Jenssen and Jorgensen, 2004; Wang and Ahmed, 2004; Hauschildt, 2004; Crossan and Apaydin, 2010). The German wine industry should therefore be far ahead in evolution from an ancient factor- via an investment- to an innovation-driven industry, with less product centricity and strong service innovation orientation

(Woodward, 2005; Prajogo and Ahmed, 2006). Wine and tourism fit into such innovation paradigm given its service nature and as it is declared as a source for innovation in the wine industry, especially in case of an integrated direct and online sales approach (Kagermeier, 2011).

A key word search in the wine specific literature database "vitis vea" on wine and innovation identified more than 170 relevant articles. About 45% of those articles are on enological innovations, 30% on viticulture, and the remaining 25% deal with marketing and business administration. These managerial articles show three focal areas of wine and innovation:

- clusters and networks as a source of innovation and competitive advantage (about 40%),
- product and marketing innovation (about 30%), and
- innovative organization and leadership (about 12%).

The dominating articles on clusters and networks illustrate the relevance in the context of wine and tourism and innovation. Michael Porter developed his highly regarded theory on clusters assessing the California wine industry (Porter, 1991). Clusters are concerted market efforts of cooperatively acting organizations of horizontal or vertical relationship unified by the joint interest to create competitive advantage. This approach is often called co-opetition since competing organizations engage cooperatively. Besides explaining cooperative strategies in industries such as automotive or IT, cluster theory based research serves to explain that emerging countries can catch-up against old economies, often using the wine business as exemplary industry (Hira, 2013; Touzard, 2010). Concerted efforts within a region via cluster approaches with joint success for the participants are indeed highly relevant in the context of wine and tourism (Giuliani et al., 2011; Kagermeier, 2011; Charters et al., 2011). Only by concerted efforts of wineries, regional tourism organizations, tour agencies, restaurants, hotels etc. will the potentials of tourism and wine be exploited. The above-mentioned efforts to better position the German wine region Franken explicitly bases on the cluster approach. This cluster approach with a strong lead partner is declared as reason for its success (Kagermeier, 2011).

With a symbiotic offer design for wine and tourism wineries can create a mix of product and service innovation. Additionally, such a business model allows to further choose between direct and indirect service delivery and close or far distant services (Khan and Khan, 2009; Antonioli et al., 2010; Caputo, 2002; Freel, 2005; Harrison, 1994; Julien and Ramangalahy, 2003; Scozzi et al., 2005). Although it's historic origination and tradition wine and tourism represents an innovative approach for wineries to position and act in the competitive market.

3.4 STRATEGIC POSITIONING OF GERMAN WINERIES

Strategic management is declared to be decisive in competitive environments (Porter, 1988). On the basis of a long-term planning process accounting for the environment, trends and changes, and competition strategic positioning is decided. The positioning allows to profile in the competitive market to win and attract clients and also to provide orientation for the organization. As a result, sustainable competitive advantages with above average returns can be achieved (see Fig. 3.2).

In the following, the strategic positioning of German wineries is analyzed to gain insights into their ambitions to be active and position in the context of wine and tourism. In line with the logic of strategic planning we consider the wineries perception of environment and challenges, generic strategies realized, actual strategic and innovation measures, and resulting impact on the performance.

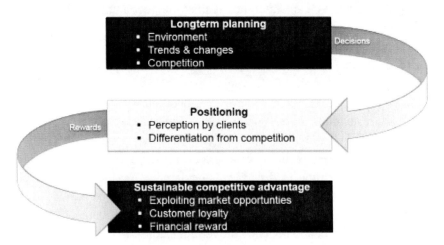

FIGURE 3.2 Essence of strategic management.

Strategic Winery Management and Tourism: Value-Added Offerings 49

An online empirical study on strategy and innovation of German wineries was realized in 2012. Out of a database of more than 6,000 German wineries about 2,000 of the wineries were randomly selected and invited to participate in a pretested online questionnaire. More than 300 valid responses could be used for the analysis.

3.4.1 CHARACTERISTICS, BASICS AND ENVIRONMENTAL PERCEPTION

The participating wineries represent the German winery population since all wine producing regions of Germany are covered, the vast majority of the participants is family owned, they are small, and the wineries exist for a long period of time. Only 2% of the interviewed wineries were established within the last ten years but 60% exist for more 25 years meanwhile 30% were established before 1850. Only 7% of the population has a size to nourish more than 10 employees with only 10% owning more than 25 hectares of vineyards. That population shows the longstanding family tradition that characterizes the German wine production.

The revenue generation of the wineries is very wine focused. 80% of the wineries state that wine sales determine 90% or more of their revenues. Less than 15% of the interviewed wineries estimate that more than one-fifth of their revenues is due to innovative offering components. Export activity seems to be interesting in the wine and tourism context since Charters observed more export oriented wineries to be less motivated in tourism. Almost half of the German wineries of the interviewed population report no export activities. For 15% of the wineries export generates up to 5% of their revenues and slightly more than one-fifth sell up to 20% to foreign countries. About 10% of the interviewed wineries report to be very active in exporting with revenues up to 50% or beyond of their revenues stemming from international business and by serving more than 5 countries (see Fig. 3.3).

Overall, the wineries tend to be small, entrepreneurial and wine focused with strong orientation for home market coverage.

Remauld and Couderc explain that environment is an important strategic variable with implication on strategic choice and innovation for the wine business (Remaud and Couderc, 2006). It should therefore also be accounted for when analyzing wineries strategies in the context of tourism.

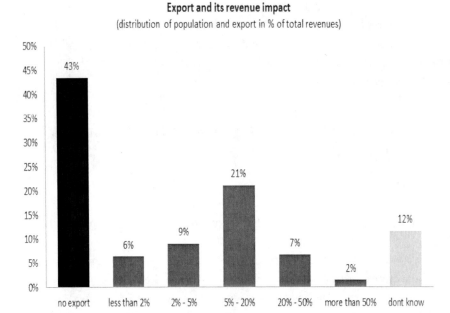

FIGURE 3.3 Export revenue contribution.

The perceived challenges of the German wineries are characterized by restriction in managerial freedom and uncertainty about future development. German wineries report that the top challenges are increased bureaucracy, changing customer behavior, and societal responsibility. Sustainability and climate change are following in importance. Such an environmental perception differs from what leaders and managers of other industries declare to be the main external factors impacting strategic measures and activities. They rank all the wineries' key challenges low in their stated environment perception. The general study on managerial challenges discovers that the general top three challenges are intensive competition, increasing complexity, and economic uncertainty (BCG, 2009), all stated with minor relevance by the German wineries. Hence, the German wine producers recognize the need to profile strategically in the light of changing customer demands but often feel restricted by regulatory environment.

The wine supply side seizes the need to adapt to the changes in the customer preferences in their downstream processes to deliver to the customers. Business model adaptations and certainly service extension or niche

Strategic Winery Management and Tourism: Value-Added Offerings 51

offers on wine and appear to be highly relevant solutions in the fierce market competition. But the wineries need to react also for their upstream processes of production given the high impact of external environment factors. As stated biological, organic, and sustainable products are increasing in market share. Vineyards with bio- or biodynamic cultivation in Germany doubled from 2005 till 2010 to cover more than 5% of total surface (Fader, 2012). Ecological strategic positioning ranges from biological focus to ecologic premium strategies and allow to integrate tradition with modern appearance and design and also profit from tourism (Siebold, 2012; Dressler, 2013c).

3.4.2 STRATEGIC LANDSCAPE OF GERMAN WINERIES AND PERFORMANCE IMPACT

The essence of strategic positioning is to sustainably outperform competitors. Despite the vast literature on strategy and strategic choices the notion of strategic grouping is less explored for industries characterized by small and medium sized enterprises (Deimel, 2008), as the German wine business. Porters' generic strategies (Porter, 2000) built the basis for the following strategic group assessment integrating insights of strategic studies with focus on the wine business. Remauld and Couderc deliver an overview on literature and empirical tests of strategic typology in the wine world (Remaud and Couderc, 2006). The authors identify three clusters in line with prospector, analyzer, and defender strategies (Miles et al., 1978) and conclude that environment interpretation (challenge vs. opportunity), strategic ambition and goal (market share vs. performance), and extend of internationalization (export) appear to be main cluster determinants. Additionally, a clustering analysis for the German wine market provided guidance for our study (Göbel, 2002). The wineries were therefore grouped based on their generic strategies on value provided to the customers (costs versus differentiation) and scope (niche vs. overall market).

The landscape of the German wine business is characterized by a rich portfolio of strategic positioning with strong tendency to profile rather close than distant to competitors (Fig. 3.4). Premium and quality strategies are pursued by more than 50% of the population of the interviewed wineries. These findings illustrates that the strategic positioning is still rather product focused. Most respondents stated to position via quality

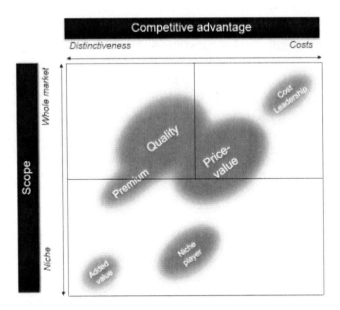

FIGURE 3.4 Landscape of generic strategic positioning.

leadership (36%) or price-value-strategy (33%) with the ambition to cover the whole market. Niche positioning (9%) and value-add strategies (3%) as strategies with strong customer focus are only stated as profiling basis by a minority of the interviewed wineries. Cost leadership is the generic strategy of 5% of the population meanwhile premium offer strategy is communicated by 15%.

Given global competition, the small business size of the players, costly and capital intensive growth or expansion ambitions, and the overall low profitability, cost leadership as generic strategy can at best be chosen by few players in the industry. It is less realized by independent wineries but rather by large wineries or cooperatives. In the light of the market fragmentation a low population of cost leadership strategies was therefore expected. But focus strategies, for example to exploit specific tourism opportunities, were expected to determine more wineries' strategies. For the German brewery landscape in comparison, 6% of cost leadership, 20% of premium and 74% of niche strategy positioning are reported (Freter, 2008).

The uncertainty about the future market development apparently impacts strategies and positioning as there is an obvious tendency to avoid niche approaches and to position close to the competitors to avoid risky decisions. The expected strong population of players to position via niche strategies, with innovation, regional scope, and hospitality as possible key levers (Touzard, 2010) is not yet characterizing the German winery landscape. These findings raise some doubt that strategic groups with explicit value-added offerings on services and tourism are recognized and realized by the wineries. Despite the variety and breadth of offer extension – adding guest rooms, new fashionable wineries, wine tastings, music or cultural events, wine paths and a lot of others – holistic strategic approaches are lagging. Furthermore, the product centrism of the communicated strategies allows for skepticism that cluster approaches are highly appreciated by the wineries or that wine and tourism represents strategic grouping focus.

An evaluation of the effectiveness of strategic positioning with their characterizing measures and the profit impact provides further insight into strategic grouping and hints for tourism or service centered strategies and their results. The cluster of cost leaders proves to be successful in regards to their financial ambitions and results. This strategy is yet less promising to win new clients in the fierce competition in Germany. Indeed, those wineries are characterized by straight forward realization of measures to optimize their business. Innovation and tourism is of less importance for such strategies as their clients and the business models require "no frills offerings." Meanwhile premium strategist score high on the success dimensions and the strategy certainly is suitable for market expansion, only 40% of the population is successfully transforming their positioning into premium prices – with negative impact for the ones not capable of doing so. Meanwhile characterized by innovation and export agility, premium strategist struggle to deliver a winning service offering to fit premium expectations of customers. Quality leadership or price-value show almost identical results supporting the notion that those product focused strategies lack adequate differentiation. Indeed, fair quality and price-value is expected for all offers. Furthermore, the targeted higher price positioning of quality leaders is often not realized.

Positioning via niches delivers best results on product and service quality and on client loyalty. Therefore, addressing focused market segments rewards when meeting the expectations of specific customer groups. Although business literature supports to offer solutions and follow value-add strategies, the cluster realizing such ambitions shows inferior performance. Meanwhile this population scores high on creativity, innovation, and strategic behavior, the transformation of value add offerings into profitable business is not satisfactory. An explanation might be that a lot of producers offer value-added services without pricing them adequately to receive attention given that their strategic approach proofs not to be sufficiently differentiating. As a result, explicit value-added services and offerings cannot be priced in the market.

Overall, the strategic profiling of German wineries is still dominated by product-centrism and the aim to be recognized rather close than distant to competitors. Niche and value-add strategies are yet in evolution as are explicit positioning or value generation on the basis of tourism. Additionally, the strategic landscape explains why a lot of publicly requested concerted efforts to foster wine and tourism activities are still lagging expectations. Only 12% of the interviewed winery population – niche and value-added strategists – might declare tourism activities as their main strategic lever. Cost leaders by nature refrain from concerted efforts to foster wine tourism to focus on low-cost delivery besides product quality. Most prime strategists focus on superiority of their wines and as documented in the interviews some apparently struggle with their service offerings. Prime strategy anxiety to jeopardize the prime strategy when pursuing joint regional efforts and therefore to blur their positioning is a further explanation of reluctance or inactivity (Menival and Han, 2013). Indeed, one flagship winery for example stated that tourists are destroying the very valuable wooden floor of the chateau dating back to the end of the 15th century. Furthermore, the export orientation and success of the prime strategist further reduces their interest in wine tourism, as Charters explored (Charters and Menival, 2011). But those flagships wineries as well as the big players are needed as innovators and promoters to attract tourists as successful wine and tourism efforts (Kagermeier, 2011).

The rather broad strategic orientations of quality leadership and price-value offerings are mainly product focused and might currently neglect profiling opportunities on services, innovation, and tourism. That winery population profits from regional touristic offers and might choose to better profile and differentiate based on tourism in the future, but so far a lot of the wineries of that population today rather piggy-back on concerted efforts than they are actively engaged and realizing them.

3.4.3 INDICATIONS FOR A TRANSITION – TOURISM AND SERVICES GAINING STRATEGIC GROUND

Looking at the current measures and strategic activities that the interviewed wineries stated to react to the environmental challenges nurture the impression that tourism based services or activities gain ground and adequate strategic profiling will follow. The reported portfolio of innovation and measures as a result of the changing customer behavior and environment is rich and diverse. One-third of the activities are product centered but following that pole position are two domains with equal attention of the wineries. Offering new services and new sales channels with each about 20% of the stated activities illustrate that there is a strong need to change the interaction with the clients, realize new approaches to win new customers or to increase loyalty, and to better profile in the market. The stated measures to increase services offered are often directly linked to tourism since they are dominated by touristic attractions or offering events.

Meanwhile the wineries stated the highest level of realized versus planned activities for new wine creation, the level of implementation for services extension was also above average for all measures stated.

The findings of the portfolio analysis (Fig. 3.5) of strategic and innovative measures with strong orientation on service extension and additionally a high level of realization of those activities support the notion of a transition within wineries to better address market needs, niches, and better exploit strategic opportunities in the future. But the low attention and overall lowest realization of adding value features in the offering indicate that more creative and holistic approaches are avoided. This observed behavior reflects the so-called bandwaggoning effect (Abrahamson, 1991, 1996) describing that innovation is rather a result of wanting to catch

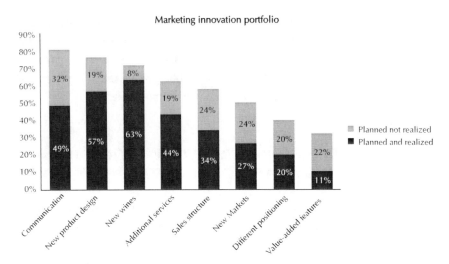

FIGURE 3.5 Portfolio of marketing innovations.

up with neighbor winery having done so and therefore not to miss out on opportunities than individual strategic approaches and positioning (Dressler, 2013b). In the following, we provide a descriptive typology for the current strategic winery behavior in regards to tourism activities.

3.5 STRATEGIC TOURISM CLUSTERS OF GERMAN WINERIES

We use the insights of the panel to draw a landscape of wineries and their tourism engagement and shed light on the generic strategies and managerial potentials in the context of wine and tourism.

3.5.1 WINERY CLUSTERS TOWARDS TOURISM

Based on our findings that most wineries do not capture the strategic benefit of tourism and wine, for some wineries such activities might even be or be perceived to be counterproductive or that windfall profits arise without individual engagement or support for tourism activities. The general public expectation that wineries should be happy about and even actively support tourism is a misperception of strategic motivation of the wineries. A differentiating typology to guide future tourism activities and

Strategic Winery Management and Tourism: Value-Added Offerings

to motivate wineries to be active is derived resulting in five clusters of strategic winery behavior in the context of wine and tourism (see Fig. 3.6).

The five strategic groups of this descriptive typology range from potentially or realistically negative impact via neutral to profiting to sustainable strategic advantage and profit impact. The groups are titled "(supposedly) negatively impacted," "free-riders," "opportunity seekers," "selective offer extensionists," and "state of the art tourism strategist." Meanwhile the first cluster of "(supposedly) negatively impacted" has no strategic motivation to engage in tourism the last one "state of the art tourism strategist" exploits tourism to differentiate and profile in the market. Hence, tourism interest and engagement intensity ranges on strategic continuum.

Some premium strategy wineries with a loyal customer base within regional proximity or strong export orientation judge tourism activities with needed investments to result in negative returns. They might dislike

Strategic winery clusters on tourism intensity

Low strategic engagement → High strategic engagement

Cluster:	Negatively impacted	Free-riders	Opportunity seekers	Selective offer extensionists	State of the art - tourism strategists
Logicr:	Tourism engagement is perceived to have negative impact on own performance	Profiting of the positive impact of others engaged in tourism without individual contribution	Situational tourism activities support or offer adaption when experiencing sales problems	Selective but long-term offer addition, often motivated by neighbour wineries' success or in case of financial incentives (e.g. funding)	Motivated by the idea and will to differentiate via tourism and to attract new customers with according offerings
Levers:	- Costs of tourism activities without proper return - Negative brand impact	- Profiting from reputational effects - Profiting from potential customer increase - Avoidance of additional costs	- Tourism as tactical sales engine - Support for central tourism activities only when sales lag expectations - Profiting from reputation effects and cluster efforts	- Winning new client or additional revenues with new show room, guest room, guest rooms, wine tours,... - Cluster initiative based motivation	- Strategic profiling - Winning wine tourism awards - Driving reputation and therefore brand development - Wine and architecture
Population:	- Prime strategists without interest to win more distant client base or mass value clients - Most big wineries or cost leaders serving indirect channels	- Some cost leaders engaged in direct sales - Undifferentiated wineries with direct sales but no tourism contribution	- Product-focussed wineries - Stuck-in the middle producers - Cost leaders in first moves to reposition to escape tough competition and import product pressure	- Quality oriented wineries extending their offering to grow or increase profit - Niche players exploring opportunities to position differently in the market	- Prime strategists positioned as regional flagships - Niche providers, value-add strategists and quality leaders with extended offer portfolio

FIGURE 3.6 Tourism based strategic winery management – explorative clusters.

mass tourism in their winery, or they could be afraid of negative impact on their brand strategy. Cost leadership on the other hand requires strong focus on permanent cost cutting and selective quality or service increase where active involvement in tourism can oppose consequent strategic orientation. Therefore, large wineries serving predominantly indirect channels or wineries with such strategic sales structure will face negative profitability and belong to the cluster of "(supposedly) negatively impacted."

Wineries characterized by more prominent direct sales to their consumers should profit of regional destination marketing since it attracts tourists and therefore feeds potential customers. But their engagement often limbs the resulting reward. The effect of free-riding on reputational effects (e.g., regional appellation and wine quality efforts) as well as indirectly profiting of cluster activities without individual contribution or activity even seems to be efficient for them, but only on a short term perspective. Surely, a lot of product focused wineries without profiling for specific target segments as well as some cost leaders avoiding investments and expenses but profiting without adequate engagement belong to the "free-riders" of the presented typology. As described in the literature, the willingness to support and be active in tourism supporting initiatives increases when sales are lagging. (Menival and Han, 2013) They then initiate short term marketing efforts to win a tourism based client population. Tourism functions as short term sales engine and can therefore be labeled as "opportunity seeking." In the light of the low profitability of the German wineries avoiding additional costs seems not only rational but also often prerequisite for survival.

The survey backs the notion that wineries are aware of their need to change and adapt especially when serving the direct wine sales channels. The wineries need to be creative and profile to keep direct relationships with their customers. While it is still common for German wineries that either consumers pick up at the winery or viticulturists deliver personally the wine purchase to their customers all over Germany, wineries are confronted with decreasing loyalty and the need to be active in social media. Optimizing web pages, creating online-shops, building interactive wine experiences, special events or tastings, but also investing into their show rooms and sales facilities to increase loyalty of existent clients and further attract customers are just examples of individual strategies to profit of experience buys ambitions of the consumers (Dressler, 2012a, 2012b).

Frequently, offer extensions targeting tourists is initially driven by neighbor wineries. "Selective offer extensionists" adapt innovation and services to not miss out on opportunities. As experienced by the panel offering additional services such as events, wine tastings, wine education, or active harvesting by the clients become basic offer elements without strategic reorientation. A lot of the product focused strategies on quality or price-value as well as wineries that are strategically "stuck in the middle" muddle through competition by adding "me-too" components. The result of that behavior is that it becomes more difficult to play such offers components to profile in the market and therefore to increase awareness for superior services or extended offerings. Even more challenging is the pricing for the wineries that intend to strategically exploit tourism-based opportunities. As a result, "added value strategies" are still lagging financial success.

Some wineries have succeeded in exploiting tourism potentials strategically and hence constitute the cluster of "state of the art tourism strategist." They realize a holistic approach offering hosting, eating, experiencing, active integration of clients, and exploiting regional differentiation. Those wineries surely diversify with increased activities or offering adaptation and therefore depend less on their wine products and therefore nature or seasonality. Additionally they can win an attractive client base and increase loyalty. Especially some flagship wineries have proven that premium strategy can profit of tourism and brand differentiation as well as value can profit of such an approach.

3.5.2 STRATEGIC OPPORTUNITIES – GENERIC STRATEGIES AND TOURISM LEVERAGE

As a result, the recognized and above-mentioned generic strategies of the German wineries can also be plotted in the context of their motivation for tourism engagement and its profit impact. Especially for the product focused generic strategy on quality, for niche positioning and for exploiting added-value creative strategic offer design a strategic approach on tourism can be highly valuable to increase performance or to outperform competitors.

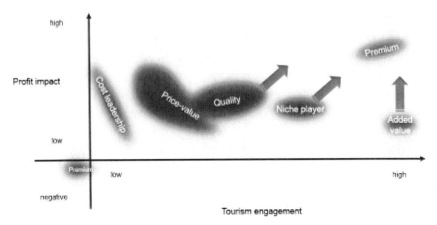

FIGURE 3.7 Generic strategies, tourism and profit impact.

Meanwhile cluster activities to market regions and its wineries are fashionable a more differentiated understanding of strategic motivation should help to further render such activities more effective (see Fig. 3.7). Cooperative behavior and cluster initiatives of wine and tourism need intrinsic motivation of all participants to be active in such partnerships and will then result in positive impact for German wine (Hall and Mitchell, 2010; Porter, 2000).

3.6 SUMMARY AND OUTLOOK

Wine and tourism draws a lot and increasing attention in literature. In that body of knowledge, the strategic winery management perspective lags the ones of destination management or consumer behavior. This article contributes findings of an empirical research on strategy and innovation of German wineries adding insights to the strategic winery management perspective in the context of wine and tourism.

The German wine industry is characterized by fierce competition. Wineries profit of a longstanding synergetic exploitation of wine and tourism since direct sales to consumers or participation in wine fairs represents important sales channels. All German wine regions are increasingly engaged to market their destination as an attractive wine and tourism region. Extending the wineries services or stronger engagement in cooperative cluster approaches bear the opportunity to differentiate via innovation and to gain new customers. Wineries are pushed especially from authorities and experts to increase tourism activities without differentiating for wineries' individual motivation or challenging profit impact besides overall roughly calculated economic effects.

Empirical insights on strategic and innovation management of German wineries indicates that there is a variety of activities or circumstances where wineries can profit of tourism – from service offerings with touristic components, direct sales to tourists, differentiation strategies on the basis of tourism or others. All of the activities contribute to value creation and support the transition of the industry to enter the stage of service and less product focus. Still, tourism-centric strategic positioning of the wineries is not yet strongly developed. Prevailing product centrism, scarce niche approaches, generic strategies like cost leadership, and anxiety that tourism activities might harm premium strategies explain why tourism potentials are still far from being fully exploited strategically by independent wineries or cooperatives. Additionally, the large wineries serving one third of the market via indirect sales channels or cooperatives with an equal strategic approach are not interested in actively supporting wine tourism activities.

A lot of German wine producers and active marketers apparently are not strategically motivated to foster activities and to increase touristic attraction. The innovation portfolio of the analyzed wineries signalizes increasing attention and activity for wine and tourism and nurtures the perception, that wineries increasingly discover tourism as an opportunity to profile and differentiate against competition. Still, reluctance towards creative approaches and problems to price such approaches are hindering full market exploitation. Financial reward is yet concentrated on few first movers turning innovative approaches into a holistic, brand value increasing profiling with more diversified revenues, new client inflow, and increased loyalty.

Five clusters of strategic wine and tourism motivation of German wineries are presented and allow to tailor regional activities, cluster initiatives, or regional programs and financial support to increase impact and therefore effectiveness. Tourism could serve for a lot of wineries to better profile in the competitive market. Still, some wineries and wine producers will not and should not foster their engagement or strategic offering.

Apparently, the German wineries profit of activities and engagements realized by the regions, the authorities, and some players actively involved. The known obstacle of free ridership therefore needs to be addressed to foster strategic thoughts and more active support for such initiatives. Tourism certainly contributes to the transition to reach a state beyond product centricity of the German wine industry since it provides opportunities to win customers, especially by profiting of the intertwined worlds of wine and tourism. But the opportunities and the future should not be jeopardized by abstract postulation or petitionary appeals. Understanding the strategic motivation with fitting, pinpointed, and targeted incentives is needed. The identified strategic groups and the developed typology should enable more effective management and initiatives.

KEYWORDS

- **direct customers**
- **discount customers**
- **food retailer customers**
- **innovation management**
- **supermarket customers**
- **variety seekers**
- **wine store customers**

REFERENCES

1. Abrahamson, E. 1991. Managerial fads and fashions: the diffusion and rejection of innovations. *Academy of Management Review,* 16, 586–612.
2. Abrahamson, E. 1996. Management Fashion. *Academy of Management Review,* 21, 254–285.
3. Abrahamson, E. 2000. Change without pain. *Harvard Business Review,* 78, 75–79.
4. Aizenman, J. & Brooks, E. 2008. Globalization and Taste Convergence: the Cases of Wine and Beer. *Review of International Economics,* 16, 217–233.
5. Alston, M. & Freebairn, J. W. 2001. Beggar-thy-Neighbor Aspects of Generic Commodity Promotion Programs. *NICPRE Quarterly,* 8.
6. Anderson, K. 2010. Contribution of the Innovation System to Australia's Wine Industry. *Giuliani, Morrison, Rabellotti (Hrsg.): Innovation and Technological Catch Up: The Changing Geography of Wine Production.*
7. Antonioli, D., Mazzanti, M. & Pini, P. 2010. Productivity, innovation strategies and industrial relations in SMEs. Empirical evidence for a local production system in northern Italy. *International Review of Applied Economics,* 24, 453–482.

Strategic Winery Management and Tourism: Value-Added Offerings

8. Arnold, R. & Fleuchaus, R. 2010. Ein Überblick zu Segmentierungsansätzen im Weinmarketing. *In:* Fleuchaus, R. & Arnold, R. (eds.) *Weinmarketing: Kundenwünsche erforschen, Zielgruppen identifizieren, innovative Produkte entwickeln.* Wiesbaden: Gabler Verlag.

9. Aylward, D. 2004. Innovation-Export Linkages within Different Cluster Models: A Case Study from the Australian Wine Industry. *Prometheus, 22 (4),* 22.

10. Aylward, D. 2006. Innovation lock-in: unlocking research and development path dependency in the Australian wine industry.

11. Barney, J. 1991. Firm Resources and Sustained Competitive Advantage. *Journal of Management,* 17, 99.

12. Barney, J. 2001. Is the Resource-Based View a Useful Perspective for Strategic Management? Yes. *Academy of Management Review,* 26, 41–56.

13. BCG 2009. Organization 2015 – Designed to win. The Boston Consulting Group.

14. Blisard, N. 1997. Generic Dairy Advertising: How Effective? *Food and Marketing, Economic Research Service.*

15. Bloemer, J. & Ruyter, K. D. 1999. Customer Loyalty in High and Low Involvement Service Settings: The Moderating Impact of Positive Emotions. *Journal of Marketing Management,* 15, 315–330.

16. Bmelv 2011. Ertragslage Obst-und Weinbau 2011. *In:* ABT. 1, R. (ed.). BMELV.

17. Brester, G. W. & Schroeder, T. C. 1995. The impacts of brand and generic advertising on meat demand. *American Journal of Agricultural Economics,* 77.

18. Brunner, K.-M. 2011. Essen, Trinken und Reisen im gesellschaftlichen Wandel – Potenziale für Weintourismus aus (wein-)soziologischer Perspektive. *In:* Dreyer, A. (ed.) *Wein und Tourismus.* Erich Schmidt Verlag.

19. Bruwer, J. & Alant, K. 2009. The hedonic nature of wine tourism consumption: an experiential view. *International Journal of Wine Business Research,* 21, 235–257.

20. Bruwer, J., Lesschaeve, I., Gray, D. & Sottini, V. A. 2013. Regional brand perception by wine tourists within a winescape framework. *7th International Conference AWBR.* St. Catherines.

21. Capitello, R., Agnoli, L. & Begalli, D. 2013. Tourism experiences and wine experiences: a new approach to the analysis of the visitor perceptions for a destination. The case of Verona. *In:* AWBR (ed.) *7th International Conference.* St. Catherines.

22. Caputo, A. C. E. A. 2002. A methodological framework for innovation transfer to SMEs. *Industrial Management & Systems,* 102, 271–283.

23. Cardebat, J.-M. & Figuet, J.-M. 2013. Expert opinions and Bordeaux wine prices: an attempt to correct the bias of subjective judgments. *AAWE,* Working paper 129, 1–31.

24. Castriota, S. & Delmastro, M. 2008. Individual and Collective Reputation: Lessons from the Wine Market. *Working Paper* (Online).

25. Charters, S. & Ali-Knight, J. 2002. Who is the wine tourist? *Tourism Management,* 23, 311–319.

26. Charters, S. & Menival, D. 2011. Wine tourism in Champagne. *Journal of Hospitality & Tourism Research,* 35, 102–118.

27. Charters, S., Mitchell, R. & Menival, D. 2011. The territorial brand in wine. *In:* AWBR (ed.) *6th international conference of the association of wine business research.* Bordeaux.

64 Strategic Winery Tourism and Management

28. Choisy, C. 1996. Le poids du tourisme viti-vinicole. *Espaces,* 30–33.
29. Cohen, E., D'Hauteville, F., Goodwill, S., Lockshin, L. & Sirieix, L. A cross-cultural comparison of choice criteria for wine in restaurants. *In:* AWBR, ed. 4th international conference, 2008 Siena. 1–18.
30. Corsi, A. M., Lockshin, L. & Mueller, S. Competition between and competition within: the strategic positioning of competing countries in key export markets. *In:* BEM, ed. 6th AWBR international conference, 2011 Bordeaux. 1–17.
31. Crossan, M. M. & Apaydin, M. 2010. A Multi-Dimensional Framework of Organizational Innovation: A Systematic Review of the Literature. *Journal of Management Studies,* 47, 1154–1191
32. Cusmano, L., Morrison, A. & Rabelotti, R. 2010. Catching up Trajectories in the Wine Sector: A Comparative Study of Chile, Italy and South Africa *World Development* 38, 1588–1602.
33. D'Aveni, R. 1994. *Hypercompetition: The Dynamics of Strategic Maneuvering,* New York, Basic Books.
34. Dana, L. P. & Winstone, K. E. 2008. Wine cluster formation in New Zealand: operation, evolution and impact. *Journal of Food Science and Technology,* 43, 2177–2190.
35. Dapd. 2012. Tourismus sichert Millionen Jobs. *Rheinpfalz,* 3.2.2012.
36. DBV 2012. Situationsbericht 2011/12 – Trends und Fakten zur Landwirtschaft. *In:* Bauernverband, D. (ed.). Berlin.
37. Deimel, K. 2008. Stand der strategischen Planung in kleinen und mittleren Unternehmen in der BRD. *Zeitschrift für Planung & Unternehmenssteuerung,* 19, 281–298.
38. Denton, D. K. 1999. Gaining competitiveness through innovation. *European Journal of Innovation Management,* 2, 82–85.
39. Dressler, M. 2012a. Innovation focus and capacity challenge of small entrepreneurs – looking at German wineries. *In:* DIJON, E. (ed.) *International Conference on Innovation & Trend in Wine Management, June 2012.* Dijon.
40. Dressler, M. 2012b. Innovative Weinwelt: der "aktive Kunde." *Der Deutsche Weinbau,* 6, 16–18.
41. Dressler, M. Customer involvement management – Empirical observations of explorative studies on enrichment activities of German wineries. *In:* AWBR, ed. Academy of Wine Business Research 7th International Conference, June 12 -15, 2013 2013a St. Catharines, Canada. Brock University.
42. Dressler, M. 2013b. Innovation management of German wineries: from activity to capacity—an explorative multi-case survey. *Wine Economics and Policy,* 2, 19–26.
43. Dressler, M. 2013c. Ö kologischer Weinbau: Positionierungsanalysen. *Der Deutsche Weinbau,* 5, 16–18.
44. Dressler, M. 2013d. Strategische Führung in der Weinwirtschaft. *Der Deutsche Weinbau,* 4, 34–37.
45. Dreyer, A., Antz, C. & Linne, M. 2011a. Wein und Tourismus – Handlungsempfehlungen und Perspektiven am Beispiel der Weinregion Saale-Unstrut. *In:* Dreyer, A. (ed.) *Wein und Tourismus.* Erich Schmidt Verlag.
46. Dreyer, A., Antz, C. & Linne, M. 2011b. Wein und Tourismus – Trends, Synergien und kooperative Vermarktung. *In:* Dreyer, A. (ed.) *Wein und Tourismus.* Erich Schmidt Verlag.
47. DWI 2003. Neues Marketing für neue Konsumenten. DWI.

Strategic Winery Management and Tourism: Value-Added Offerings 65

48. DWI 2011. Weinmarkt 2010. *In:* Weininstituts, I. D. D. (ed.) *Deutscher Wein Statistik.* Mainz.
49. DWI 2012. Deutscher Wein Statistik 2012/2013. *In:* DWI (ed.). Mainz.
50. DWI 2013. Deutscher Wein Statistik 2013/2014. *In:* DWI (ed.). Mainz.
51. Engelhard, W. 2011a. Erneuter Absatzknick. *Wein+Markt,* 18–19.
52. Engelhard, W. 2011b. Harddiscounter: Verloren und trotzdem gewonnen. *Wein+Markt,* ProWein Ausgabe 2011, 16–17.
53. Engelhard, W. 2011c. Wieder weniger Weinkunden. *Wein+Markt,* ProWein Ausgabe 2011, 14–15.
54. Ernest-Hahn, S. 2005. *Wein in der Gastronomie,* Stuttgart, Matthaes.
55. Fader, B. 2012. Aktuelle Zahlen im Visier. *Das Deutsche Weinmagazin,* 12, 28–30.
56. Fäßler, A.-M. 2008. *Dem Weintourismus auf der Spur.* Uni Wien.
57. Faugère, C., Bouzdine-Chameeva, T., Durrieu, F. & Pesme, J.-O. 2013. The impact of tourism strategies and regional factors on wine wine tourism performance. *7th International Conference AWBR.* St. Catherines.
58. Frank, B. 2010. *Die Diffusion von Rebsorten – eine globale Betrachtung,* Weikersheim, Markgraf Publishers.
59. Freel, M. 2005. The characteristics of innovation-intensive small firms: evidence from "Northern Britain." *International Journal of Innovation Management,* 9, 401–429.
60. Freter, H. 2008. *Markt- und Kundensegmentierung,* Stuttgart, Kohlhammer.
61. Frick, B. & Simmons, R. 2013. The impact of individual and collective reputation on wine prices: empirical evidence from the Mosel valley. *Journal of Business Economics,* upcoming.
62. Getz, D. & Brown, G. 2006. Critical success factors for wine tourism regions: a demand analysis. *Tourism Management,* 27, 146–158.
63. Getz, D., Dowling, R., Carlsen, J. & Anderson, D. 1999. Critical success factors for wine tourism. *International Journal of Wine Marketing,* 11, 20–43.
64. Gilinsky, A., Santini, C., Lazzeretti, L. & Eyler, R. 2008. Desperately seeking serendipity. *International Journal of Wine Business Research,* 20, 302–320.
65. Giuliani, E., Morrison, A. & Rabellotti, R. (eds.) 2011. *Innovation and Technological Catch-Up: The Changing Geography of Wine Production,* Northampton, MA: Edward Elgar.
66. Göbel, R. 2002. Erfolgsfaktoren von Weinbaubetrieben auf Basis der Erfolgsfaktoren- und Betriebsleiterforschung *Geisenheimer Berichte.*
67. Göbel, R. 2012. *Persönlichkeitsorientierte Architektur & Weinmarketing,* Gebr. Kornmeyer.
68. Govindasamy, R., Italia, J. & Thatch, D. 1998. Consumer awareness of state-sponsored marketing programs: An evaluation of the Jersey Fresh program. *Journal of Food Distribution Research,* 39, 7–15.
69. Govindasamy, R., Italia, J. & Thatch, D. 1999. Consumer attitudes and response toward state-sponsored agricultural promotion: An evaluation of the Jersey Fresh program. *Journal of Extension,* 37.
70. Grün, O. & Brunner, J.-C. 2002. *Der Kunde als Dienstleister – von der Selbstbedienung zur Co-Produktion,* Wiesbaden, Gabler.
71. Hall, C. M. & Mitchell, R. 2010. *Wine marketing,* Butterworth-Heinemann.
72. Hanagriff, R. D. & Lau, M. H. 2009. Can a State Funded Rural Economic Development Program Positively Impact the State's Economy? A Case Study Application

using Texas Department of Agriculture's Rural Tourism Economic Development Program. *Southern Agricultural Economics Association.* Atlanta, Georgia.

73. Hanagriff, R. D., Lau, M. H. & Rogers, S. L. 2009. State Funded Marketing and Promotional Activities to Support a State's Winery Business; Are There Economic Returns?: A Case study using Texas Senate Bill 1370's support of the Texas Wine Industry. *Southern Agricultural Economics Association.* Atlanta, Georgia.

74. Harrison, B. 1994. Planning in specific companies and situations – SMEs. *Long Range Planning,* 27, 180–180.

75. Haupt, D. 2010. Weinwirtschaftsbericht. *In:* Ministerium Für Wirtschaft, v., Landwirtschaft Und Weinbau Rheinland Pfalz (ed.). Mainz.

76. Hauschildt, J. 2004. *Innovations management,* München, Verlag Vahlen.

77. Hira, A. 2013. *What Makes Clusters Competitive?: Cases from the Global Wine Industry,* McGill-Queen's Press.

78. Hira, A., Giest, S. & Howlett, M. 2013. Explaining the Success of Clusters: A Framework for the Study of Global Wine Industry Dynamics. *In:* Hira, A. (ed.) *What Makes Clusters Competitive – Cases from the Global Wine Industry.*

79. Hoffman, D. 2010. Der deutsche Weinmarkt 2009. *Das Deutsche Weinmagazin,* 56–58.

80. Hoffman, D. & Szolnoki, G. 2011. Der Premiummarkt für Weine in Deutschland. Mainz: MULEWF Rheinland Pfalz.

81. Hoffman, D. & Szolnoki, G. 2012. Consumer segmentation based on usage of sales channels in the German wine market. *In:* Dijon, G. E. (ed.) *ITWM.* Dijon.

82. Hoffmann, D. 2005. Der Markt für Wein. *Agrarwirtschaft,* 54, 84–88.

83. Hoffmann, D. 2010. Stabiler Markt. *Weinwirtschaft,* 5, 167–168.

84. Holbrook, M. B. & Hirschman, E. C. 1982. The experiential aspects of consumption: consumer fantasies, feelings, and fun. *Journal of consumer research,* 132–140.

85. Jenssen, J. I. & Jorgensen, G. 2004. How do corporate champions promote innovations? *International Journal of Innovation Management,* 8, 63–86.

86. Johannessen, J.-A., Olaisen, J. & Olsen, B. 1999. Managing and organizing innovation in the knowledge economy. *European Journal of Innovation Management,* 2, 116–128.

87. Jordan, R., Zidda, P. & Lockshin, L. 2006. Behind the Australian wine industry success: Does environment matter? *3rd International Wine Business Research Conference.* Montpellier.

88. Julien, P.-A. & Ramangalahy, C. 2003. Competitive strategy and performance of exporting SMEs: an empirical investigation of the impact of their export information search and competencies. *Entrepreneurship Theory & Practice,* 227–245.

89. Kagermeier, A. 2011. Kooperationen als Herausforderung für die Weiterentwicklung des Weintourismus. *In:* Dreyer, A. (ed.) *Wein und Tourismus.* Erich Schmidt Verlag.

90. Kaiser Harry M., Myrland Øystein & Diansheng, D. 2003. Price and Quality Effects of Generic Advertising: The Case of Norwegian Salmon. *Cornell University.*

91. Kaiser Harry M. & Yuqing, Z. 2009. Evaluating the effectiveness of generic advertising versus non-advertising marketing activities on New York State milk markets. *Agribusiness,* 25, 351–368.

92. Kaiser, H. M., D. J. Liu, T. D. Mount & Forker, O. D. 1992. Impacts of Dairy Promotion from Consumer Demand to Farm Supply. *Commodity Advertising and Promotion, eds. H. W. Kinnucan, S. R. Thompson and H. S. Chang, Iowa State University Press..*

Strategic Winery Management and Tourism: Value-Added Offerings 67

93. Kaiser, H. M. E. A. 2008. The Problem of Free Riding in Voluntary Generic Advertising: Parallelism and Possible Solutions from the Lab. *American Journal of Agricultural Economics,* 90, 540–552.
94. Khan, M. & Khan, M. A. 2009. How technological innovations extend services outreach to customers – The changing shape of hospitality services taxonomy. *International Journal of Contemporary Hospitality Management,* 21, 509–522.
95. Kolesch, H. Weintourismus und Regionalentwicklung "der gefühlte Wehrwert." 2009 Veitshöchsheim. Bayerische Landesanstalt für Weinbau und Gartenbau Veitshöchsheim.
96. Kolesch, H. 2010. Franken-Wein. Schöner. Land! A Wine Tourism Concept. *Obst- und Weinbau. Schweizerische Zeitschrift fuer Obst-und Weinbau der Eidg. Forschungsanstalt Waedenswil,* 146.
97. Kolesch, H. 2013. *RE: Das fränkische Weintourismuskonzept – Maßnahmen, Organisation, Kommunikation und Qualitätsmanagement.* Type to Enology, B. O. V. A.
98. Kotler, P. 1986. The Prosumer Movement: A new challenge for marketers. *Advances in Consumer Research,* 13, 510–513.
99. Markgraf, H. 2012. Die Deutschen lieben Sekt *AHGZ online* [Online]. [Accessed 9.10.2012].
100. Mason, M. C. & Piaggiaro, A. 2012. Critical Success Factors for Wine Tourism Regions: A Demand Analysis. *Tourism Management,* 33, 1329–1336.
101. Mend, M. 2009a. Wie steht's mit dem Erfolg? *Das Deutsche Weinmagazin,* 26–28.
102. Mend, M. 2009b. Wirtschaftliche Entwicklung von Weingütern in Rheinland-Pfalz: Wie steht's mit dem Erfolg? *Das Deutsche Weinmagazin,* 12, 26–28.
103. Menival, D. & Han, J. Y. 2013. Wine tourism: futures sales and cultural context of consumption. *7th International Conference AWBR.* St. Catherines.
104. Miles, R. E., Snow, C. C., Meyer, A. D. & Coleman, H. J. 1978. Organizational Strategy, Structure, and Process. *Academy of Management Review,* 3, 546–562.
105. Miller, J. Weintourismus liegt voll im Trend. 2nd symposium of international wine tourism, 13.6.2007. 2007 Iphofen. Bayerisches Staatsministerium für Landwirtschaft und Forsten.
106. Nestlé 2011. So is(s)t Deutschland – Ein Spiegel der Gesellschaft. Frankfurt Main.
107. Nielsen 2012. Handel, Verbraucher, Werbung – Deutschland 2011. The Nielsen Company.
108. Nohl, W. 2001. Sustainable landscape use and aesthetic perception–preliminary reflections on future landscape aesthetics. *Landscape and Urban Planning,* 54, 223–237.
109. O'Neill, M., Palmer, A. & Charters, S. 2002. Wine production as a service experience – the effects of service quality on wine sales. *Journal of Services Marketing,* 16, 342–362.
110. Oberhofer, J. 2011. Agrarbericht 2011: Gewinne regelrecht eingebrochen. *Der Deutsche Weinbau,* 26–31.
111. Oberhofer, J. 2012. Faßweinbetriebe sind 2011/12 die Gewinner. *Der Deutsche Weinbau,* 22–25.
112. OC&C 2012. Erwartete Konsumentenreaktion auf Preiserhöhung je Land. *In:* 2011/2012, P. (ed.).
113. OIV 2012. Statistical report on world vitiviniculture 2012. OIV.
114. Olsen, J. & Newton, S., K. Millenial wine consumer dining preferences segmented by restaurant type – an exloratory study. *In:* School, B. M., ed. 6th AWBR International Conference, 2011 Bordeaux. 1–12.

115. Orth, U. R., ST Ö CKL, A. & AL., E. 2011. Wein & Tourismus: Determinanten und Konsequenzen emotionaler Bindung zu Regionen und deren Marken. *In:* DREYER, A. (ed.) *Wein und Tourismus.* Erich Schmidt Verlag.
116. Pilz, H. 2012. Weinimport auf Rekordniveau. *Weinwirtschaft,* 20, 9.
117. Porter, M. E. 1988. From competitive advantage to corporate strategy. *McKinsey Quarterly,* 35–66.
118. Porter, M. E. 2000. Location, Competition, and Economic Development: Local Clusters in a Global Economy. *Economic Development Quarterly,* 14, 15–34.
119. Prajogo, D. I. & Ahmed, P. K. 2006. Relationships between innovation stimulus, innovation capacity, and innovation performance. *R&D Management,* 36, 499–515.
120. Rabobank 2012. The incredible bulk. *Industry Notes.* Rabobank.
121. Remaud, H. & Couderc, J.-P. 2006. Wine Business Practices: A New Versus Old Wine World Perspective. *Agribusiness,* 22, 405–416.
122. Riviezzo, A., De Nisco, A. & Garofano, A. 2011. Understanding wine purchase and consumption behaviour: a market segmentation approach. *In:* AWBR (ed.) *6th international conference of the association of wine business research.* Bordeaux.
123. Römmelt, W. 2012. Schwierige Imagebildung trotz Wachstum. *Weinwirtschaft,* 20, 31–35.
124. Schallenberger, F. 2009. Weinbau. Made in Germany. Der deutsche Weinmarkt im Blickfeld. *In:* Bank, R.-P. (ed.). Mainz: LBBW.
125. Schipperges, M. 2013. Verbraucher offen für neue Entdeckungen. *Das Deutsche Weinmagazin,* 31.08.13, 57–63.
126. Scozzi, B., Garavelli, C. & Crowston, K. 2005. Methods for modeling and supporting innovation processes in SMEs. *European Journal of Innovation Management,* 8, 120–137.
127. Shamsuddoha, A. K. & Ali, M. Y. 2006. Mediated effects of export promotion programs on firm export performance *Asia Pacific Journal of Marketing and Logistics,* 18, 93–110.
128. siebold, H. 2012. Ö koweingut findet einen potenten Retter. *Stuttgarter Zeitung.*
129. Skinner, A. M. 2000. Napa Valley, California: a model of wine region development. *In:* Cambourne, B., Macionis, N., Hall, C. M. & Sharples, L. (eds.) *Wine Tourism Around the World, Development management and markets.* Oxford: Elsevier Butterworth-Heinemann.
130. Szolnoki, G., Heußler, N. & Bleich, S. (eds.) 2009. *Analysis of prices and geografical origins as quality indicators.*
131. Thach, L. 2007. Trends in wine tourism. *Wine Business monthly,* 14, 86–89.
132. Touzard, J.-M. 2010. Innovation Systems and Regional Vineyards. *ISDA.* Montpellier.
133. Visser, E.-J. & Langen, P. D. 2006. The importance and quality of governance in the Chilean wine industry. *GeoJournal,* 65, 177–197.
134. Wang, C. L. & Ahmed, P. K. 2004. The development and validation of the organizational innovativeness construct using confirmatory factor analysis. *European Journal of Innovation Management,* 7, 303–313.
135. Woodward, D. 2005. Porter's Cluster Strategy Versus Industrial Targeting. *ICIT.* Orlando, USA.

CHAPTER 4

WINE VERSUS WEDDINGS: WINE TOURISM IN THE EMERGING NORTH CAROLINA WINE INDUSTRY

IAN M. TAPLIN[1] and MINH-TRANG THI NGUYEN[2]

[1]*Professor, Department of Sociology and International Studies, Wake Forest University, Winston-Salem, NC 27109, USA; Bordeaux Ecole de Management, Bordeaux, France*

[2]*Wake Forest University, Winston-Salem, NC 27109, USA*

CONTENTS

4.1   Introduction 69
4.2   Clusters and Identity Formation 71
4.3   Wine Tourism in North Carolina 73
4.4   Methodology 76
4.5   Let the Weddings Begin 77
4.6   Wine Trails 81
4.7   Weddings as Wine Tourism? 83
4.8   Conclusion 85
Keywords 87
References 87

4.1 INTRODUCTION

Following the success of wine tourism in New Zealand and Australia, the topic has attracted increased interest from both researchers and winery groups in other countries (Bruwer, 2003; Mitchell and Hall, 2006; Koch et al., 2013). Wineries see tourism as a means of enhancing the visitor experience as well as creating brand loyalty and establishing customer relationship (Hall et al., 2002; Alonso et al., 2008). It provides significant opportunities for wineries to leverage their location and scenic beauty and bring new visitors to tasting rooms and more generally build awareness of the industry in a particular region. The goal is to capitalize upon the experiential aspects of wine tasting; to encourage people who value the aesthetic aspects of the winery and who might consider this a value-added activity worthy of their time and monetary investment (Bruwer and Alant, 2009). Since direct to consumer (cellar-door) sales out of tasting rooms and through wine clubs are an important feature of small wineries' business strategy, any additional way of encouraging visitors is eagerly embraced. This is particularly salient for wineries in new regions where general consumer awareness is less developed and product legitimacy less firmly established. Convincing local consumers that wine-making is a viable enterprise with a desirable finished product becomes central to promotional endeavors in such regions.

Throughout the east coast of the United States, from Georgia to New York, winery growth continues (Pinney, 2005; Riscinto-Kozub and Childs, 2012) but the liability of newness has meant it can be difficult to establish the requisite credibility for the finished product (wine) to build a regional reputation. Consequently, many wineries still struggle to gain product acceptance amongst a skeptical public; an issue further exacerbated by small batch and high production costs that translate into high retail prices. The resulting financial constraints can easily impede firm growth, especially with a product like wine where revenue streams are delayed by 3–5 years following initial grape planting. Resource rich wineries are less likely to face such limitations but then operate with up to 10-year profitability targets that enable them to focus upon brand building and enhanced product quality through the use of professionalized management (winemaker, vineyard manager, marketing and tasting room staff, etc.). However, most new wineries in these emerging regions do not have the luxury of such resources and more eagerly embrace local winery networks to capitalize upon identity building. For them wine tourism is a way to simultaneously increase sales, build their brand and foster further regional industry growth that can attract additional attention. In other words, it can be an indispensable part of their operational focus.

In this chapter, we examine how wineries in North Carolina have embraced wine tourism as a way to build brand identity. By leveraging their location within a network or cluster of wineries, they hope to gain visibility and attract visitors to their tasting rooms. This is not dissimilar to the goals of wineries in other regions, especially smaller ones that focus upon a majority of sales directly from tasting rooms, thus bypassing more costly distribution networks. However, we focus upon a specific aspect of wine tourism – the promotion of weddings, banquets and wine trails – that appears quite prominent amongst some NC wineries. We discuss the extent to which resources are allocated to such activities and how this constitutes a slightly different concept of wine tourism to that with which most people are familiar. In other words it is the pastoral setting that becomes the focus of activities, supplementing wine making both financially and quite possibly in overall strategic intent. We conclude with a critical assessment of what such endeavors might portend for the regional industry as it continues to grow.

4.2 CLUSTERS AND IDENTITY FORMATION

Studies have indicated the importance of networks and clusters of firms through which knowledge sharing and information exchange can facilitate collective organizational learning (Giuliani, 2006; Taplin, 2011, 2012; Yang et al., 2012). In turn this can lead to improved wine quality and consequently an enhanced reputation for the region's wines, which can further stimulate sales. However, that process can be lengthy and many new industry entrants face immediate problems of generating sufficient sales to meet their financial goals and even production capability. Wine tourism thus becomes a way to further leverage the clustering that is occurring, making it easy for visitors to come to a particular area and visit several wineries in geographical proximity to each other.

Although studies of clusters have indicated production benefits as quality improvements occur and the liability of newness is diminished, there has been less emphasis upon the tourism-related gains that might come from such proximity. Specific wineries can market themselves individually or via their appellation location – the latter an important regional source for brand building for established areas such as Burgundy or Napa Valley, California (Dawson et al., 2011). In emerging wine regions however, regional identity creation is simultaneously dependent upon product recognition, reputational growth and successful linkages between wineries as they cooperate. With otherwise limited resources, small wineries in such regions typically embrace wine tourism as a way to generate visitors and to maximize direct to consumer sales. In doing so, they seek to capitalize upon geographic proximity (clusters of wineries) and a distinctively cooperative approach to marketing.

Self-promotion is generally part of a broader marketing framework, often supported by state wine and grape grower organizations as well as state government commissions (Collins, 2006; Mitham, 2012). The assumption is that the more wineries exist in a particular concentrated area, the more likely visitors are to come to that area. Hence wineries promote themselves within a regional identity (AVA) and a visibility on newly established wine trails that both increases customer awareness and contributes to enhanced familiarity with the product itself (wine). Potential visitors are encouraged to spend time at numerous wineries in a particular area which has the effect of co-creating value by offering customer service attributes that do not exist at supermarkets (Hollebeek and Brodie, 2009). The more wineries there are in a particular area, the greater the visibility of the area as a distinctive wine region.

Increased visitor frequency generally improves customer service and winery retail expertise as well as adding to customer knowledge. Customers can relax as they taste wine, immersing themselves in a pastoral setting that evokes a calmer and relaxed age. This hedonic consumption experience varies from tourist to tourist (Bruwer and Alant, 2009), but the majority will buy when they visit even if it is merely one or two bottles. On site or 'cellar door' sales enables wineries to build their own brand, generate necessary revenue streams as well as build regional wine recognition (Riscinto-Kozub and Childs, 2012). This can lead to repeat visitation and customers buying more and higher priced wines, often by joining wine clubs that wineries have established. Most small wineries rely upon cellar door sales for the bulk of their income since it is often difficult for them to find appropriate distribution channels for their product. This heavy reliance means it is imperative for customers to have memorable experiences during their first visit and hence return.

In this chapter, our focus is on certain specific ways in which wineries embrace wine tourism and what the consequences are for these actions. Wineries inevitably see wine tourism as a way of increasing sales and building brand but exactly how they implement strategies to achieve this can vary. While most wineries utilize the attractiveness of their location and the aesthetic appeal of the winery as a hedonic consumption experience, others go a step further and market themselves as a site for weddings, corporate functions and other group activities (concerts, picnics etc.).

In other words 'formal' events complement the functional activities of the winery (growing grapes and making wine), subsequently providing a captive market for the wine as well as a revenue stream for the winery. But the more successful functions/events are financially, we wondered whether they might supplant the actual wine making itself. The extent to which one is prioritized over the other seemed to be an important question that merits further investigation since it is perhaps indicative of a broader tourism (and wine making) related strategy. Are some wineries leveraging location to achieve financial goals that the actual wine making is unable or only partially able to attain?

This might provide an interesting perspective on how wineries balance two mostly but not always complementary strategies. It is also a way of discerning how wineries prioritize activities in line with their resource capabilities. Are weddings and other such functions a means to build brand and attract customers; capitalizing upon facilities that offer a compelling aesthetic appeal for such romantic occasions? Or have they become the sine qua non for many wineries whose financial limitations preclude them from making the necessary commitment to winemaking? Although it is difficult to precisely determine quality outcomes of such differing positions, it is important to note that overall reputation for a sector in an embryonic industry such as wine in a new region can dramatically effect legitimacy and eventually sales.

4.3   WINE TOURISM IN NORTH CAROLINA

This research examines the growth of wine tourism in the emerging North Carolina wine region, but focuses specifically upon wineries that market themselves as sites for such formal events. It is our assertion that wineries in which there is considerable emphasis upon such events, the enhanced revenue stream from such activities has effectively cross subsidized the wine making operation. The extent to which such activities insulate the winery from concentrating upon upgrading the quality of the wine produced is a matter of conjecture that we will return to later in the chapter. Indubitably though, event functions offer a guaranteed and reasonably instant source of revenue whereas grape growing and wine-making is a longer, far less predictable revenue stream. Many new wineries underestimate the amount of capital needed for sustained production or fail to consider harvest problems that can constrain output. Faced with such pressing financial exigencies, weddings and banquets become paramount as an income source. This can provide a financial buffer but can potentially distract attention from what ostensibly was, and is, their core activity – wine making.

We chose to examine the wine industry in North Carolina because it has one of the fastest rates of new winery growth in the United States, three regional appellations which provide a cluster identity, and institutional support for and private sector involvement in wine tourism (see the web site by the NC Department of Agriculture and consumer Affairs, NCwine.org, for details). Although there is a long history of attempted and successful grape growing and wine making in the state that stretches back to the late 18th century (Taplin, 2011), the revival of the industry since the late 1970s followed by takeoff in the late 1990s qualifies it as having the second fastest growth rate of new wineries in the United States.

There are currently (2013) 116 wineries in the state and a new one opens almost every month. The industry has an economic impact of $1.28 billion and it employs 7575 workers. Most of the wineries are small (less than 2500 case production) and are owned by individuals who developed a passion for wine, sometimes growing grapes themselves and then gaining permits and bonding for a winery and tasting room; in other instances moving straight into fully fledged winery/tasting room operations. For most of these operations, the motivation was part of aspirational lifestyles – individuals were at a stage in life when they had the financial resources and level of commitment to devote to such a venture. Some worked full time at the winery; most however, retained a full time job to cross subsidize the vineyard and relied upon family members to help them with a limited opening schedule (Taplin, 2012). Most wineries were self-financed by individuals or through partnerships. Banks initially were reluctant to loan money for wineries in an area where they had limited experience.

Aside from financial resources, most wineries relied upon 'learning by doing' as a means of acquiring operating knowledge – the routine day-to-day activities associated with grape growing and wine making. Institutional support through the NC Department of Agriculture and Consumer Affairs (earlier through the NC Department of Commerce) and several local Colleges and Universities that offered enology and viticulture courses provided formal, 'codified' knowledge. Tacit knowledge, or that related to understanding local 'terroir' and distinctive regional conditions, was provided informally through the networks that emerged. Newcomers generally sought out established winery owners to learn as much as they could to supplement whatever formal education in grape growing and winemaking that they acquired. Such valuable localized information was enhanced when several resource-rich wineries established operations and their professional staff (vineyard management and winemakers) were able to proffer more structured learning (Taplin and Breckenridge, 2008). The latters' 'leadership' role has been crucial in the gradual formation of a regional identity.

Sustained industry growth since the late 1990s has resulted in firms becoming embedded in thick networks of knowledge sharing, with organizational learning as community sharing. The resulting cooperative business model has lowered some transaction costs for firms and certainly encouraged a culture of trust amongst the various wineries in a particular location. Not surprisingly, where there is a density of firms in a particular region, wine tourism has developed as other businesses saw opportunities to capitalize on emerging interest in wine and offer such services as limousine and coach tours. Wineries saw themselves as providing a product, the value of which could be enhanced if it was positioned as a broader consumer good. Instead of merely tasting wine and possibly buying it, consumers could now experience the full sensory features of the vineyard. The extent to which, and how, they have tried to capitalize upon this aura of agricultural sophistication is the subject of this chapter.

4.4 METHODOLOGY

This study relied upon secondary descriptive data as well as in-depth interviews with a sample of firms that possessed characteristics determined to be central to the question at hand. Specifically the data for this study were derived from firm web sites of every winery in North Carolina. This was supplemented with information provided by NC Department of Agriculture and Consumer Affairs, which provides booklets indicating winery location, basic facilities, opening hours and travel directions. From each source we looked for any reference to or mention of wedding or banquet promotion, and whether or not there was an indication of the winery being part of a wine trail.

We examined the web sites to see if the winery was listed as part of a regional appellation (AVA) that might drive tourist visits. We checked whether the winery indicated that tours are available in addition to a tasting room. We followed up by contacting by telephone all of the wineries in the Piedmont region which is where much of the recent growth has occurred and is the site of the three established AVAs in the state. Given the density of wineries in this region, it was assumed that wine tourism and wine trails would be most likely to exist here in an organized form and that area wineries would attempt to capitalize upon this in some form or other.

In the telephone calls we asked about their attempts to encourage and facilitate wine tourism, whether or not they were on wine trails and worked with wine tour companies. If they hosted weddings or banquets, we asked specifically about the emphasis they placed upon such activities. Those that did advertise such events were the subjects of a follow-up visit in which one of the authors asked specific, but confidential questions regarding relative financial priorities. Thirteen wineries were willing to share such information and were candid about their business strategies. These interviews typically lasted about an hour and the respondents were promised anonymity. We subsequently cross-checked their responses with whatever data we had on the winery from its web site.

For broader background information we utilized two recent studies on North Carolina wine tourism; the first by Appalachian State University in 2008 (Evans et al.), the second funded by NC Department of Commerce and prepared by UNC Greensboro, Bryant School of Business (Byrd et al., 2012). These studies examined visitor demographic profiles, tourists' level of understanding and knowledge of wine, how tourists select NC winery regions, and how wineries communicate their intentions. They are both based upon a sample of tourists to NC wineries rather than detailed analysis of winery tourism strategies, but nonetheless provide valuable data on what motivates wine tourists and their visitation habits.

4.5   LET THE WEDDINGS BEGIN

Founded in 2000 *Elkin Creek Vineyard* in the western Piedmont region publishes a small glossy brochure that states: "Elkin Creek Vineyard is proud to be able to host your entire wedding experience. Our on-site restaurant and commercial kitchen can cater to all your needs, from rehearsal dinner to your reception. We offer plated dinners and buffets style options. In addition to providing your event with fine food, we offer our excellent selection of Elkin Creek Vineyard wines. Please join us for a complimentary wine tasting to find the perfect wine pairings for you and your wedding."

There are numerous photos of smiling couples, the setting is bucolic, and there are descriptions of the floral categories that can provide the background to ones ceremony (Mountain Laurel, Rhododendron, etc.). A link to the wedding coordinator is provided. They also publish a similarly professional booklet advertising the winery that contains mention of the cabins on the property that available for rent. Come and drink, stay and get married is the abiding message.

Nearby is *Grassy Creek Vineyards and Winery*, founded in 2003, that uses its cabins as a central part of the wedding promotion and visitor experience. "Klondike Cabins at Grassy Creek Vineyard and Winery are a beautiful spot to host your wedding or special events. Accommodation, the grounds, and of course our winery and special wines have all of the necessary components to stage a magical time." Photos of happy couples follow.

Also in the western Piedmont area is *Uwharrie Vineyards*, set in 50 acres of vines on rolling hills near Charlotte, NC. According to their web site

A small intimate affair or a grand event, let Uwharrie vineyards be the location of your wedding celebration and/or rehearsal dinner. Our bridal consultant, event planner, professional chef, winemaker and staff members are here to assist you in your event planning and be available to help facilitate your needs.

The web site mentions that they have hosted 120+ wedding weekends thus far and it contains numerous wedding photos. Elsewhere there are details about their wine-making philosophy, as well as full information about visits and tours, wine club membership and the numerous health benefits associated with wine consumption.

In the western Piedmont is also located *Autumn Creek Vineyards*. The site of an old tobacco farm, it was purchased by the current owners in 2000 and the first vines planted in 2001 (currently there are 17 acres under cultivation). Their professional looking website[1] describes Cabins, Weddings and Tasting Room (in that order). "Autumn Creek Vineyards offers the perfect location for weddings and receptions. Our rustic and elegant Pavilion is the ideal location for your reception celebrating your newly married life with family and friends" they go on to emphasize. In fact the home page has rotating photos of weddings and events and none of the winery. There are cabins (including rental rates) listed prominently and the only photo of the winery is one of the outside of the tasting room with a brief mention of the wine varietals made.

Finally, in the eastern Piedmont is *Rock of Ages Winery* whose web site unambiguously states that they designed the winery with wedding ceremonies and corporate events in mind. Rock of Ages is designed in an old English style with hints of Italian and Western lodge influences.

This symphony of natural colors and textures is surrounded by 26 acres of vineyards and a 4-acre lake. Ideal for an outside wedding and corporate events in one of the most picturesque wineries in the United States. We have our own kitchen, chefs and staff. Let Rock of Ages Winery make your next event one that will be remembered by all forever.

The photos follow. Construction of the winery began in 2005 and the owner, having obtained a degree in viticulture and enology from Surry Community College, is also the winemaker.

---

[1] As one can imagine in an industry with very different levels of resources, the quality of the web sites varied: some were sophisticated visual extravaganzas, some merely informational with photos, others providing a brief history of the owners (and their pets!), in 4 instances the web site didn't work, and 1 winery did not even have a website.

The above examples were selected from the two Piedmont regions as wineries for which weddings are a central part of their 'branding' strategy. Each is illustrative of the particular focus that some wineries place upon wedding promotions. Thirty 7% of wineries in the western Piedmont and 35% in the eastern Piedmont made weddings central to their web sites; respectively 13% and 0% had an indirect reference to weddings (no direct link or photos but a comment that events such as weddings could be arranged in situ). In the mountain region, 11% emphasized weddings directly and 28% made a reference to their possibility. For the coastal region, it was respectively 29% and 14%. Table 4.1 below provides a summary of these data.

Two of the four 'resource rich' wineries (*Childress and Raffaldini*) directly advertise their facilities as wedding sites but the winery and their wine are the prominent features on their web sites. The other two in the region (*Shelton and Raylen*) do not even indirectly refer to weddings. In the mountains, *Biltmore Estates* clearly sees itself as a site for weddings but then mainly in conjunction with the adjacent Biltmore House. The other major winery, *Duplin*, in the coastal region does not reference weddings but does have a restaurant and offers banquet facilities.

In our follow up in-depth interviews and site visits with owners, we randomly selected ten in the western Piedmont (50%) and three in the eastern Piedmont (43%) who had made weddings a central part of their winery promotion. Of these, all but 2 indicated that weddings were a crucial part of their operating budget, a way of ensuring profitability in most years as opposed to a loss.

The costs of providing the facilities (converted barns, old mill house, cabins, landscaping lake, etc.) were capitalized up front and depreciated against the ensuing revenue stream over varying multi year periods. After estimating the number of weddings and average cost/revenue for each

TABLE 4.1 Wineries That Directly and Indirectly Promote Weddings

Region	Number of wineries	Directly promote weddings	Make reference to their possibility
Mountains	18	2 (11%)	5 (28%)
Western Piedmont	54	20 (37%)	7 (13%)
Eastern Piedmont	20	7 (35%)	0
Coastal	14	4 (29%)	2 (14%)

event, they were able to develop a budget that was a crucial part of their overall operating expenses. This enabled them to balance any losses in winemaking (important for newly established wineries that were waiting for vines to mature and yield fruit) and yield a positive financial balance. In other words, the weddings accounted for the cash flow whilst the wineries (they hoped) were the revenue stream.

Their owners were unambiguous in their commitment to weddings. When asked directly to prioritize, each said that weddings were the focus of their operation, the wine making a distant second. They clarified by saying that they built the winery because they liked the idea of owning a winery but realized that to make money they needed a solid and predictable income stream that wine could not necessarily guarantee. So the facilities were designed explicitly to have an aesthetic appeal that could conjure the romance of a pastoral setting for a wedding. They even admitted that their winemaking was probably not as good as it could be if they had the resources to devote to it; one even went so far as saying that quality didn't matter since wedding parties were required to use the winery's wine so it was a captive (and not necessarily discerning) market.

Other wineries that focused upon weddings said that they were merely a way to supplement their income and feel that it didn't affect their winemaking ability. Half of the wineries said that weddings (and banquets/private parties) account for 10–15% of their margins – an important revenue source that contributes to the winery being profitable. Of the others, some said that it helped and was "a little extra on the side" (western Piedmont winery owner); one said that it "kept them above water," another that it was a nice way to move some of their backlog of wine from earlier vintages.

When asked why they decided to pursue weddings, four indicated that early in their development they had received so many enquiries about staging weddings ("something about a winery setting that appears now to be a popular wedding destination" one owner told us) that they decided to adapt their facilities to meet this need. In some cases this could be a marquee on the property; in others an adjacent barn was hastily converted or a new structure constructed. Others said that it seemed a logical thing to do when others were doing it. One said: "we have a beautiful setting with several old barns, a small lake and gentle rolling hills. The tasting room has a great view over all of this, and since we have a kitchen, glasses and lots of wine, why not offer this type of formal catering." Another commented that they had done small banquets for their wine club members so it made sense to branch out and offer more formal receptions that they could personally cater. Such activities generated considerable profit, they noted – at least compared to wine making! About one third of the wineries has hired special wedding planners or merged that position with tasting room staff. These tend to be wineries that offer weddings on a regular basis between May and October. Others arrange it on a more informal basis, doing in-house catering often by one of the owners.

Many owners said that the newly constructed or adapted facilities proved useful as multi-purpose – several putting their temporary bottling lines in these structures. When asked if they thought that weddings might eventually attract new customers to the winery they all concurred. More specifically, one said that it generates somewhere between 20 and 25% of new customers – people who had attended the wedding and then returned to visit the winery and subsequently buy wine. Another indicated that it definitely brought new customers because people would comment that they had earlier visited the winery for a wedding. Others were more circumspect or had not been able to measure any gains.

4.6   WINE TRAILS

Given the recent importance of wine trails as a way of attracting customers to groups of wineries as well as an indication of cooperation amongst wineries, we examined web sites to ascertain whether such information was available. We also analyzed the web sites for other information about local accommodation, restaurants, local attractions, etc., that might be construed as encouraging visitors. Table 4.2 summarizes this information for the four regions in North Carolina.

A surprisingly small number of wineries in each of the regions promoted wine trails or were listed as being part of one. The possible exception was in the eastern Piedmont where 25% of the wineries had a link and in each case it was to the Haw River AVA of which they were a part (see also McCluney, 2011).. According to one local winery owner, the Haw River AVA has helped the wine business grow. A member of the NC wine

TABLE 4.2 Wine Trails and Other Tourist Related Activities Listed by Wineries

Region	Number of wineries	Wine trails links	Other tourist related activities (accommodation, etc.)
Mountain	18	0	2
Western Piedmont	54	12	19
Eastern Piedmont	20	5	1
Coastal	14	0	4

and Grape Council added "Tourists will still pass a few tobacco patches in the area, but the Haw River AVA enhances our state's wine tourism product and brings hikers, bikers, float trippers, restaurants, festivals and, of course, wine tasters" (quoted in McCluney, 2011).

In telephone interviews and site visits, each of these wineries said that they had attempted to define themselves as part of this AVA. They believed that their collective identity would help promote sales and build a local brand as it had done in the first NC AVA, Yadkin Valley. There was little or no expense to make the listing or link and they believed by doing that and indicating local accommodation they were making visits easier and convenient. Several said that they liked the idea of other wineries being in close proximity as that actually might encourage visitors.

In cases where there was no link, wineries indicated that this was not something they felt they needed to do. Private companies were developing wine tours and since they pre-booked at the winery, there were little that the winery itself needed to do. Also they believed that wine trails are in their infancy and not that well known. Or they said there were not any in their area, so there was nothing to promote.

We did investigate the provision of private tour organizations that offered limousine service for groups of visitors. One such example in the western Piedmont is Yadkin Valley Wine Tours (www.yadkinwinetours. com). Established in 2005 it is the largest education wine tour company in North Carolina, providing tours to the Yadkin Valley from nearby cities such as Winston-Salem, Charlotte and Raleigh. Other smaller local companies provide similar tours, basically transporting small groups to pre-booked tastings at a select number of wineries in a particular locale.

Wine Versus Weddings: Wine Tourism in the Emerging North Carolina

When asked about their response to such tours, all the wineries said they liked them as long as they could accommodate the numbers. However, they noted that people on such tours tend to be more discerning about wine and are likely to buy when they visit a winery. Such tours also provide a somewhat more reliable revenue stream for wineries from group tasting fees. It is difficult to ascertain exactly how many such companies exist because there is no central business record on them. However, anecdotal evidence suggests that the numbers are rising in part because of the increased numbers and density of wineries in certain areas; they are also most likely to be in the western and eastern Piedmont region where the majority of the wineries are located.

Links to accommodations and restaurants were seen as important but only if it was felt that the accommodation was appropriate to the image they were trying to create at the winery. For example Bed and Breakfast Inns in an area were more likely to be listed than typical highway motels; similarly family owned restaurants as opposed to fast food outlets. When probed about this, the wineries that did list or link with such sites were trying to embellish the rural charm and sophistication of such a setting as being consistent with their own brand image.

4.7 WEDDINGS AS WINE TOURISM?

According to published studies, wine tourism is growing in NC, with many repeat visitors as peoples' knowledge of the product improves (Byrd et al., 2012). Customer service is an important feature determining satisfaction and the likelihood of returning for such visitors, which is not surprising. However, the recommendations of this report and a previous tourism study (Evans et al., 2008) are for wineries to capitalize upon proximity to other wineries in the area and develop or enhance special events. With this explicit encouragement it is perhaps not surprising that new wineries embrace this multi-facetted approach to self-promotion as part of their market focus.

What is axiomatic about our research findings is that many wineries, of different sizes and resource capabilities, see weddings and private functions as a valuable source of revenue and are therefore partially redefining the notion of wine tourism. For some of the smaller wineries it is a necessary component of their operating budget; for others a supplemental income source. All recognize that their physical surroundings have precisely the aesthetic appeal that is in demand by a group of customers who are in search of an appropriately romantic, or in the case of banquets, a peaceful pastoral setting. In many respects, to not offer such facilities that are conceivably under-utilized does not make good business sense.

Not surprisingly many of the wineries that have embraced this strategy are recent start-ups, making weddings and wine trails a central part of their overall operating philosophy. More widespread information about practices (knowledge transfer but in this instance not about winemaking but about event planning) reduces start-up snags. The dissemination of information about such events and the wineries is more widespread, and public enthusiasm for such settings more accepted and entrenched.

An example of this trend can be found in the newest winery in the western Piedmont, Yadkin Valley AVA. *Medaloni Cellars* just opened with 22 acres, a tasting room and cabins for rent. They are already planning to host several weddings and in a recent newspaper article covering the opening, the owner Joey Medaloni said: "We come from the hospitality background. So I'm trying to combine hospitality with the wine country." (Hastings, *Winston-Salem Journal*, May 22, 2013). They have created a wine trail and plan on building a restaurant this summer. In other words they have wholly embraced the idea of combining a winery with weddings and other forms of entertainment.

If marketing weddings at one's winery has become practically de rigueur, how does this fit with the information we have regarding tourist demographics? Might the profile of the person planning a wedding be similar to that of a wine tourist? From various studies of wine tourism we know that the average wine tourist is relatively affluent. In the case of North Carolina, they are predominantly white educated females averaging 45 years of age, with just over a third having household incomes in excess of $100,000. Seventy three percent were from within state, 38.7% stayed overnight in the area and two thirds were repeat visitors (Byrd et al., 2012). Given that the average cost of a wedding is

$23,000–26,000, there is certainly a similarity in the wedding and tourist demographic groups.

4.8 CONCLUSION

This study examines how wineries in an emerging wine region have used weddings and formal functions as part of their operating and growth strategy. Not only have such activities provided valuable revenue streams, they have also helped build a local brand and encouraged greater awareness of wineries in this particular region. While such strategies might not necessarily have improved the reputation of winemaking in North Carolina, they have nonetheless made more people aware of the existence of a wine industry in the state. In this respect, such activities play a nuanced role in tourism development, bringing people to wineries, some of whom might not otherwise make a visit. Such findings are consistent with studies that argue that a variety of activities within the winery encourage wine tourism (Dawson et al., 2011), as well as the importance of strategic marketing in emerging wine regions (Koch et al., 2013).

There has been a question as to whether the enthusiasm for wedding promotion might have adverse effects upon winemaking and the quality of the wine. In an embryonic industry, with a steep learning curve for new entrants, the fear amongst some wine critics is that weddings might divert attention and resources away from the core activity of wine making. This could damage the reputational aspects of the region at a time when its identity is still in the formative stages. Whilst it is difficult to determine exactly how much this has occurred it is interesting to note the number of wineries who unabashedly acknowledge the priority that weddings take in their operation.

Conceivably attributable to the liability of newness, underestimation of the resources necessary for successful wine production, or even a naïve assumption that the beauty of the setting might cancel out shortcomings in wine quality, it is nonetheless an issue that merits further investigation. Because it is still in a growth stage with widely varying levels of quality in the finished wine, some within the industry locally are arguing for improved quality benchmarks as a way to ensure continued growth and enhanced legitimacy. The NC Wine and Grape Growers Association recently introduced quality panels to assist wineries in objectively assessing their product; not mandating such testing but encouraging wineries to utilize such services as part of their ongoing professionalization. The extent to which wineries submit wines to such panels and accept the findings, remains to be seen. The wine price points for smaller wineries will probably remain high, given the lack of economies of scale.

Consequently, the need for quality is paramount if the industry is gain more than a localized reputation. Unfortunately because many of the winery owners are new to the industry, they often lack the critical self-evaluation that can enable them to recognize flaw in their product. Or, as one winery owner told us, they could not afford to rectify what he noticed was a problem, and continued selling the wine as long as customers bought it.

We also surmised that wine trials would be an important component of brand building for wineries but this proved less salient. Fewer than expected wineries capitalized upon such trails, despite the fact that they are used as a marketing tool by state agencies promoting the industry. On the other hand, the idea of wine trails appears to have been enthusiastically embraced by private companies specializing in regional tours. This has indirectly aided wineries by bringing groups to tasting rooms and contributed to sales revenue. New wineries appear more cognizant of this activity and promote it; older ones less so.

Finally we should note the limitations of our study with the absence of counter factual evidence. Since we concentrated on analyzing wineries that enthusiastically embraced weddings, we did not explore in detail those that did not make such activities a central part of their brand development. To assume that they were and are endowed with greater resources would be simplistic (especially since at least two that did promote weddings were amongst the biggest in the area). We can only surmise that their focus was on winemaking with a few ancillary activities, or that their site was lacking in the aesthetic appeal to generate wedding interest. Our aim, however, was to focus upon why a certain group of wineries had developed a particular tourist focus and hopefully the above discussion provides answers to this question.

KEYWORDS

- **cellar door**
- *Childress*
- *Raffaldini*
- **terroir**
- **wine tourism**

REFERENCES

1. Alonso, A. D., Fraser, R. A., Cohen, D. A. (2008). 'Exploring wine tourism in New Zealand: The visitors' point of view,' *Tourism Analysis*, 13/2: 171–180.
2. Bruwer, J. (2003). 'South African wine routes: some perspectives on the wine tourism industry's structural dimensions and wine tourism product,' *Tourism Management,* 24/2002: 423–435.
3. Bruwer, J., Alant, K. (2009). 'The hedonic nature of wine tourism consumption: An experiential view,' *International Journal of Wine Business Research,* 21/3:235–257.
4. Byrd, E. T., Canziani, B. Hsieh, J., Debbage, K. (2012). Study of visitors to North Carolina wineries. University of North Carolina Greensboro, Bryan School of Business and Economics.
5. Collins, R (2006). 'NY wine trails are pathways to dollars,' *Wines and Vines*, September.
6. Dawson, D., Fountain, J., Cohen, D. A. (2011). 'Place-based marketing and wine tourism; creating a point of difference and economic sustainability for small wineries,' paper presented at 6th AWBR International Conference, Bordeaux Management School, 9–11 June.
7. Evans, M. Pollard, C., Holder, GT. (2008). Discover North Carolina Wines: A wine tourism profile study. Boone: Appalachian State University.
8. Giuliani, E. (2006). 'The selective nature of knowledge networks in clusters: Evidence from the wine industry,' *Journal of Economic Geography,* 7, 139–168.
9. Hall, M, Sharples, L. Cambourne, B., Macionis, N. (2002). Wine Tourism Around the World – Development, Management and Markets, 2nd edition, Oxford: Butterworth-Heineman.

10. Hollebeek, L. D., Brodie, R. J. (2009). 'Wine service marketing, value co-creation and involvement: Research issues,' *International Journal of Wine Business Research,* 21/4:339–353
11. Koch, J. Martin, A., Nash, R. (2013). 'Overview of perceptions of German wine tourism from the winery perspective,' *International Journal of Wine Business Research,* 25/1:50–74.
12. Kunc, M. H. (2009). 'Forecasting the development of wine tourism: A case study in Chile, ' *International Journal of Wine Business Research,* 21/4:325–338.
13. Mitham, P. (2012). 'Woodinville wine country to focus on tourism,' *Wines and Vines,* July.
14. Mitchell, R., Hall, C. M. (2006). 'Wine tourism research: the state of play,' *Tourism Review International,* 9, 307–332.
15. Pinney, T. (2005). History of wine in America: From prohibition to the present. Berkeley, Ca.: University of California Press.
16. Riscinto-Kozub, K., Childs, N. (2012). 'Conversion of local winery awareness,' *International Journal of wine Business Research,* 24/4:287–301.
17. Taplin, I. M. (2011). The Modern American Wine Industry. (London: Pickering and Chatto).
18. ——— (2012). 'Innovation and growth in a new 'New World' wine region: The case of North Carolina, *Journal of Wine Research.*
19. Taplin, I. M., Breckenridge, R. S. (2008). 'Large firms, legitimation and industry identity: The growth of the NC wine industry,' *Social Science Journal,* 45, 52–60.
20. Yang, N., McCluskey, J. J., Brady, M. (2012). 'The value of good neighbors: A spatial analysis of the California and Washington State wine industries,' *Land Economics,* 88/4: 674–684.

CHAPTER 5

WINE TOURISM IN BORDEAUX

TATIANA BOUZDINE-CHAMEEVA,[1] CHRISTOPHE FAUGÈRE,[2] and PIERRE MORA[3]

[1]*Professor, Kedge Business School, Bordeaux, France, E-mail: tatiana.chameeva@kedgebs.com*

[2]*Professor, Kedge Business School, Bordeaux, France, E-mail: christophe.faugere@kedgebs.com*

[3]*Professor, Kedge Business School, Bordeaux, France, E-mail: pierre.mora@ kedgebs.com*

CONTENTS

5.1 Introduction 90
5.2 Brief History of Bordeaux's Traditions in Wine Making and Trading 93
5.3 Key Figures of the Bordeaux Region Wine Tourism 95
5.4 Wine Tourism and Culture in the Extant Literature 97
5.5 Wine Tourists' Perceptions and Expectations Regarding Their Experience at Bordeaux Wineries 99
5.6 Wine Producers' Perception Regarding Wine Tourists: Bordeaux vs. Other Famous Wine Producing Regions 103
5.7 Managerial Implications 110
5.8 Conclusions 111
Keywords 113
References 113

5.1 INTRODUCTION

InFocus: This chapter focuses on wine tourism in the Bordeaux region; a region that is well-known for a wine-making tradition covering the last two millennia.

Brief description: We compare and contrasts findings from two separate recent studies: the first one about testimonials of foreign and local tourists visiting wineries in the region and the second about the perceptions of wine tourists by wine producers in Bordeaux vs. other wine capitals. We use known categories describing types of wine tourists visiting French properties (Atout France, 2010) and implement a comparative analysis. This allows us to point out areas of inconsistencies in the way Bordeaux Châteaux conceive of their wine tourism activities and services.

Main goal: To understand better the challenges of wine tourism in Bordeaux and the interference of traditions on the development of this sector.

> The real voyage of discovery consists not in seeking new landscapes, but in having new eyes.
>
> *Marcel Proust*

> In water one sees one's own face, but in wine one beholds the heart of another.
>
> *French Proverb*

Bordeaux is a unique French city who gave its name to the color of its wines and to a special wine style known all over the world. The city, listed as a UNESCO World Heritage Site since 2007, enjoys its unique prestige in the heart of wine country. According to TripAvisor[1], Bordeaux (and the larger Aquitaine region), Napa Valley and Tuscany secure the top 3 spots among the top 10 wine destinations in the world, followed by French Champagne-Ardenne region and Australia's Barossa Valley. Saint-Emilion, a UNESCO World heritage village, and the Medoc area are the two destinations that attract the most wine tourists to the region (see Fig. 5.1).

---

[1] http://www.travelblissful.com/where-the-wine-is-divine-top-10-grape-destinations/

Wine Tourism in Bordeaux

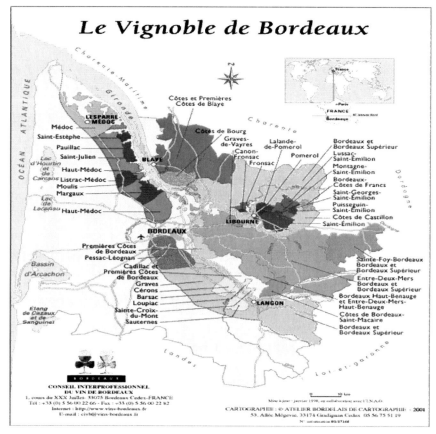

FIGURE 5.1 The Bordeaux wine region areas.[2]

In 2010, worldwide wine tourism generated about $17 billion annual revenues. Other wine producing countries such as Australia, New Zealand, South Africa and California have extensively invested in this new business model for at least two decades now, with a majority of wineries operating at least a cellar door/sales shop and bigger wineries offering restaurants and accommodation services as well as other tourist attractions. Curiously, while France is one of the top wine producing and wine consuming country in the world, and the first tourist destination on

---
[2] Source: https://www.bordeauxprof.com

the planet, it has not been a leader in the wine "oeno" tourism movement. The country lags behind other wine producing countries of the New-World with only 5.2 million wine tourists, half of them foreigners, out of a total 83 million tourists visiting the country, according to the figures of the French Ministry of Agriculture (2012). France became interested in this activity quite recently, mainly because of the growth of global competition on world wine market and the 2008 global financial crisis (Lignon-Darmaillac, 2009). An analysis of profits generated during these last 5 years shows that wine tourism has become a new economic and strategic trend in the French wine regions. World wine consumption is nowadays mostly dominated by countries like China, the US and Russia. Wine tourism when geared towards attracting younger generations and more women, can become a viable counterweight to the steady drop of wine consumption in France over the last decade. Wine tourism drives direct sales up for wine Châteaux and at the same time helps to solidify their market position internationally.

In this regard, wine tourism today turns out to be an unexpected bounty in terms of promoting the Bordeaux wine region. It is no more a passing fad. It has become the cutting edge of the global economic development of the region. Although not as widespread in the Bordeaux region, a number of leading Châteaux have begun to welcome visitors either by appointment or at allotted times. Nowadays, there is a growing population of producers rivaling with the best from the New-World by offering accommodations, restaurants, shop sales and impressive tour experiences of underground cellars/caves. More and more producers realize that the development of wine tourism can be a successful means of generating and diversifying sales revenues (Barney, 1991; Peteraf, 1993; Getz and Brown, 2006). It is an economic asset for vineyards, a new form of enhancing wine knowledge through direct sales and an effective means of promoting customer loyalty. Pleasing customers is important, but it is clear that wineries are sometimes not active enough in shaping their own customer service strategy. Wineries may have a natural tendency to embrace the unique natural, human and historical capital of their region, but by the same token inherited traditions can slow down the need to adapt to a new clientele (Alant and Bruwer, 2004; Brunori and Rossi, 2000; Bouzdine-Chameeva, 2011).

5.2 BRIEF HISTORY OF BORDEAUX'S TRADITIONS IN WINE MAKING AND TRADING

Back when ancient Rome was occupying the south of France, the Graves region, upstream the river Garonne and southwest of Bordeaux, accounted for the largest part of the Bordeaux region wine production. The production went as far east as the vineyards known today as Saint-Emilion. The advent of the Médoc region's wines for example, only occurred during the nineteenth century. Since the Middle-Ages, Bordeaux owes much of its prosperity to the close relationships of its vineyards with the United Kingdom. From the 11th century on, beginning with Aliénor d'Aquitaine, Queen of France and England, a special bond with England was created. Indeed, during the Hundred Years War, the majority of Aquitaine, and the port of Bordeaux in particular, were occupied by the English. At that time, the French market, including Paris, was closed to Bordeaux producers. Furthermore, sea trade was considered safer than ground transportation. Bordeaux wines enjoyed a quasi-monopoly on the vast British market. The great historian of the vine and wine Raymond Dumay argues that the Bordeaux region focused more on producing large quantities of wine in order to meet the expected volume of exports. Later, an orientation towards quality became the rule during the twentieth century. The British imperial power over all the oceans allowed the global expansion of Bordeaux wines. Free trade was a convenient way for Bordeaux wines to get around the oppressing "centralism" of the French State.

An innovation of Bordeaux at the time was the blending of varietals, which was a consequence of a diverse "terroir" (or soil specificities), unlike what has been done in typically in the Burgundy region. The fact that Bordeaux is today known around the world for being a product or a brand and not a city, is due to the English genius for exporting and trading their products (standardized or elitist) to the four corners of the world. Today 25% of Bordeaux wine production is exported. This percentage is much higher for the Grands Crus wines. The commerce network known as *La Place de Bordeaux* (see Fig. 5.2) is based on the tradition that the Châteaux from the area (132 Grands Crus today) produce wine but do not really sell it. Over time they have built relationships with brokers, the "Maisons de Négoce" or merchants of Bordeaux who market wines on

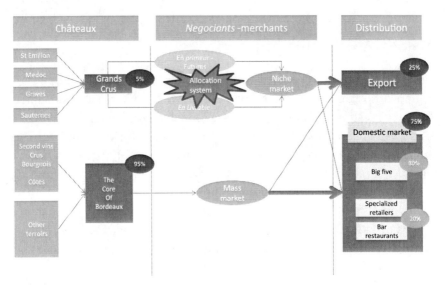

FIGURE 5.2 La "Place de Bordeaux."

the domestic and export markets. Each year, during the April campaign, "primeur" or young wines are sampled and their potential worth is gauged and priced. A few days later, the "allocations" are proposed, that is, the number of bottle cases and the prices at which the various Châteaux will sell to merchants. After agreeing on a price and quantity, the trader/merchant will wait eighteen months during which the wines are aged in oak barrels in the cellars of the Châteaux. This system guarantees future purchase prices for the traders and ensures that producers receive the cash they need to budget their upcoming operational expenses.

Merchants have specialized in the acquisition of detailed and valuable knowledge of local and distant markets, which would be costly for Châteaux to obtain. This activity specialization between producers and traders indeed has helped Bordeaux wineries with their maintaining and sometimes expanding their market shares. Often, merchants themselves select, assemble and even create signature brands. Today, a clear trend towards the concentration of production and distribution of wines continues in Bordeaux. Nevertheless, this region has been able to maintain a strong diversity in an area of 8,000 Châteaux and Domains, with about 300 merchants on Bordeaux and 57 Controlled Appellations, all of whom can proudly claim a unique brand identity, with some varying degree of visibility on the global wine market.

5.3 KEY FIGURES OF THE BORDEAUX REGION WINE TOURISM

The number of tourists visiting wine Châteaux in the Bordeaux region during the period from January to August in 2007 was 11,355 visitors, and in 2013, the figure was over 14,000 visitors. This constitutes a 30% increase in spite of the tight economic environment caused by the 2008 financial crisis. Today, the tourism industry employs in Aquitaine more than 35,000 employees on the permanent basis and about 70,000 during the summer period. These activities account for more than 5% of wage-earners in the region. Every year over 10,000 visitors in Aquitaine spend about €3 billion between May and September. According to Atout France (2010) more than 6 million tourists visit French wine cellars per year. For the Aquitaine region with 6299 facilities (6230 Châteaux and 69 wine-growers coops) 5.09 million visitors were recorded between 2010 and 2012 (3.6 million visits for the Bordeaux area). Wine tourism represents almost 7% of all business revenues generated in Bordeaux (Office du tourisme, 2012).

In 2009 about 80% of tourists in Aquitaine were French, the rest were foreigners. However during the last 3 years, Bordeaux has welcomed more and more foreign tourists. This trend is strengthening, and in 2013, already more than 35% of visitors were coming from other countries. These visitors are mainly from United Kingdom, Spain, USA, Germany, Australia, Italy, Japan, and Netherlands (Office du tourisme, 2012). Since 2010, France has recorded a 15% annual rise in the number of tourists coming from China. Bordeaux has indeed become one the most cherished destinations for Chinese tourists. In the past 5 years, more than 60 prestigious wine Châteaux have also been purchased by Chinese investors who are interested not only in meeting a growing Chinese demand for Bordeaux wines but also in taking advantage of this increasingly lucrative niche of the tourism market. There are several internationally recognized events in the region linking wine with arts, culture and even sports! VinExpo founded in 1981 by the Bordeaux Chamber of Commerce and Industry is held every other year in Bordeaux. It has turned out to be the world's leading trade show for wine and spirits professionals.

The 17th edition in 2013 attracted more than 50,000 visitors from 148 countries. Another big event is Le Marathon du Médoc[3], a race with more than 9,000 runners, one-third of them being foreigners. The marathon snakes its way through more that 50 wineries, among them many famous Grand Classified Growth as Beychevelle or Haut-Bage. Runners go from Château to Château. They can stop for tasting wine and are serenaded by piped-in Mozart concertos. This colorful event is cherished by wine producers of the region, artists, 2800 volunteers and sportsmen and women from 50 different countries.

Since 1998, Bordeaux City Hall organizes the Bordeaux Wine Festival along the Garonne riverside. The event is run over 4-days in the last weekend in June. Young and old learn more about the art of wine making and tasting in the joyful atmosphere. The event includes a parade of Bacchus floats, wine tastings, vineyards tours and wine barrel races; spectacular riverside fireworks illuminate the night sky on the last day. This festival features more than 50 stands, 100 chateaux represented and many others open for tours; a dozen of great food facilities are open for the visitors on the festival's grounds. Each festival has the city guest of honor – after Porto, Munich, Fukuoka, Saint-Petersburg, Quebec and Hong Kong, Los-Angeles will play this role in 2014. Out of a total budget of €2 million, 30% come from public grants and subsidies. Attendance is continuously record breaking approaching 500,000 visitors in 2012. The gross revenue totaled over €3.4 million that year. The wine tourist business growth in the Bordeaux region has been supported by an expansion of wine tourism services. More than 480 wine Châteaux, cooperatives and wine trade houses open their doors to visitors, year around. Each week more than 40 specialized tours offer wine tasting and Châteaux visits and more than 20 others offer weekend-stays that bring together wine, historical heritage, spa and golf. Numerous strolls and trails exist in vineyards around Bordeaux. There has been an increased availability of oenological and gastronomic activities in the region. Bordeaux has launched the €63 million project of a new museum – *The City of Wine Civilizations*. It should open its doors in 2016 to welcome 400,000 visitors per year in a space of 10,000 square meters.

---

[3] http://fr.wikipedia.org/wiki/Marathon_du_Médoc

During the last ten years, a new trend has emerged. A fierce competition has started in the region among the leading chateaux of the classified first growths vineyards regarding the construction of *modern* cellars. The most famous French architects have been hired for these new concepts – Portzamparc, Nouvel, Foster, Wilmotte, Botta, Bofill, Pei.., to name a few. They have not only created architecturally beautiful chef-d'oeuvres (works of art) but they also have designed exceptional décor with amazing acoustics for music concerts featuring world-class musicians. It would be reasonable to assume that all these investments and strategic choices are based on a keen understanding of the type of visitors that come to the Châteaux. It is nevertheless worth using the scientific method to find out what the key motivational factors are that attract visitors to the region. A good understanding of the profile and aspirations of Bordeaux wine tourists may help us determine whether or not wineries respond well to these expressed needs and preferences.

5.4 WINE TOURISM AND CULTURE IN THE EXTANT LITERATURE

Getz (2000) and Hall et al. (2000) define wine tourism as "touring vineyards, wineries, wine festivals, and wine exhibitions, where wine tasting and/or experiencing the attributes of the wine region are the principal factors of motivation for the visitors." The activity of wine tourism is an extension of the rather complex relationship between a wine region as a tourist destination, the local wineries, and the tourist/consumer (Bruwer and Lesschaeve, 2012). Wine tourism or visits to wine regions is a phenomenon that has undergone close academic scrutiny in the last decade. According to Mitchell and Hall (2006) there are seven themes prevalent in the emergent body of research studies: the wine tourism product, wine tourism and regional development, quantifications and segmentation of winery visits, behavior of winery visitors, the nature of the winery visit, biosecurity and wine tourism. Carlsen and Charters (2006) in turn identify five thematic groupings in academic publications: wine tourism culture and heritage, wine tourism business, wine tourism marketing, wine tourists and wine tourism systems. Tourists have a multitude of reasons for visiting wineries. Indisputably, the core-motivating factor has to do with the consumption of wine. However, this is not enough, as otherwise these people could just buy wine at the store. The wine tourist aspires to explore both the wine and location where wine is produced. In a broader context, wine tourism may also be linked to other lifestyle activities and to travel per-se (Bruwer & Alant, 2009). Pearce (2005) suggests that the core factors to all travel, regardless of previous experience are "three dimensions of motivation functions: ... novelty, escape/relax and relationship [strengthen]..."... The "novelty" factor relates to motives of varying experiences including interests and fun, while the "escape/ relax" factor motives relate to getting away and resting and the relationship (strengthen) factor motives focus on companionship of family and friends in experiences.

Thus wine tourists may be looking for a multi-layered experience that encompasses broader touristic, recreational, educational and social activities (Pearce, 2005). They may also seek multi-sensorial hedonistic experiences via for aesthetic beauty and the pleasure of gourmet food (Alant and Bruwer, 2004; Bruwer and Alant, 2009; Hall et al., 2000; O'Mahony et al., 2005). The search for pleasure is indeed a deep-seated human characteristic, which can be greatly motivational (Goossens, 2000). Visitors seek relaxation, rest, education, and appreciation of rural landscape and scenery (Carmichael, 2005). Some of them yearn for a romantic experience (Getz and Brown, 2006). Wine region visitors' motivations at the macro level (which region to visit) and micro level (which winery(ies) to visit and what experiences to have there) may well fit these some or all of these reasons (Alant and Bruwer, 2010).

The greater the motivation of visitors for tasting wine, the more intent they are to seek activities beyond tasting and buying wine, like learning and cultural experiences, but that this varies across regions and cultures (Charters and Ali-Knight, 2002). These authors find that there is neither one type of wine visitor nor a clear unilateral definition of wine tourist behavior. Tourists are not a generic group of people (Pearce, 2005) and hence wine tourist behavior can vary in different regions and cultures. Carlsen and Charters (2004) put forth a broad palette of the internal (motivation, attitudes and beliefs, life styles and personality types) and external (demography, dynamics and group cultures) factors influencing wine tourist's consumer behavior: wine purchasing, brand image, loyalty, expert views and evaluations, recent consumer experiences of visits (hedonic nature, atmosphere, service quality). Certain studies emphasize considerable gaps with respect to expectations and actual wine visits – the lack of information on wines, or the deficiency of attention towards different levels of consumer knowledge (Famularo et al., 2010; Bruwer and Alant, 2004).

There are more and more ongoing research on wine tourist behavior focusing on their expectations (Orth et al., 2005), on segmentation in relation to tourist origins, age and/or specific generation, life style (Carlsen, 2008). Researchers are particularly interested in the role of tourism experiences in consumer attachment to regional brands (Orth et al., 2011). The results of these studies are not homogenous and strongly depend on the context of consumption, and on national or cultural differences. Furthermore, along with similarities there are striking differences opposing the expectations of local and non-local tourists (Bouzdine-Chameeva and Durrieu, 2010).

5.5 WINE TOURISTS' PERCEPTIONS AND EXPECTATIONS REGARDING THEIR EXPERIENCE AT BORDEAUX WINERIES

A recent study entitled "Tourism and Wine" (Atout France, 2010) proposes a four socio-groups typology for wine tourists in France: *epicureans*, *classic*, *explorers*, and *experts* (see Fig. 5.3). These categories were identified through aspirations and different consumption patterns. According to this study, an "epicurean" wine visitor relates to wine as exaltation of all senses; for a "classic" tourist, wine is the heart of local historic, cultural, architectural and gastronomic heritage; a wine tourist "explorer" perceives the magic and alchemy in wine, which he/she identifies as a work of art; while an "expert" wine visitor has a more scientific approach and intends to investigate wine through the prism of know-how and technical competences with their specific codes, terroir, and rules...

Each socio-group possesses its own expectations and demonstrates a diverse behavior towards the choice of wine tourism activities. The study concludes that the goal of wine tourism activities is to find the right balance among sensorial, cultural, emotional and rational dimensions. The characteristics of Bordeaux wine visitors are quite representative of the national level: the epicureans constitute 39% (compared to 40% on national level); the group of classic tourists accounts for 27% (versus 24% on the national

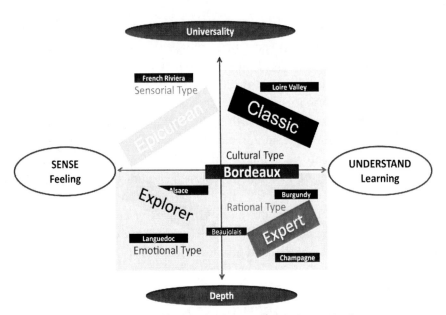

FIGURE 5.3 The perception of the Bordeaux Region by wine tourists[4].

level); the explorers represent 19% (20% on the national level) and the experts' group accounts 15% (versus 16% on the national level). The three major motivations for visiting the Bordeaux region are to learn about wines and vineyards; to discover this world famous region and enjoy the gastronomy around authentic labels of terroir (see Table 5.1). From this 2010 study, the findings are that Bordeaux wine visitors line-up mostly on the two dimensions of being "experts" and "classic" consumers of wine.

Relying on these categories of wine tourism experiences, we will study how the wine tourism regional structures meet the needs and expectations of Bordeaux wine visitors in terms of accommodation, food services, and different activities offered in the region. The perception of various wine regions of France by a wine visitor differs, and Bordeaux is viewed by most as the most symbolic, iconic and ambivalent region in terms of its image and attractiveness. The cultural and rational dimensions are more prevalent dimensions in the perception of Bordeaux by wine tourists.

A sample of 450 tourist surveys visiting six different wine areas of Bordeaux region (including Saint Emilion, Medoc Graves, Sauterne, Cotes

---
[4] Adapted from "Tourisme et vin," Atout France, 2010, p.43.

Wine Tourism in Bordeaux

TABLE 5.1 Reasons and Motivations of Wine Tourists in the Bordeaux Region

The tourists' motivations are:	All tourists	Foreign tourists	French tourists
Discovery of wines and vineyards	40%	50%	34%
Fame of region	26%	27%	25%
Gastronomy and local authentic products	21%	21%	22%
Family ties and attachment to the region (friends, memories, families…)	20%	14%	24%
Cultural and architectural heritage (museums, sites…)	17%	17%	17%
Weather/Climate	14%	15%	14%
Nature and natural landscape	13%	12%	14%
Regular visits to a site or previous stays in the area	10%	9%	11%
Trails, walks, cycling, biking	9%	8%	9%
Visiting a particular site	6%	3%	8%
Coming to a cultural event (festival, concert, exhibits)	2%	1%	2%

*In percent of tourists – the total may be above 100% as these are multiple choice questions.

de Bordeaux and Entre-deux-Mers – Fig. 5.1) was analyzed in a recent study (Bouzdine-Chameeva, 2011). The goal of that study was to define the obstacles and incentives associated with wine tourism, the types of activities to be offered, the profile of wine tourists in Bordeaux and their wine knowledge. The survey contained 129 questions as part of a broader international study (Orth et al., 2011) of 15 wine regions in 9 different countries: Germany, Australia, Austria, Spain, USA, France, Hungary, Italy and Switzerland. The respondents filled the questionnaire on their way out of wine cellars' tasting or in the buses bringing them back to the city after wine Châteaux visits. The survey was conducted during the period from November 2009 to March 2010, which is considered as a quiet time in the tourist season, despite the fact that the number of visitors remains relatively high throughout the year. This study (Bouzdine-Chameeva, 2011) essentially adds to the findings published in 2010 by Atout France. It allows us to identify the deep-seated motivations as well as profile differences of wine visitors coming to Bordeaux vineyards in high and low seasons.

The sample was gender balanced (52.2% were men and 47.8% were women). The majority age range of tourists was under 30-years old followed by those currently in their 40s and 50s. This implies that wine tourism in the Bordeaux region attracts more a dynamic and active young population, particularly during the low season. Most respondents lived less than 2000 km from the Bordeaux region and came for a short-stay visit of 3 days at maximum. The public interested in wine tourism in the region is predominantly French (84%), although 23 countries are represented in the sample. With respect to habits and wine knowledge of respondents, 20.4% of them are regular consumers of Bordeaux wines (the age range concerned is less than 30 and 40–50 years old); only 8.2% do not drink wine or drink it rarely. The level of knowledge about the Bordeaux wine region and the consumption frequency are partly correlated; and there is relative consensus concerning fair pricing of Bordeaux wines (41.3%). Nevertheless consumers' indifference in this regard (28.7%) may indicate that price is not a decisive criterion for them when buying wine. Tourists do not seem to be sensitive to fashion trends in respect to wine. They consider wine prices as a sign of quality and the selling price of wine in certain cellars maybe revised upwards as long as psychological barrier is not surpassed.

Visitors perceive the Bordeaux region as being rather exclusive with its high quality wines. More than 75% of respondents were attracted by its charm, character and personality. However the opinions of respondents strongly differ with respect to hospitality and the warmth of welcome. They point to the lack of information about the range of existing activities and services related to wine tourism. More than 50% of the surveyed considered that the onsite services offered good value for money, whilst about 25% of respondents were indifferent. 75% of the interviewed tourists find that their stay matched their expectations about the Bordeaux region even if less than half consider coming back for future vacations.

Further analysis by age range resulted in the following key findings:

- The youngest age group of less than 30-years old seeks vacations with dynamic cultural, sportive and festive activities and attaches considerable importance to the nightlife around;
- The group between 30 and 40-years old favors rural get-away holidays with children appreciating cultural and sports activities, in particular amusements parks, concerts, museums without neglecting shopping in local boutiques;

- Those who are in 40s to 50s range, are in line with the previous group on cultural interests, but they appreciate more walking, biking and cross-country cycling;
- The age group between 50 and 60-years old definitely places less emphasis on shopping or nightlife but focuses more on cultural events;
- The oldest group of over 60-years old takes far more into account gastronomy and relaxation, and prefers going out to a lunch or dinner or to the movies.

5.6 WINE PRODUCERS' PERCEPTION REGARDING WINE TOURISTS: BORDEAUX VS. OTHER FAMOUS WINE PRODUCING REGIONS

While getting direct testimonials from tourists regarding their winery visit experience is a key step for understanding the wine tourism market, it is also interesting to get the other side's perspective; that is, winery owners/managers' perceptions of their visitors. By comparing the two perspectives, one can infer whether or not Bordeaux wine producers do indeed respond well to the needs and expectations of their visitors and thus demonstrate a strong commitment to expanding their wine tourism business. Here, we report on producers' perceptions using a study of wineries members of the Great Wine Capitals Global Network. The Great Wine Capitals (GWC) is a network of nine major cosmopolitan cities in both the northern and southern hemispheres. These cities are the business hubs for their nearby famous wine regions.

A survey of winery owners or general managers was administered during winter 2011 and spring 2012. A sample of 186 wineries responses was collected covering six wine major wine capitals of the world: Mendoza (Argentina), Bordeaux (France), Mainz (Germany), Firenze (Italy), Porto (Portugal) and Cape Town (South Africa). To contrast Bordeaux winery owners/managers' attitudes with those of other regions, we split the sample into two groups: Group 1 Bordeaux (95 wineries) and Group 2 composed of Mendoza, Mainz, Florence, Porto and Cape Town with a total of 91 wineries. The survey questionnaire was designed to elicit the winery's owners' (or general managers') perception of visitors as well as several indicators of wine tourism business performance (not covered in

104 Strategic Winery Tourism and Management

this chapter).[5] Table 5.2 below shows the list of possible predefined alternative answers to the question "How would you characterize the type of tourist who comes as visitor?" For assessing the owners' perceptions, the coded variables are polychotomous with five survey responses choices

TABLE 5.2 Glossary of Terms Used in Figures 4 through 7

How would you characterize the type of tourist who comes as visitor?	Abbreviated variable
The average visitor knows about wine	VKnowsWine
The average visitor comes because of aesthetic beauty of winery or surrounding landscape	AestheticB
The average visitor comes because winery offers unique experiences (separate from wine tasting)	UniqueExp
The average visitor shows genuine curiosity about our wine	Curiosity
The average Visitor comes because of the recommendation from other businesses	RecomBus
The average visitor seeks a sophisticated sensory experience	SphstctedExp
The average visitor appreciates and shows a deep respect for our traditions	DeepRspct
The average visitor comes because our winery is on a wine route	WineRoute
The average visitor comes because our winery is part of an organized tour	BcsOrganizedTour
The average visitor comes because our winery is famous in the region	WineryFamous
The average visitor comes because our winery is in tourism brochures and magazines	BrochMagazines
The average visitor comes because our winery is listed on internet	LstdInternet
On average, visitors come back to visit us	RptCustomers
The average visitor comes because he/she wants to introduce winery to friends or relatives	FriendsRelat
The average visitor come because they are attracted by our wine making philosophy based on environmentally friendly methods	PhiloEnviro

---

[5] The full-blown study linking activities to performance can be found in Faugère, Bouzdine-Chameeva, Durrieu & Pesme (2013).

for each answer: Strongly Agree, Agree, Neither Agree nor Disagree, Disagree or Strongly Disagree.

Figures 5.4 and 5.5 below show mean response rates for all alternative answers given by Group 1 (Bordeaux) wineries. First, we note that a majority of Bordeaux owners testify that visitors are genuinely curious and come foremost to their winery in order to discover their wines. They strongly agree that visitors show a "deep respect" for their winery and its traditions. Owners are less in agreement regarding the assessment that their visitors already know about wine before coming onsite and that they seek a unique experience beyond *just* wine tasting. Overall, they are more dubious that visitors are familiar or resonate with their "wine-making philosophy." They are evenly split in terms of agreement/disagreement about the statement that their visitors are looking for a sophisticated experience. The self-image of the winery being famous in the region definitely plays an important role in the owners' minds as a wine tourist attraction. By contrast, the aesthetic beauty of the winery and its surrounding landscape are not very important factors to the owners' eyes. In their judgment, wine tourists come to a great extent because they wish to visit the winery with

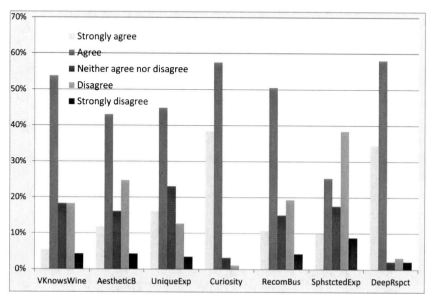

FIGURE 5.4 Perceptions of visitors by Bordeaux wineries (I).

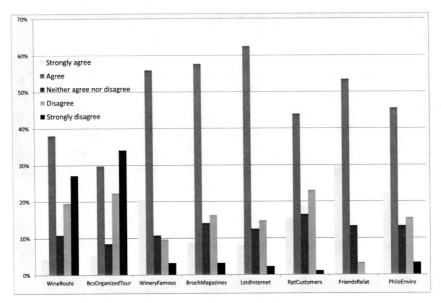

FIGURE 5.5 Perceptions of visitors by Bordeaux wineries (II).

family and friends. There is overall agreement with the proposition that many visitors are repeat customers.

Recommendations by other businesses are very important as a perceived determinant of visits. Media such as the Internet and brochures and magazines are also perceived as having largely a positive effect on attracting visitors. On the other hand, and this might be an issue specific to the Bordeaux region, wineries are evenly split with respect to the proposition that tourism business is generated by wine routes, and they are largely in disagreement that organized tours help generate business.

In order to bring forth an international perspective, we now compare the (Strongly Agree + Agree) response rates from Bordeaux with that of the other Great Wine Capitals. Figure 5.6 and 5.7 below show a direct comparison between Bordeaux and Group 2 capitals: Mendoza, Mainz, Firenze, Porto and Cape Town. First, we find that Group 2 capitals tend to consider in greater proportion that their visitors are indeed educated about wine; that they seek a sophisticated sensory experience and an experience that goes beyond just wine tasting. This is further stressed by Group 2 owners being in broader agreement with the proposition that visitors

Wine Tourism in Bordeaux

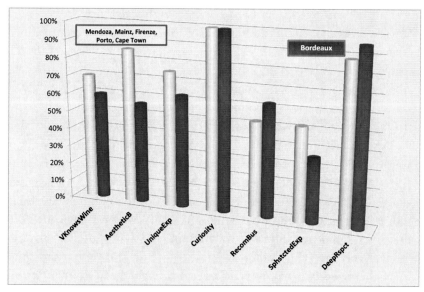

FIGURE 5.6 Perceptions of visitors by GWC wineries (I).

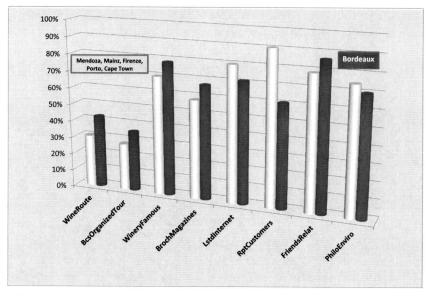

FIGURE 5.7 Perceptions of visitors by GWC wineries (II).

appreciate the aesthetic beauty of the winery and landscape. Group 2 winery owners also emphasize more strongly the perception that many of their visitors are repeat customers. The aspects of curiosity and respect for traditions are also as important in their judgment, not so different from the results reported for Bordeaux wineries.

The winery owners' perceptions might be influenced to a great extent by the type of activities they offer. Figure 5.8 shows the main activities offered onsite. It is not very surprising to find that most wineries in the overall sample offer wine tasting and guided visits as the main onsite activity. We find that Group 2 wineries tend to focus more on gastronomy, lodging and cross-selling of regional produces than Bordeaux region wineries. On the other hand, Bordeaux wineries consider arts (painting and photo) exhibits and entertainment activities such as concerts relatively more important.

Thus, to a certain extent it is not surprising that Group 2 wineries feel that their visitors are seeking an experience non-exclusively focused on wine tasting, given the holistic nature of the services they offer. However, it is surprising that Bordeaux wineries would not consider (as much) that their visitors seek a sophisticated experience, given that the owners emphasize more cultural and entertainment exhibits. In that respect, it seems that Bordeaux wineries hold a paradoxical view of that their visitors are sophisticated about the arts and

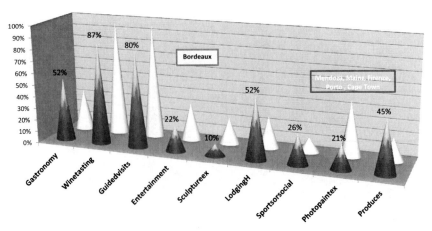

FIGURE 5.8 Key activities offered.

Wine Tourism in Bordeaux

at the same time that they are not very sophisticated about wine appreciation. This observation is however consistent with the Atout France (2010) categorization of wine tourists in the Bordeaux region as being more "intellect driven" while at the same time not having a deep prior knowledge about wine.

Figure 5.9 shows the main marketing tools used by our sample of GWC wineries. Wineries were asked what were their top 3 main marketing tools. By far, the top marketing tool used across the sample is a winery's Own Website. However, this does not mean that this category where wineries deploy the most resources or that it is their most effective tool. Tourism Offices are intensely used by Group 1 (Bordeaux) wineries by contrast with wineries in Group 1. Brochures in Hotels as well. By contrast, Tasting Events, Travel Agents, Tour Operators and Newsletters appear to be marketing strategies that are used more intensively by Group 2 wineries. From these findings we can infer that Group 2 wineries put more emphasis on a holistic tourism experience with the wine experience as one of the key components. They use more tour operators and other means of connecting with their clientele and thus appear to want to create an emotional

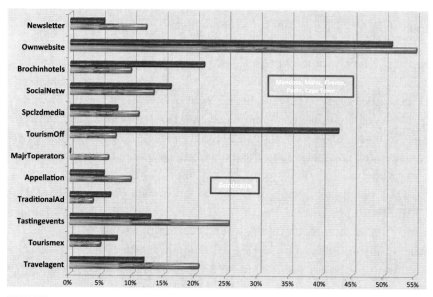

FIGURE 5.9 Main marketing tools.

attachment with their wineries. Bordeaux wineries put more emphasis on investing in the cultural and educational aspect of the wine experience and use more traditional means of marketing which do not necessarily seek to establish a long-term relationship with the visitor.

5.7 MANAGERIAL IMPLICATIONS

As a first exploratory study, the 2010 Atout France survey findings are enlightening. The profile of an average Bordeaux wine tourist is that of an "expert" and "classic," not that of an "epicurean" or "explorer." To a certain extent, this correlates with the perception of wine growers in the Bordeaux region regarding their visitors. Nevertheless, there are some discrepancies. Bordeaux winery owners/managers do not seem to believe that their visitors are "experts" and therefore do not treat them as such. They strongly emphasize the educational aspect of their job when dealing with visitors. The depiction of the average tourist as "classic" in the Bordeaux regions may also be deceivingly oversimplified. It appears that many visitors seek multi-layered and sophisticated experiences, which encompass other activities than just wine tasting and culture. Bordeaux wineries do not seem to reach a consensus with respect to recognizing this specific segment of touristic demand. This is the demand for well-being activities: a combination of eating well, staying in nice accommodations, other social activities, with a friendly hospitality. Testimonials by Bordeaux visitors, at least show that there is room for progress in the latter category. The weight of tradition can be observed with the strong emphasis that Bordeaux Châteaux place on the fact that their visitors show a "deep respect" for their traditions. This sentiment can certainly taint the overall interaction between winery staff and visitors and create a feeling of "distance" for the visitor.

The international study of Great Wine Capitals (Faugère, Bouzdine-Chameeva, Durrieu and Pesme, 2013) finds that other world famous wine regions tend to take a more holistic and personalized approach to wine tourism. This is because on average, they offer a more diversified portfolio of activities and use marketing tools that aim at cultivating a long-term relationship with the client. On the other hand, Bordeaux wineries rely more on the goodwill capital that comes from the region and the

Châteaux's fame (Bouzdine-Chameeva, 2011). They also tend to use more classic marketing tools. With respect to managerial implications we consider that specific marketing strategies should target the groups of those who are in their 30s and their 50s – these two age ranges consume less wine than other groups. One of the strong motivations of wine tourists in the Bordeaux region is the desire to acquire knowledge in oenology, and this should be taken into consideration when elaborating novel vacation packages. Night clubs, extreme sport activities in wine areas would attract the youngest group seeking more dynamic vacations. The group of those over 60-years old prefers vacation offers focused on well-being including spa, vino therapy and gastronomy, including cooking classes, for example.

Wine tourists testify that several dimensions of the winery experience are missing because many Bordeaux wineries do not really need to commit resources and train staff for these activities. However, many smaller properties relying on direct selling as a key revenue source have caught on with this new wave, and furthermore the positive fallouts in terms of promotional goodwill cannot be underestimated, especially when social networks reign supremely in today's world.

5.8 CONCLUSIONS

The world-wide reputation of the Bordeaux name is a double-edge sword. The attractiveness of the Bordeaux wine region for wine tourists is primarily due to the image of icon Bordeaux wines, to the historical, cultural and architectural heritage, to the inherent landscape and vineyards. Riding on this reputation may on the other hand prevent Châteaux to get fully committed to wine tourism, as other sales channels provide the lion's share of their revenues and investing in new infrastructures (lodging/restaurants) is a costly hurdle. There is a danger for Bordeaux wine producers to view wine tourism activities simply as an opportunity for direct wine sales, and not as a different and comprehensive approach to doing business.[6] For a flourishing wine tourism business, the relationship between wine producer,

---

[6] As an example, Chateau Franc-Mayne in Saint Emilion sells around 80percent of their wine in direct to the consumers through wine tourism and online/mail, bypassing therefore the traditional intermediaries of merchants and maximizing their profit margin (Lacey, 2012).

the product itself and wine consumer has to become a finely balanced long-term partnership, in the context of the strong global competition on the wine market. Producers should be aiming to get as close as possible to their final consumers to ensure future success.

A recognition of wine tourism as a modern, economically based construct embedded in consumptive behavior is slowly spreading in the Bordeaux region today. As in all other wine regions of the world the primary motivations of visitors to winery cellar doors remain "to taste wine" and "to buy wine." The challenges for the development of wine tourism in Bordeaux include the difference in viewing a wine Château as the home of the brand, while in the New world (in Australia or USA) tasting rooms are the home of the brand. Bordeaux wine producers assume that their consumers already have a relationship with Bordeaux brand, which is more or less correct. They see their role as that of simply displaying the existing history and reputational winemaking quality that has endured over the centuries. Hence the "selling" of wine is not strongly emphasized during visits. By contrast, in the New World, the focus is more on getting the visitor to buy wine or other regional goods on the premises. Hence, the focus in Bordeaux is on leaving visitors with the memory of unforgettable wines, traditions, etc.... rather than on the visitor's total experience.

This approach necessarily leads to obvious infrastructure issues. As with any successful company or organization there is a need to adapt to new market conditions and demands in order to stay profitable. The Bordeaux wine region, whilst possessing a long history and tradition, has to adapt to changes in the modern market place. There is no doubt that Bordeaux is a success story having produced some of the world's most iconic, desirable and expensive wine products. Nevertheless, in terms of wine tourism, the region is in some sense polarized. The producers at the top level have great success via the traditional sales channels, while the smaller ordinary wine producers struggle at the bottom and need to continually adapt using new sales strategies because of their lesser-known brands. Wine tourism in the Bordeaux region exhibits a substantial potential for growth, for example with Chinese tourism. This growth can be built upon the great cultural and intangible heritage of its wine sites. It is a robust and positive force that a region with such a glamorous wine reputation can tap into while preserving its values and heritage.

KEYWORDS

- **Bordeaux wines**
- **Bordeaux's traditions**
- **infrastructure**
- **wine tourism**

REFERENCES

1. Alant, K. and Bruwer J. (2004). "Wine tourism behavior in the context of a motivational framework for wine regions and cellar doors," Journal of Wine Research, Vol. 15, No 1, pp. 27–37.
2. Alant, K. and Bruwer J. (2010). "Winery visitation sets: intra-regional spatial movements of wine tourists in branded regions," International Journal of Wine Business Research, Vol. 22, No. 2, pp. 191–210.
3. AMS Conseil (2010). "Etude sur œnotourisme dans la région bordelaise," Rapport d'analyse, sous la direction de T. Bouzdine-Chameeva. Equipe de recherche "Marchés des vins et des spiritueux," BEM – Bordeaux Management School, 72p.
4. Atout France (2010). Tourisme et Vin, Paris: Editions Atout France, 98p.
5. Barney, B.J. (1991). "Firm resources and sustained competitive advantage," Journal of Management, Vol. 17, No 1, pp. 99–120.
6. Bouzdine-Chameeva T. (2011). "L'œnotourisme: portrait du secteur en 2010 des vignobles bordelais" Dans l'ouvrage collectif, J-F Trinquecoste (eds): "Le Vin et ses Marché: Annales 2011" Edition Dareios – Pearson, pp. 46–60.
7. Bouzdine-Chameeva T., Durrieu F. (2010). "The winery as an experiential stimulation: differences between passage and proximity tourism" Proceedings of the 5th International Academy of Wine Business Research conference, Auckland, NZ, February pp. 8–10.
8. Brunori, G. and Rossi, A. (2000). "Synergy and coherence through collective action: some insights from wine routes in Tuscany," Sociologia Ruralis, Vol. 40, No 4, pp. 409–423.
9. Bruwer, J. and Alant, K. (2009). "The hedonic nature of wine tourism consumption: an experiential view," International Journal of Wine Business Research, Vol. 21, No 1, pp. 235–257.
10. Bruwer, J. and Lesschaeve, I. (2012). "Wine tourists' destination region brand image perception and antecedents: conceptualization of a winescape framework," Journal of Travel & Tourism Marketing, Vol. 29, No 7, pp 611–628.
11. Carlsen, J. and Charters, S. (2004). Ed., Introduction, in J. Carlsen & S. Charters (Eds.), Global Wine Tourism: Research, Marketing and Management, Wallingford: CAB International, pp. 1–16.

12. Carlsen, J. and Getz, D. (2008). "Wine tourism among generations X and Y," Tourism, Vol. 56, No 3, pp. 257–269.
13. Carmichael, B. (2005). "Understanding the wine tourism experience for winery visitors in the Niagara region, Ontario, Canada," Tourism Geographies, Vol. 7, No 2, pp. 185–204.
14. Charters, S. and Ali-Knight, J. (2002). "Who is the wine tourist?" Tourism Management, Vol. 23, pp. 311–319.
15. Famularo B., Bruwer, J. and Li, E. (2010). "Region of origin as choice factor: wine knowledge and wine tourism involvement influence," International Journal of Wine Business Research, Vol. 22, No 4, pp. 362–385.
16. Faugère, C.; Bouzdine-Chameeva, T.; Durrieu, F and Pesme, J-O. (2013). "The impact of tourism strategies and regional factors on wine tourism performance: Bordeaux vs. Mendoza, Mainz, Florence, Porto and Cape Town," Proceedings of the 7th International Academy of Wine Business Research conference, Canada.
17. Getz, D. (2000). Explore Wine Tourism: Management, Development & Destinations. New York: Cognizant Communication Corporation.
18. Getz, D. and Brown, G. (2006). "Critical success factors for wine tourism regions: a demand analysis," Tourism Management, Vol. 27, No 1, pp. 146–158.
19. Goossens, C. (2000). "Tourist information and pleasure motivation," Annals of Tourism Research, Vol. 27, No. 2, pp. 301–21.
20. Hall, C.M.; Johnson, G.; Cambourne, B.; Macionis, N.; Mitchell, R. and Sharples, L. (2000). Wine Tourism around the World. Oxford: Butterworth Heinemann.
21. Lacey S. (2012). "Factors and trends affecting the Bordeaux wine market," CIVB documentation accessible at http://www.wsetglobal.com/
22. Lignon-Darmaillac, S. (2009). L'oenotourisme en France: Nouvelle Valorisation des Vignobles: Analyse et Bilan. Ed. Féret, 256 p.
23. Office du Tourisme de Bordeaux (2012). Rapport d'activité: exercice annuel 2012. 32pp http://www.bordeaux-tourisme.com/
24. O'Mahony, B.; Hall, J.; Lockshin, L. and Brown, G. (2005). "Understanding the impact of wine tourism on future wine purchasing behaviour: wine tourism experiences and future behavior," University of South Australia, Adelaide.
25. Orth, U. R.; Wolf, M.M. and Dodd, T.H. (2005). "Dimensions of wine region equity and their impact on consumer preferences," Journal of Product & Brand Management, Vol. 14, No 2, pp. 88–97.
26. Orth, U. R.; Stöckl, A.; Bouzdine-Chameeva, T; Brouard, J; Cavicchi, A.;, Durrieu, F.; M. Faraoni, M.; Larreina, M.; Lecat, B.; Olson, J.; Pesti, A.; Rodriguez-Santos, C.; Santini, C.; Veale, R.; Wilson, D. (2011). "The Role of tourism experiences in attaching consumers to regional brands," Proceedings of the 6th International Academy of Wine Business Research Conference, Bordeaux, France, June 9–11.
27. Pearce, P.L. (2005). Tourist Behaviour – Themes and Conceptual Schemes. Channel View Publications, Clevedon.
28. Peteraf, M. A. (1993). "The cornerstones of competitive advantage: a resource based view," Strategic Management Journal, Vol. 14, No 3, pp. 179–191.

CHAPTER 6

EMERGING ISSUES IN WINE TOURISM

LIZ THACH

Professor of Wine Business and Management, Department of Business Administration, Sonoma State University, California, USA

CONTENTS

6.1   Introduction...115
6.2   #1: Environmental Impact More Critical....................................117
6.3   #2: Understanding Consumer Motivations and CRM Becomes More Important...118
6.4   #3: Social Media Grows in Importance for Wine Tourism..........119
6.5   #4: GPS/Mobile Technologies Increasingly Helpful 120
6.6   #5: Increased Winery Partnerships With Other Types of Tourism.. 120
6.7   #6: Rise of Asian Wine Tourism 121
6.8   #7: Risks of Saturation and Increasing Competition 122
6.9   #8: More Sophisticated Wine Tourism Measurements 123
Keywords 125
References... 125

6.1 INTRODUCTION

There are a number of emerging issues in the world of wine tourism, and many of these are spawned not only by the growth in global wine regions, but by innovative practices and expanding wine tourism research. This chapter explores this growth and innovation, and then identifies and describes eight emerging issues that are beginning to impact wine tourism today and will continue to do so in the future.

Wine tourism is expanding around the world, with the number of new wine regions and wineries increased rapidly in the past decade. In the US alone, the number of bonded wineries has grown from 3469 in 2002 to 8806 in 2012 (Wine Institute, 2013). This expansion trend is also witnessed in other parts of the world, especially Asia where the number of Chinese wineries has increased to over 600 in the past several years from a very small base (Johnson & Robinson, 2013). At the same time, France still reigns supreme as one of the countries with the largest number of wineries, totaling over 10,000 in the Bordeaux region alone, and attracting more tourists than any other country in the world (Carlsen & Charters, 2006).

Perhaps in a response to the growth of wine regions, research in wine tourism has also expanded. Today there are more than 300 peer-reviewed articles in the *International Wine Marketing and Wine Tourism Database* at the University of South Australia, and over 160,000 books and articles on tourism in general cataloged in the CIRET database of the *International Center for Research and Study on Tourism* (CIRET, 2013). This research not only describes the various wine regions around the world, but also focuses on how to establish wine tourism, economic impact, strategy, marketing, wine tourist behavior and systems. With the World Tourism Organization reporting that international tourism generated $1.3 trillion in 2012 export earnings (UNWTO, 2013), it is understandable why so many researchers are focused on this.

Wine tourism is not just expanding, however, it is also evolving and becoming more sophisticated. Consumers are seeking more innovative experiences and expect more than just a traditional tasting. Many wine regions are combining the wine visit with culinary, environmental, and architectural offerings amongst others. For example, in Sonoma County, California, Kunde Winery advertises dog walks in the vineyard followed by a wine tasting, and at Saturna Island Winery in British Columbia, wine tourists not only taste wine, but are invited to go kayaking and search for whales (Thach, 2013). This type of unique involvement is reflected in the *Best of Wine Tourism Awards of Excellence*, which are bestowed each year to wineries and regions which provide the best service, innovative experience, and art, architecture or culture features (Greatwinecapitals.com, 2013).

Due to the growth and innovation in wine tourism, it is natural that there are multitudes of emerging issues. Following are descriptions of eight of some of the most relevant topics. These include: (i) Environmental Impact, (ii) Changing Consumer Motivations and CRM, (iii) Growth of Social Media, (iv) GPS/Mobile Technology, (v) Innovative Partnerships, (vi) Rise of Asian Wine Tourism, (vii) Increased Saturation and Competition, and (viii) Advanced Measurements.

6.2   #1: ENVIRONMENTAL IMPACT MORE CRITICAL

The environmental impact of wine tourism is becoming increasingly important. As more tourists flock to wine regions, the pressure on infrastructure and environment grows. Additional vehicles create more air pollution, and a larger number of visitors effects water and energy use. Wine regions need to plan carefully for the impact of an increasing number of tourists, because too much growth and success in a short period of time can have negative consequences.

Napa Valley has been one region that has experienced this, and has managed to handle the problem well. With almost 3 million visitors in 2012 spending $1.4 billion (Visitnapavalley.com, 2013), Napa Valley is more popular than Disneyland, and has been forced to expand the number of hotels, resorts and restaurants to accommodate the crowds. At the same time, they have limited the number of new wineries that can be built, and have strengthened their environmental protection efforts. They are the first wine region in the US to have an Agriculture Preserve, and the Napa Valley Vintners focus on preserving open space and preventing future over development (NVV.org, 2013). They also have implemented a Climate Action Plan to reduce greenhouse gas emissions, and developed Napa Green, a program to certify wineries and vineyards in sustainable practices. Local hotels are also involved in environmental conservation efforts through programs such as Green Certified Hotels. These types of efforts are necessary in successful wine regions in order to create a positive balance between tourists and environment.

Global warming is also expected to impact wine regions around the world, with some vineyards becoming cooler whereas others are expected to have temperature increases (Hannah et al., 2013). This will impact the type of grapes that can be grown in the different regions as well as quantity. This may also have an effect on the number of tourists who decide to visit the region or not, based on changes to the climate. In some extreme cases, it is predicted that some current wine regions may have to stop growing grapes and identify alternative crops to match the new climate due to global warming (Hannah et al., 2013).

6.3   #2: UNDERSTANDING CONSUMER MOTIVATIONS AND CRM BECOMES MORE IMPORTANT

Wine tourism research has already shown that wine tourists differ in their motivations to visit wineries (Carlsen & Charters, 2006). Some go to learn about winemaking, varietals, and to develop their tasting ability. Others are more interested in the cultural and heritage aspects, whereas different consumer segments visit wineries for fun and to experience wine in connection with food, art, romance, the environment, architecture, and even health reasons. Furthermore, research shows that wine tourism motivation differs by country, with tourists in Europe more interested in cultural reasons (Tassiopoulos & Haydam, 2006).

It is expected that consumer motivations will continue to evolve, and as new wine consumers are introduced to wine from different parts of their world, such as India and Asia, that palate differences may also become more important. For example, some consumers prefer sweeter wines, whereas others like dry wines with bigger tannins. In order to match consumer preferences, wineries can elect to produce different types of wines, or they may decide to only produce a distinctive regional style. The question of whether to produce wine for consumers or to produce wine according to a terroir style will become more important in the future.

Linked to understanding consumer motivation and palate is the ability to track consumer preferences in winery databases. By asking wine tourists to sign-up for mailing lists, email lists, or wine clubs, wineries have the opportunity to gather more information about their likes and dislikes.

The use of Customer Relationship Management (CRM) allows them to respond to individual differences and offer wine solutions and activities, such as special events, to fit each customer.

6.4 #3: SOCIAL MEDIA GROWS IN IMPORTANCE FOR WINE TOURISM

With the advent of social media in the mid 2000's, ushering in a realm in which consumers can share their viewpoints on products and services they purchase, the impact on tourism has been profound. As one regional tourist director reported, "With people only scheduling one or two vacations per year, they want to make sure they are going to a good place with decent hotels and restaurants. Therefore, we find they turn to social media such as Trip Advisor and Yelp. If we have bad reviews for the hotels, wineries, and restaurants in our region, then we will lose money. Therefore, we are focused on training all service providers in hospitality and making visitors feel welcome (p.1, Zahner, 2013)."

Tourists not only read and place reviews on social media platforms such as Trip advisor and Yelp, but they also use other social media forms such as sharing vacation photos on Instagram and Pinterest, videos on YouTube or Vimeo, and tweets and updates on Twitter, Facebook, and other social networking sites. They read wine blogs to see which wineries to visit, and use wine apps to decide what to buy, how much a wine costs, and to find coupons to save on tasting room fees.

Interestingly statistics show that wine drinkers are heavy users of social media, with more than 300 iPhone apps for wine and 7000 tweets per day about wine (Newman, 2010). Google Analytics (2012) reports that wineries are the third most popular subject on Pinterest and one of the most widely searched product categories on Google search engines (Rosenberg, 2011). Facebook stats reveal that more than 90% of wine drinkers use Facebook 6.2 hours per week (Breslin, 2013). Furthermore, there are more than 1300 wine blogs in more than 10 different languages (Quint, 2012).

Because of this, developing a proactive social media strategy will become increasingly important to wine regions and individual wineries. It will become part of their marketing and public relations mix, and require staff to be trained on how to implement and monitor. Already many destination-marketing organizations (DMO's) have created new departments to focus on social media, and some wineries have as well.

6.5 #4: GPS/MOBILE TECHNOLOGIES INCREASINGLY HELPFUL

Related to the increase of social media is the advent of mobile technologies and GPS (geographical position systems), which allow tourists to find wineries more easily. Traditional wine maps will still be important for a time, but consumers will also rely on GSP on their phone or other mobile device, and/or in their car to help them locate wineries, hotels, and restaurants.

Another advantage of mobile technologies is the ability to easily network with friends using the social media platforms described above, since many of these are available on mobile phones. In this way wine tourists can "advertise" where they are via "check-in" apps such as Facebook, Foursquare, or Foodspotting in a restaurant setting. They may also elect to upload photos of a winery they are visiting at that moment. Furthermore other friends in the area may see where they are and elect to join them.

Because of the growth of mobile technologies and GPS, it is important for wineries to make sure they are listed on maps and can be easily located with these types of platforms. They can also choose to advertise on some of these systems to bring more wine tourists to their destination. At the same time, traditional signage to assist visitors in finding different wineries, as well as safe road conditions are still important for wine tourism.

6.6 #5: INCREASED WINERY PARTNERSHIPS WITH OTHER TYPES OF TOURISM

As wine tourism experiences become more innovative and unique around the world, wineries and regions will continue to develop new partnerships with other types of tourism. This is already apparent in the areas of culinary tourism with wine regions in Italy, Spain, France and Mexico

Emerging Issues in Wine Tourism 121

excelling in this area, as well as eco-tourism where visitors enjoy wine tasting while appreciating the great outdoors. Examples of ecotourism experiences paired with wine can found in New Zealand, Canada, and parts of the USA, Argentina, Chile and Australia.

Other types of partnership may include sports, such as golf and wine, or spas and wine. South Africa and Napa Valley have done a good job of linking these activities in beautiful resorts that offer all three. Agritourism and wine may a nice partnership for visitors who want to learn about the agriculture of a region. The New York Fingerlakes wine region has done a good job of promoting this, as has the many agritour-ismos in Italy that provide lodging, food, and an opportunity to learn about the vineyard, olive orchards, wheat fields, and other agriculture in the surrounding region.

Innovative partnership may also include financial arrangements such as Sonoma Vintner's relationship with VISA credit card, which benefits not only the partners but also the wine tourists. For tourists who use a Signature Visa card, they can visit more than 100 wineries in Sonoma County for free with no tasting fees. In addition they receive a discount on purchases. This encourages wine tourists to visit these wineries, and VISA benefits by the use of their card. Sonoma County Vintners benefits by a percentage of sales from VISA.

As wine tourism expands, and competition between regions increases, it is expected that innovative partnership like these will spread. The fact that many wineries are now using more sophisticated consumer databases and engaging in CRM (Customer Relationship Management), allows them to learn more about their consumers and what they like. Linking consumer preferences in other activities to wine creates a healthy atmosphere for innovation and new partnerships.

6.7 #6: RISE OF ASIAN WINE TOURISM

In the past decade wine has become more popular in China, South Korea, Japan, and Hong Kong. Indeed, in China, the Chinese government has encouraged the adoption of wine as a means to wean the population off of the more potent rice liquors (Qin, 2006). Therefore the number of Chinese vineyards and wineries has grown dramatically over the past few years and

China is now the 6th largest producer of wine in the world (OIV, 2013), and the fifth largest consumer of wine after the US, France, Italy and Germany, respectively (Vinexpo, 2013). Indeed from 2006 to 2011, the Chinese wine market grew by 20% each year, and by the year 2015, it is forecasted to grown an additional 54% (Lodge, 2011). China is also investing in and purchasing foreign wineries in Bordeaux and the Napa Valley.

In 2012 wine sales increased in South Korea, Japan, and Vietnam from 2–6%, with young adults adopting wine in increasing numbers (Euromonitor, 2013). Hong Kong, with its 0% tax on wine imports became the world's largest market for fine wines at auction. In Southeast Asia there is also a growing wine industry in Thailand, Singapore, and Indonesia.

This new interest in wine from Asian consumers is already having an impact on wine tourism in France and California, with an increased number of visitors from these countries. Furthermore, China is investing it in own wine tourism infrastructure, especially in its up and coming wine region of Ningxia where the local government is providing training to officials on how to promote wine tourism to bring Chinese tourists to the region (Qin, 2012). Ningxia, located in the center of China, is home to over 30 wineries and the location of Chateau Helan Winery that won the Decanter Award for one of the 100 best international wines in 2011.

6.8 #7: RISKS OF SATURATION AND INCREASING COMPETITION

As the number of wineries increase around the world, some experts have raised the question of how many wine regions can one country sustain? For example, Napa Valley now has 480 wineries, whereas Sonoma County next door has 370 wineries, and new ones are opened every year (NVV. org, 2013; SCV.org, 2013). With the increase in wine brands, competition increases and it is very difficult for a new unknown brand to obtain distribution in national and global markets (Wagner et al., 2010).

Direct-to-consumer sales (DTC), known as cellar door sales in other countries, are often the only option for small-unknown wineries and wine regions. Therefore, they rely heavily on wine tourism to bring

Emerging Issues in Wine Tourism   123

visitors to the region in order to purchase wine so that the wineries can survive. The wine regions must invest in infrastructure such as wine routes, websites and advertising; work in partnership with local restaurants and hotels; develop a calendar of events to attract visitors; and insure that everyone who interfaces with tourists has completed hospitality training.

Once a wine region has established itself and has become known as a positive tourist destination, then it must continue to "refresh" its strategy and promotion to keep visitors coming back. This is because in some saturated wine countries or states, established wine regions are now competing against other newer regions. Therefore more sophisticated wine tourism tactics are needed to sustain the livelihood of the local wine businesses and supporting establishments.

6.9   #8: MORE SOPHISTICATED WINE TOURISM MEASUREMENTS

Another emerging trend is more advanced measurement tools for wine tourism. These measurements can take place at the country, state, regional, and individual winery level. The statistics may be used not only to attract tourists by verifying the area is popular, but can also be used to obtain funding and grants from local and national government programs designed to promote tourism.

At the state and regional level, statistics can be gathered by analyzing lodging, restaurant and tourism tax data, as well as by employment records. Common measurements include:

- number of visitors per year to state/region;
- annual revenues from tourism;
- amount ($) per tourist;
- taxes to state/region due to tourism;
- number of tourist-related jobs in state/region;
- economic Impact to due to tourism.

Wine regions can also gather data directly from tourists by asking them to complete short surveys about their visit. Incentives to complete the survey may include being entered in a raffle to win a prize. Common questions include:

- reasons why tourists come to state/region;
- percentage that come for wine;
- percentage that would return;
- percentage that would tell their friends to visit state/region.

At the individual winery level, tourism data may be gathered by asking questions during the tasting and/or by encouraging visitors to provide contact information for future follow-up. This may be done by requesting them to sign-up for a mailing list, drop their business card in a raffle bowl, or take a photo at a kiosk and send to friends via email. Common measurements at individual wineries include:

- number of visitors to winery each year and by month;
- sales revenue from wine tourists;
- $ on wine;
- $ on wine merchandise;
- number of wine club sign-ups;
- wine club attrition;
- favorite wines;
- what they like best about the winery.

Once the visitors are in the customer database of the winery, employees can follow-up in a number of ways to evaluate customer satisfaction and brand loyalty. They can even ask consumers to participate in short surveys to determine perception of brand image, post visit sales online, in restaurants or retail stores, and if they tell their friends about their winery visit or the brand. By tracking and analyzing these types of more sophisticated measurements, wine tourism can be enhanced at the country, state, region, and individual winery level.

In conclusion, wine tourism is growing around the world. This brings both opportunities and challenges as new issues emerge. However, since tourism is one of the largest industries in the world (UNWTO, 2013), it behooves wineries and wine regions to focus on attracting visitors in a way that is sustainable. This includes all three levels of sustainability: economic, environmental, and equitable to all employees.

KEYWORDS

- **CIRET database**
- **emerging issues**
- **environmental impact**
- **measurement tools**
- **wine tourism**

REFERENCES

1. Breslin, K. (2013). Presentation on Constellation Digital Marketing in 2013. San Francisco, California, November 2013.
2. Carlsen, J. & Charters, S. (2006). Global Wine Tourism: Research, Management & Marketing. Oxford: CABI.
3. CIRET. (2013). The Encyclopedia of Worldwide Tourism Research. Retrieved on Nov. 25, 2013 at http://www.ciret-tourism.com.
4. Euromonitor. (2012). Country Reports on Wine in South Korea, Vietnam and Japan. Published by Euromonitor. http://www.euromonitor.com/wine-in-vietnam/report.
5. Google Analytics (2012). Mobile Analytics Statistics. Available at: http://www.googleanalytics.com.
6. Greatwinecapitals.com (2013). Best of Wine Tourism Winners. Retrieved on Nov. 25, 2013 at http://greatwinecapitals.com/best-of/landing.
7. Johnson, H. & Robinson, J. (2013). The World Atlas of Wine, 7th edition. London: Mitchell Beazley.
8. Lee Hannah, Patrick R. Roehrdanzb, Makihiko Ikegamib, Anderson V. Shepardb, M. Rebecca Shaw, Gary Tabord, Lu Zhie, Pablo A. Marquetf, and Robert J. Hijmansj. (2013). Climate change, wine and conservation. PNAS Journal. Retrieved on Nov. 26, 2013 at: http://www.pnas.org/content/early/2013/04/03/1210127110.full.pdf+html
9. Lodge, A. (2011). US Tops Global Wine Consumption. Retrieved on http://www.thedrinksbusiness.com/2012/01/us-tops-global-wine-consumption-chart/
10. Newman, K. (2010) "How Wine Lovers Use Social Media: Wine and social media have created an incredible force within the industry."
11. NVV.org. (2013). About Us. Available at: http://www.nvv.org
12. OIV. (2013). Global Wine Statistics. Retrieved on Nov. 27, 2013 at http://www.oiv.org.
13. Qin, M. (2006). Opening Remarks at First Chinese Wine Marketing Conference, Beijing, China, August 2006.
14. Qin, M. (2012). Presentation at Ningxia Wine Festival, Yinchuan, China, August 2012.

15. Quint, B. R. (2010). Wine Education Network – Market Enablers – Information Overload.
16. Rosenberg, J. (2011). Presentation on Social Media & Wine Tourism. First National Wine Tourism Conference, Napa Valley, CA, Summer 2011.
17. SCV.org (2013). Above Us. Available at: http://www.scv.org
18. Tassiopoulos, D. & Haydam, N. (2006). Wine Tourists in South Africa: a Demand-side Study. In Carlsen, J. & Charters, S. (2006). Global Wine Tourism: Research, Management & Marketing. Oxford: CABI.
19. Thach, L. (2013). "12 Best Practices in Global Wine Tourism – Parts 1& 2. *Fine Wine & Liquor*, No. 71, pgs. 44–47, Jan 2013 issue. (Published in Chinese and English.)
20. UNISA, (2013). International Wine Marketing & Wine Tourism Database. Retrieved on Nov. 25, 2013 at http://www.winesea.unisa.edu.au/
21. UNWTO, (2013). World Tourism Statistics. Retrieved on Nov. 28, 2013 at http://www.unwto.org
22. VINEXPO, (2012). "Current trends in the international wine and spirits market and outlook to 2016." VINEXPO Industry Economic Study.
23. Visitnapavalley.com (2013). Visit Napa Valley: Research and Statistics. http://www.visitnapavalley.com/research_statistics.htm.
24. Wagner, P., Olsen, J. & Thach, L (2010). Wine Marketing & Sales: Success Strategies for a Saturated Market, 2nd edition. San Francisco, Wine Appreciation Guild.
25. Wine Institute (2013). Number of California Wineries. Retrieved on Nov. 25, 2013 at http://www.wineinstitute.org/resources/statistics/article124.
26. Zahner, T. (2013). Personal Interview, Santa Rosa, California, Nov. 2013.

CHAPTER 7

WINERY TOURISM IN CHINA

JINLIN ZHAO

Professor, Director of Graduate Programs, Director of Asia and Pacific Development, Chaplin School of Hospitality and Tourism Management, Florida International University, 3000 NE 151 Street, North Miami, FL 33181, USA, Phone: 305-919-4540; Fax: 305-919-4555; E-mail: zhaoj@fiu.edu

CONTENTS

7.1 Introduction 127
7.2 The History of Chinese Alcoholic Beverages 128
7.3 The History of Jiu 128
7.4 Chinese Jiu and Wine Culture 129
7.5 The Wine Industry in China Today 130
7.6 Chinese Wine Production and Import 132
7.7 Winery Tourism in China and Beyond 133
7.8 Information Sources for the Chinese Wine Industry
      and Winery Tourism 141
Keywords 142
References 142

7.1 INTRODUCTION

In this chapter, the author will discuss the history of Chinese alcohol beverages; the wine and food culture of the Chinese people; the Chinese wine industry today in terms of production and customer consumption; Chinese winery tourism destinations; and trends of winery tourism. The author will also provide a selection of Chinese wine-related websites.

7.2 THE HISTORY OF CHINESE ALCOHOLIC BEVERAGES

7.2.1 DEFINITION OF JIU

There is one word –*jiu*– representing all alcoholic beverages in China. It is further classified into distilled alcoholic beverages – *bai jiu* – which stands for spirits and liquors, which are transparent in color, high in alcohol content (38% to 75%), and made of all kinds of grains, especially, sorghum; and fermented alcoholic beverages, such as *putao jiu*, which stands for grape wine; *guo jiu*, which include all fruit wines (apple, pomegranate, pear, cherry, plum, and lychee, and many other wines; *pi jiu,* or beer; and *huang* (yellow) *jiu*, which is Chinese rice wine.

7.3 THE HISTORY OF JIU

Chinese jiu production can be traced back 6000 years. The Chinese learned to ferment grains and fruits into jiu, alcoholic beverages, at that time. In the Xia Dynasty (1600 BC), Du Kang improved the process of jiu production, and the Chinese later regarded him as the forefather of jiu.

Using grapes to make wine was recorded in *Shi Ji* by Si Maqian (145 to 90 BC). It described that Zhang Qian (164 to 114 BC), on a diplomatic mission in the Western Regions (Middle East) during the Han Dynasty (202 to 8 BC), found that people were making wine from grapes. After he came back from his mission, Zhang Qian introduced grape growing and wine making skills to Central China.

Grape winemaking was at its peak in the Tang Dynasty (618 to 907 AD). The winemaking skills and production were widely spread among ordinary Chinese. People from Western Regions opened wine shops in Chang An, the capital during the Tang Dynasty. The Yuan Dynasty (1271 to 1368) was another golden period for winemaking and trading in Chinese wine history. The government at that time encouraged farmers to plant

Winery Tourism in China

grapes and make their own wine, and the wine made was tax free. The ancient government used wine to entertain foreign diplomats and to enjoy at official banquets. Ordinary people made their own wines and enjoyed them with family and friends.

In the modern age, winemaking started in China when Mr. Zhang Bishi (1841–1916), a diplomat in the Qing Dynasty (1636–1912), invested three million *liang* in silver to build the Changyu Wine Company, the first wine production firm in China. Today it is the tenth largest wine company, with a production of nine million tons of wine annually.

7.4   CHINESE JIU AND WINE CULTURE

Jiu, including Putao jiu (wine), Pi jiu (beer), and Bai jiu (liquor and spirits), plays a significant role in Chinese culture. Jiu is a part of the Chinese meal. Today, many baby boomers or elders may have two shots per day at a meal. At the dinner table, men commonly prefer bia jiu (liquor), while women prefer fruit wine, guo jiu. Younger people, especially white collar professionals, are starting to prefer wine as their alcoholic beverage at parties. The Chinese have a saying: "If there is no jiu, there is no banquet, no get-together, no reunion, and no celebration!" Nowadays, at any banquet or at parties with family or friends, one will see that both liquor and wine are present on a table. However, most participants will choose wine instead of liquor for health reasons.

The Chinese use jiu to celebrate many festivals. The biggest festival with the largest consumption of alcoholic beverages is the Chinese Lunar New Year. The sale of alcoholic beverages during the Chinese New Year counts for 40% of annual sales. The Mid-Autumn Festival and Chinese National Day (a Golden Week holiday) are two other big festivals for alcoholic beverage sales. Alcoholic beverages are also used to commemorate the dead in the Qingming Festival. Jiu is consumed at the Lantern Festival and the Dragon Boat Festival. Young Chinese are embracing Western festivals and prefer having wine and beer on Valentine's Day, Mother's Day, Father's Day, Christmas, and New Year!

Jiu is also used to celebrate many other occasions. The day when a newly born baby passes his or her first month, the family hosts a party for parents and other family members, relatives, and friends to celebrate the baby's first month, and alcoholic beverages are served at the party. When the baby celebrates its hundredth day, there is another party with food and drinks for family and friends. At any adult birthday parties, alcoholic beverages are served. When a young person is admitted to a college or university; when the young person gets a job; when someone gets promoted, married, or moves into a new house, jiu is at these parties.

In the long history of China, many poets drank jiu when writing poems. Li Bai (701–762), a poet in the Tang Dynasty, wrote about jiu in many of his poems: "hope moonlight will pour into my golden cup when I am drinking and singing." Du Fu (712–770), Bai Juyi (772–846) and Du Mu (803–852) in the Tang Dynasty also mentioned jiu in their poems. Du Mu wrote "When I ask where is a "Jiu" shop? A herd boy points Xinghua (Apricot Blossom) Village further on the way!" Sushi (1037–1101), in the Song Dynasty, also praised jiu in his poems. He wrote "When will the moon rise? I ask the god with my wine cup in my hand" Even in modern times, many songs praise jiu and express happiness with beautiful wine.

It is a custom or tradition for anyone to bring a bottle of high quality jiu as a good gift when visiting parents, other family members, relatives, friends, and, of course, the boss. However, the current Chinese government has taken significant measures to fight corruption. Thus officials now are afraid to accept high-priced liquor or wine, or go to any private parties where high-quality, high-priced liquor and wine are served. Nowadays, lower ranking staff will also think twice before they present a liquor or wine gift to their boss! This has definitely affected the sale of wine in the last two years!

7.5 THE WINE INDUSTRY IN CHINA TODAY

There are 1,537 counties in China, and almost all the counties have some jiu production facilities. In China bai jiu production was 12.26 million tons, and the national per capita consumption was 8.43 liters in 2013. China's pi jiu (beer) production ranked No. 1 in the world in 2013. It produced 50.61 million tons, and the national per capita consumption of beer was 37.2 liters in 2013. In 2011, China had 560 thousand hectares of grapes for winemaking (OIV, 2012) and over 940 wineries in operation. Putao jiu (wine) production was 1.17 billion liters, and ranked No. 7 in the world in 2013. According to Vinexpo, the Chinese consumed 155 million nine-liter cases (1.87 billion bottles) of red wine, ranking them No. 1 in the world in 2013. This total marks a 136% increase from five years ago and surpasses France and Italy for red wine consumed in the same year. Eighty-three percent of the consumption of the wine by the Chinese was produced in China (Chow, 2014).

In the 40 some years after the founding of new China, the consumption of wine played a minor role (only 1%) in all alcoholic beverages among Chinese consumers. The production and distribution of wine were not well regulated. However, the sales of wine products have increased dramatically in recent years.

In 1987, the Chinese government held the National Alcohol Drinks Industry Conference. The conference resolved to implement four changes for alcoholic beverage production: Change from high alcohol content to low alcohol content; change from distilled alcohol to fermented alcohol production; change from low-quality alcohol to high-quality alcohol beverages; and change from heavily grain-based alcohol to fruit-based wine. The government promoted wine industry development and encouraged the Chinese people, for better health, to drink more grape wines than liquors and spirits.

The Chinese gradually have learned that red wine is a heart-healthy alcoholic beverage. Red wine has some antioxidants that help prevent heart disease by increasing levels of good cholesterol and protecting against artery damage. Also resveratrol in red wine may prevent cancer. All the medical benefits have made Chinese wine consumption increase from 0.25 liter in 2002 to 1.3 liters per capita in 2012, and to an estimated 1.9 liters to 2.0 liters per capita by 2015, according to Robert Beynat, CEO of Vinexpo (2012).

Moreover, millions of Chinese have studied and worked in the United States, France, United Kingdom, Italy, Australia, Spain, South Africa and Chile. While studying and working, they also have learned the eating and drinking cultures of those countries. When they return to China, they continue to desire to drink wine, and this has driven a tremendous demand for and sale of wine in recent years. Plus, the Chinese government has gradually reduced taxes on the import of wines from 48% to 14% since China entered the World Trade Organization in 2001.

On the other hand, the sales of liquors and spirits have decreased. Some brands, such as Fenjiu, Yanghe, and Shede decreased 50% in sales in 2013.

Even the most famous liquor company, Maotai, built a joint venture with Changli Winemaker to make Maotai Wine in 2002.

7.6 CHINESE WINE PRODUCTION AND IMPORT

The total area for vineyards is 560,000 hectares in China in 2012. The production of wine increased from 367.3 million liters in 2004 to 665.1 million liters in 2007, to 1,088.8 million liters in 2010, and to 1,178.3 million liters in 2013 (see Chart 1 below). Twenty-three provinces or autonomous regions have wine production. In 2013, the top wine production provinces are Shandong (37.8%), Jilin (22.7%), Henan (11.7%), Hebei (5.5%), with the total of 1,178.3 million liters of wine in China (Fig. 7.1). Four well-known domestic wine brands are Changyu, Great Wall, Dynasty and Weilong.

The import volume of wine was 304.8 million liters in 2010. It was 360 million liters and paid 1.4 billion US dollars in 2011. The import increased to 425.7 million liters and 2.57 billion US dollars in 2012. The Chinese consumed 1.68 billion liters of wine in 2013 (VIO report, May, 2014). A wine import research group predicts that Chinese wine consumption will increase 14.5% to 22.6% in the next 10 to 15 years (www.qianzhan.com, June 2014).

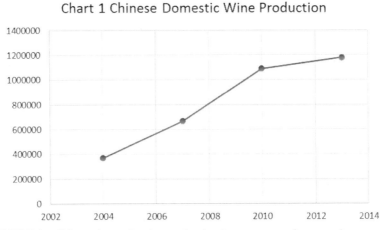

FIGURE 7.1 Chinese domestic wine production (source: www.chyxx.com).

7.7 WINERY TOURISM IN CHINA AND BEYOND

With the fast economic development of China in the last 30 years, the Chinese have more disposable income to travel within the country and abroad. In domestic travel, both numbers of trips and receipts have seen a double-digit increase in recent years. Within China, the Chinese made 2.33 billion trips in 2010, 2.64 billion trips in 2011, 2.95 billion trips in 2012m, and an estimated 3.3 billion trips in 2013. The domestic tourism receipts were 1,561.9 billion Yuan (RMB) in 2010, 1,930.5 billion in 2011, 2,270.6 billion in 2012, and an estimated 2,600 billion in 2013. Although the majority of tourists have visited historical cities, and well-known mountains, rivers and lakes, more and more travelers have sought out adventure tours and theme tours. As increasing numbers of Chinese have started to like wine, they have made winery tourism a very popular segment of domestic tourism. Many wine industry companies, real estate companies and rich individuals have invested in vineyards and built chateaus in many parts of China (Table 7.1). Domestic Chinese winemaking companies have invited many of the world's well-known wine makers to join them in building these vineyards and chateaus or work as consultants, brand representatives, and wine examiners.

Many of the vineyards and chateaus in Shandong, Ningxia, Xinjiang, Gansu and Hebei, China are situated at latitude 44 degrees north, the best location in the world for winemaking.

7.7.1 JIAODONG PENINSULA, SHANGDONG

Penglai City is known for its vineyards and chateaus. It has more than 10,000 hectares of vineyards. It has12 chateaus that have attracted one million visitors. The city received revenue of one billion Yuan from winery tourism in recent years.

7.7.2 CHANGYU

In 1992, long before all the developments of chateaus in China, Changyu built its Changyu Wine Museum and opened to the public. It exhibits the

TABLE 7.1 Known Chateaus in China

Wine Making Area	Chateaus	Remarks
Jiaodong Peninsula, Shandong	Changyu Castel, Junding, East China Baili, Duanshilin, South Mountain, Reifeng Auzias, Bodega Saina, etc.	Yantai government plans to invest one billion Yuan to build 16 more Chateaus. Yantai area eventually will build over 105 Chateaus, 6 wine villages in the future.
East Helanshan, Ningxia	Pernod Ricard Winemakes (France), Jade lake, Bacchus, Helan Qingxu, Saint Louis-Ding, east Helan, Yuhuang, and Yinchuan Plateau	Besides Changyu, Dynasty, Great Wall all have their own chateaus in the area. The area will have almost 100 chateaus being built or in planning
The Old Course of Yellow River, Henan	Century, Oldmanwine	
Changli and Huailai, Hebei	Langes, Huaxia Sanggan, Rongchen, Matin, Longhui	Hotel and spa at Langes in Changli, Jishi, Haiyawan, Jiatai in constraction in Changli,
Liaoning	Golden Ice Wine Valley by Changyu	
Tianjin	Dynasty	
Wuwei, Gansu	Muogao International	Plan to build 10 Chateaus by 2020
Xinjiang	Xintian International, West Regions	Chateau Changyu Baron Balboa
Shangxi	Grace	
Runnan	Red	

history of modern Chinese wine-making; it has many local and international samples of grapes on display; it has taste rooms and a 1,976 square-meter cellar, which was built 100 years ago; and it has a sales hall for its branded wines. In 2005, the museum received about 200,000 visitors and made 14 million Yuan.

In 2002, Changyu and the France Custer group invested 70 million Yuan to build a joint-venture Chateau Changyu Custer (Fig. 7.2) in Yantai, China. This destination offers a tour of the winemaking process. The Chateau occupies 140 hectares, of which there are five hectares of various grape plants, such as Chardonnay, Cabernet Gernischt, Riesling, etc. It has a cellar of 2,700 square meters with 1,600 oak barrels from France, Spain and Portugal. Tourists can tour the facility, learn more about winemaking, and enjoy relaxing and tasting the branded wine.

In 2006, Changyu Wine Company and a Canadian company built the joint venture- Golden Icewine Valley in Liaoning.

FIGURE 7.2 Chateau Changyu Custer.

In 2007, Changyu Wine Company also attracted 700 million Yuan from the U.S., Italy, Portugal and France to build joint-venture vineyards – Chateau ChangyuAFIP, in Beijing.

In 2012, Changyu Wine Company invested 6 billion Yuan to build another vineyard with seven attractions. It plans to attract a million visitors per year. The project will be completed in 2016.

In 2013, Changyu Wine Company opened three more Chateaus: Chateau Changyu Baron Balboa in Xinjiang, Chateau Changyu Moser XV in Ningxia, and Chateau Changyu Reina in Shanxi.

Moreover, Changyu took over Roullet-Fransac in Cognac, France, in 2013. In recent years, Changyu has also built brand alliances with Chateau Liverrsan, in Bordeaux; and Chateau Philippe Le Hardi, in Burgundy, France; Chateau Changyu Pioneer, in Sicily, Italy; and Chateau Kely, in New Zealand.

Also, China Oils and FoodStuffs Corp. (COFOC) invested 300 million Yuan to build Chateau Junding (Fig. 7.3.) and a vineyard in Yantai.

FIGURE 7.3 Chateau Junding.

It provides tours, relaxation, business meetings and hotel rooms to its tourists. In Jiaodong Peninsula, there are also East China Baili, Duanshilin, South Mountain, Reifeng Auzias, and Bodega Saina chateaus. Chateau Duanshilin established its own tourist office and its website to promote its grape pick festival and tour programs. There are many more under construction.

7.7.3 EASTERN HELAN, NINGXIA

In 2010, Ningxia Autonomous Region had 25,000 hectares of grape-growing vineyards, which harvested 13,000 tons of grapes. The region has more than 20 winemaking companies, which contributed 1.1 billion Yuan to the region's economy. Eastern Helan is located at the same altitude as Bordeaux, France. The temperature, sun, rain, and quality of soil are the best for grape growing and wine making. In 2012, there were 18 chateaus opening to the public and 14 were under construction. In two or three more years, there will be more than 100 chateaus in Ningxia (Zhang, 2013). Many companies, including domestic and international winemaking companies and non-winemaking companies, have all rushed to build wine production facilities and chateaus, such as Pernod Ricard Winemakes (France), which has a wholly-owned vineyard in Ningxia. Changyu opened its Chateau Changyu Moser XV, Ningxia in 2013 (Fig. 7.4).

COFOC's Great Wall Wine Company, Changyu, and Dynasty, have all have built vineyards in Ningxia. There are many local chateaus, such as Helan Qingxu, Saint Louis-Ding, East Helan, Yuhuang, and Yinchuan Plateau.

Besides Jiaodong Peninsula in Shandong and East Helan Mountain in Ningxia, as mentioned in Table 7.1, many regions and areas also have built chateaus in Hebei, Henan, Liaoning, The Old Course of Yellow River, Tianjin, Xianjiang, Shanxi and Yunnan. For an example, Grace Vineyard in Shangxi, attracts winery tourists to visit its over 600 hectares of vineyards and gain knowledge about Chardonnay, Chenin Blanc, Merlot, Cabernet Franc and Cabernet Sauvignon that grow there. Tourists also visit the winemaking facility, which produces 3,000 tons of wine annually. All the vineyards and chateaus in various provinces and regions try

FIGURE 7.4 Chateau Yuanshi owned by Zhihui Group: (a) the entrance, (b) the wine cellar and (c) winetasting lounge.

to provide Chinese wine tourists their winery tours, help them gain more knowledge of wine-making, encourage them to taste locally made wines (a few chateaus have restaurants, so the visitors can learn to pair local food with the chateaus' wines in the chateau restaurants), and boost wine sales. There are also many wine exhibitions, shows, wine festivals and conferences in which wine lovers can participate. One can easily find these events on Chinese wine websites.

The author visited several chateaus in Penglai and Yantai in May 2013. He could clearly see the fast development of vineyards and chateaus. However, the author questions whether the pace of chateau development is too fast and overheated, as he observed that there were not many visitors whenever he visited. The service quality needs to be improved at those chateaus. The staff at the chateaus definitely needs more service and knowledge training. The prices of the chateau wines were very expensive from a U.S. perspective. Moreover, with the fast development of the wine

industry, it is high time to improve wine-related education programs so more highly trained wine makers, marketers, and distributors, and winery tourism professionals can work in the wine industry.

Nowadays, Chinese wine tourists not only visit domestic vineyards and chateaus, but also venture overseas to tour wineries and chateaus in France, Italy, the United States, and Australia each year. One can find on Chinese wine websites Chinese travel agencies that promote overseas winery tours.

What is more, rich Chinese are not only touring international chateaus and vineyards, but also buying vineyards and chateaus overseas. In 2008, Mr. Cheng Zuochang, Hailong International Trade Corp., Shandong, was the first Chinese to take over Chateau Latour Laguens, Bordeaux, France, for two million Euros. Actress Zhao Wei spent four million Euros to buy Chateau Monlot. Mr. Shen Dongjun of Lingtong Jewelry Company, Jiangsu Province, acquired Laulan-Ducos for 10 million Euros in 2011. Mr. Zhang Jinshan, Ningxia Hong Wine Company, purchased Chateau du Grand Mouey for 10 million Euros as well. Mr. Zhang wants to make the

Chateau into a tourist destination with a nine-hole golf course, a tennis court, a Western and Chinese restaurant, a spa and a swimming pool. As May of 2014, Chinese companies and rich persons bought more than 83 chateaus and vineyards in France (South Daily, June 6, 2014). Yao Ming, a National Basketball Association star, also took over a Vineyard in Napa Valley, California, in 2011. This indicates that U.S. chateaus and vineyards will be the next targets for rich Chinese to take over. The author believes that the purposes of those purchases are: real estate investment; winemaking

Winery Tourism in China

overseas and selling the wine back to China; and building tourist destinations to attract Chinese out-bound travelers.

7.8 INFORMATION SOURCES FOR THE CHINESE WINE INDUSTRY AND WINERY TOURISM

There are many Chinese wine-related websites. The websites provide all the information about domestic and international wine industry news, market news, vineyard investments, wine products, wine festivals, exhibitions and shows, training programs, wine culture, wine competitions, and winery tourism programs at home and abroad. However, these websites are in the Chinese language. The selected websites as following:

www.winechina.com

www.wine-world.com

www.wines-info.com

www.9winetour.com

www.12580wine.com

www.winekee.com

www.wine.cn

www.zgnj.org

In summary, although the Chinese have a long history of jiu as well as winemaking, they have only recently started to develop a taste for wines. The potential development of wine- making and winery destination is enormous. More and more Chinese will explore both domestic and international vineyards and chateaus in the future. The food and drinking culture of the Chinese is changing as the world changes. The volume of wine consumption of the Chinese will increase continuously, which will drive the Chinese wine industry to develop at an even faster pace. In the meantime, import wine from overseas will have a great potential as Chinese wine consumption grows 5 times between 2002 and 2012. Many foreign wine makers and distributers should seize the opportunity to further promote their wines in this fastest-growing Chinese market. These companies should learn how Coca Cola has gradually gained its market share in China from giving free Coca Cola samples in the early 1980s. Today the company has 16% of the

$69 Billion Chinese soft drink market. The Chinese wine industry and winery tourism have a very bright future.

KEYWORDS

- **Chinese alcohol beverages**
- **Chinese wine industry**
- **Chinese winery tourism**
- *guo jiu*
- *jiu*

REFERENCES

1. Chinese liquor and spirit data (2013). http://www.chyxx.com/data/201301/193245.html
2. Chinese beer production (2013). http://www.chinese.rfi.fr/
3. Chow, Jason. (2014). China is now the world biggest consumer of red wine. Wall Street Journal, Life & Style (Jan. 29, 2014).
4. Du, Y. (2013). Taste six chateau brands, Penlai build its path for the full development of wine making. http://gb.cri.cn/42411/2013/05/20/6112s4120789.htm
5. Kate Chan Research (2012). Marketing U.S. wine in China. USDA Foreign Agricultural Service.
6. Jourdan, A. (2014). Coca-Cola says to invest over $4 billion in China in 2015–2017, Reuters, http://www.reuters.com/article/2013/11/08/us-cocacola-china-idUS-BRE9A704H$_2$O131108
7. Li, B. (2013). Chateaus in Chinese Style, www.xincaijing.com
8. Li, H., Li, J. & Yang, C. (2009). Review of Chinese grapes and Chinese wine industry in 30 years after the open door policy. Modern Food Technology. 25 (4). 341–347.
9. Ma, H. & Sheng, Y. (2014). Chinese bought more than 60 chateaus in France. (Jan. 16) http://finance.sina.com.cn/money
10. Noppe, R. P. (2012). Rise of the Dragon: The Chinese Wine Market. Unpublished master thesis, Cape Wine Academy, South Africa.
11. Reiss, S. The Chinese wine market and industry analysis. http://www.wineeducation.com/chinadet.html
12. South Daily Report (June 6, 2014). U.S. may be the next target f chateaus for rich Chinese to take over. http://www.9winetour.com/News/2014–06–06/58611.html
13. The EU SME center. Wine market in China.
14. Yu, X. (1997). Chinese Wine Culture, The contemporary Chinese Press.
15. Zhang, J. (2013). The status, policies and future of East Helan chateau development. http://wenku.baidu.com/view/d6d052d1195f312b3169a5d1.html

CHAPTER 8

ANALYZING THE EFFECTS OF SHORT- AND LONG-TERM CUSTOMER RELATIONSHIP ON THE WINE CUSTOMER LIFETIME VALUE

MICHAEL R. SANTOS and VINCENT RICHMAN

Professor, School of Business and Economics, Sonoma State University, California, USA

CONTENTS

Abstract 143
8.1 An Introduction to Customer Lifetime Value 144
8.2 Wine Marketing and the Industry 145
8.3 Wine CLV Techniques and Practice 146
8.4 Conclusion 153
Keywords 154
References 154

ABSTRACT

This chapter analyzes the short- and long-term effects of a wine firm's customer relationship on the Customer Lifetime Value (CLV). It is shown that the longer is the duration of a wine firm's relationship with its customers, the higher is the CLV. Furthermore, the wine firm gains most of the feasible CLV in about just 10- to 25-year-long customer relationship. However, achieving long-term customer relationship may require significant marketing investment to create brand loyalty. A positive wine-tasting room experience may support this goal by creating long-term customer relationship as well-as supporting short-term wine tourism.

8.1 AN INTRODUCTION TO CUSTOMER LIFETIME VALUE

Everyone in marketing discipline agrees that creating brand loyalty requires significant investment. The problem lies at finding sufficient funds and deciding on the optimal levels of the spending. Unfortunately, there are no easy benchmarks, metrics, or rule of thumb to determine the optimality. A straightforward economic logic would suggest that marketing manager stops spending when marginal revenues of the marketing spending is less than its marginal cost. However, formulating marginal revenues and marginal costs can be a challenging task.

The main idea behind CLV concept is that not all customers provide equal value to a firm. Therefore, it is suggested that firms should use its resources to serve the most profitable and loyal customers. The classification of customers in high and low profitability groups is due to an empirical observation that 80% of firm profits are generated by 20% of customers; called 80/20 rule. Furthermore, Nelson (1970) and Levy and Weitz (2007) propose that it is necessary to discourage low profitability customers by applying increased service fees. However, there is a chance that discouraging the less profitable customers may inadvertently hurt a firm's future profits in an environment where the word of mouth and social networking are important marketing tools.

A capital budgeting process may be more appropriate for determining the optimality of marketing projects. This process discounts the future expected cash flows of a marketing project to determine whether the project should be accepted or rejected. Therefore, an accurate projection of the expected cash flows over the life of the project is essential for the reliable CLV estimations to show the contribution of a typical customer in her lifetime. The CLV calculations require the projection of the total revenues from one customer as well as the cost of acquiring the same customer and maintaining her business (repeat purchases) for long-term. A related concept of Customer Equity (CE) is also defined as the total value of CLV for both current and future customers of a firm (Gupta et al., 2006).

8.2 WINE MARKETING AND THE INDUSTRY

Wine product is unique and known as "experience good" because there is difficulty in assessing the quality of wine before it is consumed. Thus, building consumer loyalty or brand name in wine business is challenging to wine producers. Researchers in wine marketing suggest that non-advertising promotional activities such as positive and emotional wine-tasting room experience, informative labeling with wine attributes, coupons, free samples, catalogues, wine club member-only invitations, supporting community-based programs, and food pairing knowledge classes may be more effective to build customer loyalty than traditional media advertising (Vlachvei, et al., 2009). Especially, wine tourism is dependent on these promotional activities at individual wineries, wine festivals, and wine shows. Nowak, Thach, and Olsen (2006) found that 70% of the customers visiting wineries purchased wine. Even though the significance of one-time purchase cannot be understated, CLV value is significantly higher if the duration of customer relationship lasts many years and the customers make repeat purchases. Recently, Carmichael (2005) and Huang (2011) emphasize wine-tasting room experience in building customer loyalty and long-term customer relationship for the growing millennial population (sons and daughters of baby boomers). Also, there is a growing link between wine tourism and the establishment of wine tasting rooms as a vehicle for marketing, branding, and wine education (Alonso et al., 2008). Cellar-door environment is seen as an essential step to encourage wine tourism and brand equity (O'Neill & Palmer, 2004).

In addition, wine firms can use market segmentation information to target high-value customers as well as creating value from less profitable customers. In this context, it was suggested that wine purchase behavior is not gender neutral and it may be easier building brand loyalty among men. For example, Barber (2009) claims that men rely on the self-assessed wine knowledge and therefore limit other sources of information in wine purchase decision.

Building brand loyalty in wine business leads to higher repeat purchases by wine customers and thus increasing CLV to a wine firm. However, according to Vrontis and Paliwoda (2008) and Vrontis et al. (2011), the international fragmentation of wine industry together with recent increases in quality of wine production all around the world provides additional branding challenges for wine producers. To overcome this challenges and further promote wine industry, Houghton (2008) and Gómez et al. (2013) suggest that increasing support from wine organizations and regulators may be needed by focusing the efforts to increase wine quality as well as organizing complementary events through wine festivals, wine and food symposiums collaborated by universities and other culinary schools to help improve regional brand image.

Finally, there are concerns over small winery operations and their ability to compete in both local and global markets. There is a chance that small brand wineries may not be sustainable if they fail to build a niche market translating to high brand loyalty. In general, the challenge for small wineries is the low repeat purchase rates of their customers resulting in low brand loyalty according to Jarvis and Goodman (2005) and Tipples (2008).

8.3 WINE CLV TECHNIQUES AND PRACTICE

In most of the Anglo-Saxon countries, the goal of a firm is shareholders' wealth maximization. Gupta et al. (2006) has shown that the higher is the CLV, the higher will be the firm value. Further, a hypothesis can be developed to show that the longer the duration of a firm's relationship with its customers, the larger will be the CLV for the firm. Thus, the longer duration of customer relationship enforces higher firm value.

Even though there is wide-spread application of CLV ranging from more advanced discounted value estimations to simple one-point value estimations in many industries, wine industry has been slow to recognize CLV as a tool in marketing. CLV application may be most useful if market segmentation allows firms to distinguish its most valuable customers. However, the less profitable customers may still provide sufficient CLV

Analyzing the Effects of Short- and Long-Term Customer Relationship 147

if the relationship last longer and provides repeat purchases. Using market segmentation to identify and discourage less profitable customers may reduce overall firm value and CLV since the wine industry is highly dependent on word of mouth through customers recommending wine products to each other.

Fortunately, the relatively simple applications of CLV models from other industries can be easily translated into the wine industry. More advanced models may require the data about consumer purchasing habits and different retention rates among market segments. After determining the market segments, a wine firm may be able to quantify one customer's average number of purchases and dollar spending in a year. The more difficult part is the translation of consumer brand loyalty into the duration of the relationship (number of years) between the wine firm and its customers. Further, the average consumer acquisition and retention costs are needed for a successful CLV application. Finally, the availability of statistics for cross-selling (expansion) opportunities to wine customers may enhance forecasts of future cash flows.

A simple one-point CLV model has the following components:

CLV = (Average Price) × (Number of Visits in a Year) × (Average Number of Units Purchased per Visit) × (Number of Years) – Initial Cost of Acquiring and maintaining a customer

For example, assume that there are two segments in the wine market with Consumer 1 being identified as high profitability and Customer 2 as low profitability:

Customer 1 (high profitability): visits a vinery 2 times a year, purchases 4 bottles of wine at each visit and pays $20 per bottle. Assuming this customer is acquired with an initial cost of $200 and retained for 5 years with a $50 additional spending by sending flyers, wine catalogs, emails, etc. Then,

The CLV = ($20) × (2) × (4) × (5) – [200 + 5 × $50] = $350.

Customer 2 (low profitability): is a wine tourist and visits a vinery only once a year, purchases 4 bottles of wine at the visit and pays $20 per bottle. Assuming Customer 2 is acquired at lower initial cost of $50 with a $0 additional spending because no flyers, wine catalogs, emails, etc., are being sent. Then,

The CLV = ($20) × (1) × (4) × (1) – [$50 + $0] = $30.

Even though, serving Customer 1 is desirable with higher CLV, serving Customer 2 will be important if Customer 1 and Customer 2 communicate through word of mouth or social networking sites by exchanging wine tasting experience and recommendations. Therefore, market segmentation and the treatment of customers in different segments require a special attention when the information flows from market segments are not independent.

The Customer 1's experience is more elaborate and therefore a model incorporating time value of money is more appropriate than the one-point CLV model shown above since the duration of customer relationship is expected to last many years.

The following tables show Customer 1's experience one-point experience over 5 years and therefore it takes the time value of money into account. The only additional assumption is a 10% discount rate applied to the future expected cash flows of the wine firm. Our estimations are similar to Dev and Stroock (2007).

Table 8.1 presents Customer 1's repeat buys for 5 years without changing its assumptions from year to year. It is assumed that the wine firm spends initially $200 at time 0 and $50 for 5 years to acquire Customer 1. Afterwards, starting at Year 1, Customer 1 visits the winery for 5 years and repeats her purchases every year. Total annual revenues are $160 [(2 visits per year) × (4 bottles purchased at each visit) × ($20 paid per bottle)] and the retention expense is $50, and therefore annual surplus is $110 each year. Thus, having an initial spending of $200 against the $110 surplus over 5 years provides a CLV of $217. This result is obtained by Customer 1's purchasing habits identical. There is a possibility that the wine firm may do cross-selling and market other products to Customer 1 over the 5-year relationship, therefore increasing CLV. However, this possibility is hard to quantify and not incorporated into the calculations. Therefore, we can assume that the 5-year CLV of $217 represents the lower limits of CLV with the given assumptions.

Figure 8.1 provides different CLV over the 5-year period. The duration of relationship lasting slightly longer than 2 years provides positive CLV to the wine firm. This is positive news to any wine firm that the CLV benefits accumulate quickly over the years.

Analyzing the Effects of Short- and Long-Term Customer Relationship 149

TABLE 8.1 Lower Limit with 5 Year-Time Horizon Assumption

Years (Duration of Relationship)	0	1	2	3	4	5
Number of Visits per Year	0	2	2	2	2	2
Quantity Purchased per Visit	0	4	4	4	4	4
Q = Total Quantity (items) Purchased in a Year	0	8	8	8	8	8
P = Price per Unit	$0	$20	$20	$20	$20	$20
P*Q = Total Revenues	$0	$160	$160	$160	$160	$160
Initial Cost of Acquiring One Customer and Retention Cost	$200	$50	$50	$50	$50	$50
Surplus = Total Revenue – Total Cost	–$200	$110	$110	$110	$110	$110
CLV of One Customer [NPV assuming R = 10%]	$217					

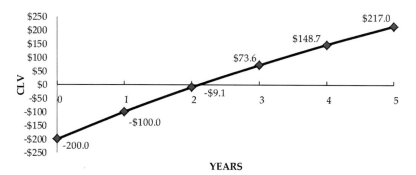

FIGURE 8.1 Short-term customer relationship and the CLV.

Further, it should be pointed out that the duration of customer relationship is the only variable among all the other variables (price, quantity, customer purchase frequency) that a wine firm can control with its marketing policies. As a result, the higher is the duration, the higher the CLV will be. Thus, we can theoretically explore the highest levels of CLV if we assume a multi-generational relationship (infinity), as it is estimated in Table 8.2.

Table 8.2 preserves the previous assumption about Customer 1 and the wine firm. The only change to our earlier assumptions is that Customer 1 will stay with the wine firm to infinity. Thus, the theoretical limit of CLV can be calculated to be $900.

Information from Tables 8.1 and Table 8.2, and Figure 8.1 shows that the CLVs range from a low level of $217 to a theoretical high level of $900. Obviously, how high of the CLV, a wine firm can reach will depend on their ability to establish long-term relationship with its customers.

Figure 8.2 shows that a theoretical level of $900 of CLV can be reached in 105 years. However, it is good news that the largest gains of CLV can be achieved in the first 25 years of the relationship. The CLVs are -$200 at Year 0, $217.0 at Year 5, $475.9 at Year 10, $636.7 at Year 15, $736.5 at Year 20, and $ $798.5 at Year 25. It is not surprising that more than half of the CLV is obtained in just 10 years of the customer relationship. This example illustrates that wineries should target a multi-generational relationship with its customers to maximize the CLV. Therefore, any promotional activities to create brand loyalty will help to maximize CLVs such as establishing frequent contacts with wine customers, a positive wine-tasting room experience, or online wine-selling may help to develop the long-term customer relationship.

Furthermore, Table 8.3 provides a sensitivity analysis by assuming a 20% increase in all variables such as quantity (either increase in the number of Visits per Year or in the Quantity Purchased Per year), Price Per Unit, Initial Cost of Acquiring One Customer, or Retention Cost.

A 20% increase in either Price or Quantity (# of visits or Quantity Purchased per Visit) has the largest effect (55.90% increase) on the value of CLV. This validates that wine pricing or market share are important variable to increase CLV. However, it is unlikely that a wine firm can increase its price or quantity comfortably without scarifying from the total revenue. Therefore, the elasticity of price for the wine firm should be considered

TABLE 8.2 Long-Term Customer Relationship and the Feasible CLV

Years (Duration of Relationship)	0	1	2	3	4	5	6	=> ∞
# of Visits Per Year	0	2	2	2	2	2	2	
Quantity Purchased Per Visit	0	4	4	4	4	4	4	
Q = Total Quantity (items) Purchased in a Year	0	8	8	8	8	8	8	
P = Price Per Unit	$0	$20	$20	$20	$20	$20	$20	
P × Q = Total Revenues	$0	$160	$160	$160	$160	$160	$160	
Initial Cost of Acquiring One Customer and Retention Cost	$200	$50	$50	$50	$50	$50	$50	
Surplus = Total Revenue – Total Cost	–$200	$110	$110	$110	$110	$110	$110	
Continuing Value (CV)						$1,100		
CV + Surplus for the first 5 years	–$200	$110	$110	$110	$110	$1,210		
CLV of One Customer [NPV assuming R = 10%]	$900							

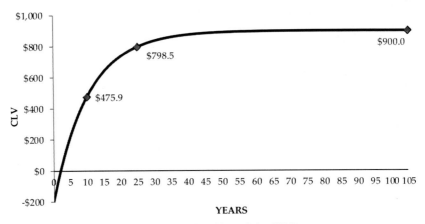

FIGURE 8.2 Long-term customer relationship and the CLV's convergence.

TABLE 8.3 Changing the Assumptions with a 20% Increase in the Variables

	Initial Assumptions	20% Increase	New NPV	% Chance
# of Visits Per Year	2	2.4	$338	55.90%
Quantity Purchased Per Visit	4	4.8	$338	55.90%
Q = Total Quantity (items) Purchased in a Year	8	9.6	$338	55.90%
P = Price Per Unit	$20	$24	$338	55.90%
P*Q = Total Revenues	$160	$192	$338	55.90%
Initial Cost of Acquiring One Customer Only	$200	$240	$177	−18.43%
Maintenance Cost Only	$50	$60	$179	−17.47%
Both Initial Cost and Retention Cost Together	$200, $50	$240, $60	$139	−35.90%
Duration of Relationship	5 Years	6 Years	$279	28.62%
Initial NPV			$217	

before making such a decision. It can be claimed that the elasticity of price for wine is higher at the lowest price ranges than highest price ranges. While brand loyalty lowers price elasticity of wine, other factors such as the customer perception of fairness in pricing may affect price elasticity of wine and the demand (Nowak & Washburn, 2002).

Also, a 20% increase in the initial cost of acquiring one customer or retention cost reduces the value of CLV by −18.43% and −17.47%, respectively. A strategic decision to reduce these costs may have similar percentage gains in magnitude. Thus, while cost-cutting measures can be considered, these changes will provide minimal. CLV gains.

Lastly, a 20% increase in the duration of the relationship between a wine firm and a customer boosts CLV value about 28.62%. This is a significant result implying that when wine market is competitive, the profit margins are tight; a wine firm can still increase its CLV by investing in resources to prolong the duration of its relationship with its customers.

8.4 CONCLUSION

Wine tasting experience and wine tourism is growing all around the world creating opportunities as well as challenges to wine producers in creating brand equity and staying sustainable. Marketing investment efforts towards building customer loyalty should be seen as an effort to increase CLV. Subsequently, CLV calculations require understanding of wine market segmentation and wine customer preferences. Even though the concept is new in the wine market, the CLV calculations based on wine market segmentation and wine customer preferences can provide: (i) the estimations for firm value, and (ii) optimum investment level for the promotional activities to establish customer loyalty.

There are several implications of CLV calculations to wine marketing managers. First, the longer the relationship lasts with wine customers, the higher the CLV and firm value become. In an environment where there is growing competition and increased wine quality all around world, making changes to both price and quantity (consumption of wine) are limited. However, prolonging the relationship of wine customers is an achievable goal for any wine firm. To establish and prolong relationship with wine customers, a positive wine tasting room experience is essential due to achieving direct contacts with the customers and providing cellar-door selling activities. Second, wine managers can assess the value contribution of each customer from the different segments of the wine market.

Therefore, the promotional activities can be focused to those customers with the highest CLV but should not disregard the less profitable customers. Because, the wine managers should be aware of that the success in building customer loyalty in the wine industry may be dependent on word of mount through social-networking recommendations more than ever, and a positive wine tasting experience will enhance brand loyalty among wine customers.

Third, wine marketing managers can focus their marketing efforts beyond wine customer acquisition and retention to increase cross-selling (expansion) activities. Mostly likely that wine customers who are satisfied with the service and quality of the products and are in a long-term relationship with a wine firm will be open to try new wine products from the same firm.

KEYWORDS

- **customer equity**
- **customer lifetime value**
- **marketing**
- **wine tourism**

REFERENCES

1. Alonso, A.D., Sheridan, L., & Scherrer, P. (2008). Importance of tasting rooms for Canary Islands' wineries. British Food Journal, 110(10), 977–988.
2. Barber, N. (2009). Wine consumers information search: Gender differences and implications for the hospitality industry. Tourism and Hospitality Research, 9(3), 250–269.
3. Carmichael, B. (2005). Understanding the wine tourism experience for winery visitors in the Niagara Region, Ontario, Canada. Tourism Geographies, 7(2), 185–204.
4. Dev C. S., & Stroock L. M. (2007). Rosewood Hotels and Resorts: branding to increase customer profitability and lifetime value, Harvard Business School Cases. Retrieved from http://cb.hbsp.harvard.edu/cb/product/2087-PDF-ENG.
5. Gómez, M., Molina, A., & Esteban, Á. (2013). What are the main factors attracting visitors to wineries? A PLS multi-group comparison. Quality and Quantity, 47(5), 2637–2657.

6. Gupta, S., Hanssens, D., Hardie, B., Kahn, W., Kumar, V., Lin, N., Ravishanker, N. & Sriram S. (2006). Modeling Customer Lifetime Value. Journal of Service Research, 9(2), 139–155.
7. Huang, L.C. (2011). The Measurement for the Service Quality of Rural Wineries. Journal of Marketing Development and Competitiveness, 5(5), 29–45.
8. Houghton, M. (2008). Classifying wine festival customers: Comparing an inductive typology with Hall's wine tourist classification. International Journal of Culture, Tourism and Hospitality Research, 2(1), 67–76.
9. Jarvis, W., & Goodman, S. (2005). Effective marketing of small brands: niche positions, attribute loyalty and direct marketing. The Journal of Product and Brand Management, 14(4/5), 292–299.
10. Levy, M., & Weitz, B. A. (2007). Retailing Management (6th ed.). Boston, MA: McGraw-Hill Irwin.
11. Nelson, P. (1970). Information and Consumer Behavior. Journal of Political Economy, 78(2), 311–329.
12. Nowak, L., Thach, L., & Olsen, J. E. (2006). Wowing the millennials: creating brand equity in the wine industry. The Journal of Product and Brand Management, 15(5), 316–323.
13. Nowak, L.I. & Washburn, J.H. (2002). Building brand equity: consumer reactions to proactive environmental policies by the winery. International Journal of Wine Marketing, 14(3), 5–19.
14. O'Neill, M. A., & Palmer, A. (2004). Wine Production and Tourism: Adding Service to a Perfect Partnership. Cornell Hotel and Restaurant Administration Quarterly, 45(3), 269–284.
15. Pride, W. M., & Ferrell O. C. (2008). Marketing (14th ed). Boston, MA: Houghton Mifflin Company.
16. Tipples, R. (2008). Cottesbrook's New Zealand Sauvignon Blanc wine to Tesco. British Food Journal, 110(4/5), 444–459.
17. Vlachvei, A., Notta, O., & Ananiadis, I. (2009). Does advertising matter? An application to the Greek wine industry. British Food Journal, 111(7), 686–698.
18. Vrontis, D., Thrassou, A., & Czinkota, M. R. (2011). Wine marketing: A framework for consumer-centered planning. Special Issue: Branding Across Industries, European Journal of Brand Management, 18(4–5), 245–263.
19. Vrontis, D., & Paliwoda, S. J. (2008). Branding and the Cyprus wine industry. Journal of Brand Management, 16(3), 145–159.

CHAPTER 9

DESIGNING FOR SALES: WINERY DESIGN AND THE VISITOR EXPERIENCE

DOUGLAS THORNLEY

Principal, Gouldevans, San Francisco, CA, USA

CONTENTS

9.1 Introduction 157
9.2 Creating Memorable Visitor Experiences 158
9.3 Building Customer Loyalty 159
9.4 Design Elements That Maximize the Visitor Experience 160
9.5 Case Studies 161
9.6 Conclusion 164
Keywords 165
Reference 165
Appendix 165

9.1 INTRODUCTION

People are drawn to wineries. The experience of driving through vineyard landscapes, learning about the mysteries of wine-making, and of course tasting the wines, draws more and more wine country visitors each year. Winery tourism is also part of the growing Slow Food and Farm-to-Table movements, where the source, purveyors, and processes behind the products are as important as the quality.

Fortunately for consumers, the wine industry is continuing to expand, partly due to wine's growing appeal to younger generations. According to Mark Freund, managing director of Silicon Valley Bank's wine division, Millennials have discovered wine at a younger age than previous generations, which might have a significant effect on wine sales as their earning power increases. Freund says that while Baby Boomers have the greatest concentration of wealth, Generation Xers spend the highest proportion of their income on wine (see, Appendix).

Capturing these consumers is becoming a big business in itself. With the large number of wineries in most wine regions, proprietors are looking for ways to differentiate themselves from the competition and create loyal customers out of casual visitors. Winery owners know that if visitors have a great afternoon and enjoy the wines, they will want to take some of that experience home with them, and will purchase the wines on-site. These direct-to-consumer (DTC) sales benefit both consumers and sellers: they offer the opportunity to extend a memorable experience to consumers while building customer loyalty and brand recognition. By eliminating the middle-man in the traditional three-tiered model of wine sales–producer to distributer to consumer–and selling directly to the consumer, wineries also dramatically increase their profits.

Successful winery sales grow out of three factors: great wine, a knowledgeable and friendly staff, and a memorable environment in which to enjoy the wine. An inviting physical environment makes people want to stay, learn more from the staff, and drink more wine. Satisfied consumers not only buy the wine they've just tasted, they join wine clubs, and make plans to visit again.

As a result of this emphasis on the visitor experience, winery design has grown beyond accommodating operations to finding ways to welcome visitors so that they want to stay–and return. Wineries looking to increase their profits and grow their business are now looking for outstanding architectural design to help.

9.2 CREATING MEMORABLE VISITOR EXPERIENCES

Winery operations can be considered analogous to theaters: there is the front-of-house experience that most visitors have, and the back-of-house – or

Designing for Sales: Winery Design and the Visitor Experience 159

production – experience that is primarily for employees, but is increasingly of interest to dedicated consumers.

The front-of-house experience includes tasting, views of the surroundings, indoor/outdoor movement, and comfort. With the beauty and mild climate of most wine regions, views out and movement from inside to outside are strong factors in visitors' perception of a place. Comfort can have a similar effect. Do visitors have to stand or can they sit? Are they in crowded tasting rooms or are private rooms available? Lastly, the front-of-house experience can include an invitation to experience the winery's deeper identity through interpretive exhibits or displays of the winery's assets. These can include information about the family's or winery's history, environmental business practices, their role in the local community, and art collections.

Predictably, the back-of-house experience is much more industrial. Production, storage, and operations are not traditionally alluring, but as people's interest in wine grows, their interest in understanding the process behind what they drink is growing as well. Wineries are starting to merge these experiences through private tours, where visitors are invited to view the wine-making process, participate in barrel tastings, and make a connection to the winery that not everyone has. Because these tours are part of connecting consumers more deeply to a winery, the design of operational spaces that can accommodate visitors has taken on an importance almost equal to the design of tasting rooms.

9.3 BUILDING CUSTOMER LOYALTY

There are four primary types of winery visitors. The first is *casual visitors* who happen to be in the area and drop in on a whim. *Winery tourists* have already made a connection to certain wineries and go back regularly or repeatedly. *Wine country aficionados* plan out their visits to wine country and are seeking particular qualities in their wine and their winery experience. Lastly, there are *wine collectors*, who visit a winery specifically to add to their wine library.

A winery's goal is to transform the casual visitor to an aficionado, thereby greatly increasing visits and on-site sales revenue. This transformation can come through a variety of experiences for the consumer, beginning with a memorable and distinctive winery that enhances the experience of the wine itself. The siting of the building, arrival sequence, architectural design, tasting environment, and landscape design all contribute to a visitor's sense of place.

In addition, wineries build loyalty through programs and special offerings such as barrel tastings, behind-the-scenes visits, educational experiences, wine clubs and VIP options for repeat customers, and marketing events. They can also encourage their staff to build a rapport with customers, offering interested visitors free tastes of wine not on the tasting list and other perks.

9.4 DESIGN ELEMENTS THAT MAXIMIZE THE VISITOR EXPERIENCE

A beautiful building will attract visitors once, but without a carefully thought-through design that facilitates a memorable experience, it will not bring them back. Four main elements contribute to the visitor experience at wineries: the arrival, the tasting room, facilities for VIPs or club members, and the production areas.

The entrance and approach to a winery are the first opportunity the design has to welcome the visitor and create the promise of a memorable experience. This includes a clear announcement from the road that the visitor has arrived at their destination, an attractive drive to the parking area, and a defined and compelling procession from the vehicle to the tasting room. Common features of successful tasting rooms include a recognizable entry; a sense of place; natural daylight and ventilation; pleasing acoustics, so that they are not loud when crowded; access to an exterior space; views of the winery or vineyards; comfortable furnishings that go beyond standing at a bar; and architectural character that fits its context and region.

VIP and club-member experiences, with their privacy and separation from the public spaces, provide an aspirational alternative to what the average visitor will have. Access to the production areas and opportunities for barrel tasting need to be carefully designed to not interfere with operations while making the visitor feel like they are in the middle of the production activities.

Designing for Sales: Winery Design and the Visitor Experience 161

More and more winery visitors are responding positively to architecture that is "authentic"–reflective of the time it was built and responsive to the context of the site and its surroundings. While medieval castles and faux French chateaus will continue to be built, the more serious wineries aspire to build in a timeless manner that will continue to be fresh, interesting, and less thematic for new winery visitors 20 years into the future.

9.5 CASE STUDIES

The wineries in the following three case studies wanted to improve the visitor experience throughout their estates–from the entrance through production–and hired our architectural firm, Gould Evans, for a significant rethinking and redesign of their facilities.

9.5.1 CUVAISON ESTATE WINES

With no clear arrival spot, visitors to this winery in Napa had a hard time finding the tasting room. Most would turn around and drive away without parking and trying to find the facility. Those who made it to the tasting room found themselves in a converted vintner's office that was too small and not at all designed for visitors. Exposure to high winds outside made going outdoors an undesirable alternative.

Our firm's goals for this design included creating a world-class environment to celebrate the brand; designing an indoor/outdoor experience that was sheltered from the wind; creating a clear sense of arrival from the road and a new entry that told visitors they had arrived; separating VIP and club members from the public tasting area; and incorporating sustainable design into the buildings to reinforce the environmental goals of the winery.

To draw people into the winery, we completely redesigned the arrival and entry experience. The original two structures and production building exuded an image of a working farm, but did not welcome visitors. Starting at the road leading to the winery, we designed an eye-catching perimeter fence that draws people to a well-marked entry. Once in the driveway, visitors see an entry canopy that rises up from the tasting room building, clearly indicating an entry point. By using glass throughout the structure, we allowed people to see that there was activity in the building and they were welcome to join it. We placed wood siding on the tasting room building and metal siding on the barrel building to clearly distinguish visitor spaces from production activities.

By creating multiple venues for tasting, we allowed VIPs and club members to enjoy the benefits of their loyalty to the winery, and simultaneously produced an environment that made becoming a club member desirable to the public. The private tasting room is separated from the public by frosted glass doors, with clear glass used at the top and bottom to show movement, activity, and continuity of use, and to entice the public to become club members to take advantage of the private space. Setting the tasting rooms within the vineyard and creating a sheltered outdoor seating area brought the beauty of the setting into the wine tasting experience.

Cuvaison also charged the design team with developing sustainable solutions for the new tasting room. They view themselves as good shepherds of the land and integrate green initiatives. According to Jay Schuppert, president of Cuvaison Estate Wines, "At Cuvaison there is a shared concern from the staff about climate change and we feel compelled to do what we can to reduce Cuvaison's impact on our environment. Going solar and being certified Napa Green creates the most visual and obvious initiatives, but they are only a few elements of what we are trying to achieve." The final design incorporated water-management systems, integrated natural ventilation and light, and utilized sustainably farmed wood products.

The results for Cuvaison have been remarkable. They have greatly increased the number of visitors, including visitors who come multiple times with friends. Their direct-to-consumer sales have increased, and the increase in profits has exceeded their business model. The industry has also recognized the design with several awards, including the Great Wine Capitals Best of Wine Tourism Award.

9.5.2 LYNMAR ESTATE

Lynmar Estate, in Sebastopol, California, had been in business since 1990 but was only a production facility, and a hard-to-find one at that. Having developed a successful brand of Pinot Noir and Chardonnay wines and a loyal following of committed wine enthusiasts, Lynmar wanted to have a destination that would allow their dedicated fans access

Designing for Sales: Winery Design and the Visitor Experience 163

to the vineyards from which their famous wines came. Located within a rolling vineyard landscape typical of the Sonoma Valley, the property was also in a rural residential area. The new visitor center needed to respect the surrounding uses while also drawing visitors.

Listening to our client's needs, we created a program that included a tasting room/hospitality center; envisioned a building that reflects the scale of the neighboring residential structures while clearly communicating that this is a winery; fashioned a multitude of outdoor spaces, including a courtyard, a porch, and a veranda; and incorporated the flexibility to expand spaces for large events. It was essential to create an iconic architectural image, since architecture is such an important part of Lynmar's identity they feature their building on their wine labels.

The new entry features a trellis tower whose vertical form was inspired by the silos and water towers commonly found in Sebastopol's agrarian setting. This prominent marker allows guests to easily navigate their way from the parking area to the tasting room. Once inside, there are several different tasting venues that can open onto one another with sliding panels–the private tasting room can open up to the public tasting room, which can open onto the courtyard–or remain closed for specific individual experiences.

The indoor/outdoor lifestyle is celebrated by the courtyard tasting area and views of the vineyards to the south and east. Lynmar has two vineyards, Pinot Noir and Chardonnay. We sited the tasting building at the juncture of the two, allowing the views and offering the opportunity to educate visitors about the all-estate-grown wines.

Lynmar Estate has seen similar results to Cuvaison since the redesign of its facilities. Where Lynmar originally sold most of its wine to third-party distributors, its sales are now focused at the winery. Wine club memberships have greatly increased, with the majority of sales going to wine club members. In addition to the increase in DTC sales, the winery's brand recognition has significantly expanded.

9.5.3 PARADUXX WINERY

The owners of Paraduxx bought a vineyard with a ranch house and barn, but no winery. Tasked with starting from scratch, we embraced the agrarian vernacular, designing groupings of buildings instead of one big production and visitor structure. This led to the unique approach of having

164 Strategic Winery Tourism and Management

several production buildings with different functions, which in turn allows guests to experience some of the production facilities on tours.

To celebrate the fermentation building and make it a visual focus from the tasting room, we took the owner's fascination with round barn buildings to the next step, designing a decagonal (10-sided) building with exposed wood and steel framing. This allowed the fermentation tanks to sit around the perimeter of the room, creating a beautiful space that became part of the visitor experience. The building expresses the concept of hand-crafted design as a metaphor for the craft of wine making. Visitors are visually invited over to the fermentation building from the tasting room by the views through the tasting room's large wall of glass.

Another production facility, the lower barrel chairs, reflects the winery's interest in Bordeaux-style wines and traditional winemaking methods, which involve more handwork and less machinery. This building stores premium wines in hand-stacked barrels. The design originally had the building fully below-ground, which complicated production that didn't rely heavily on machines. As a compromise, the building was sunk four feet into the ground, allowing for the thermal benefits from the earth while accommodating the use of hand-carts with gentle ramps. It also allows visitors to feel that they are going into a cellar as they descend the ramps, and allows them to experience old-world production methods first-hand.

Exposing visitors to the production side of a winery has proved very successful for Paraduxx. The numbers of visitors and wine club members have exceeded their expectations, and they have gained a reputation as a unique place to taste wine and be educated about its production.

9.6 CONCLUSION

Wineries have always been focused on making good wines that people want to buy. In recent years, however, the experience of wine tourism has become as important to sales as the quality of the wines, and wineries know that they now have to attract visitors to attract more consumers. This new focus on experience has brought design to the forefront of wineries' marketing efforts and turned it into a differentiator.

By welcoming visitors from the entrance through, in some cases, the production facilities, wineries are offering guests experiences well above finding their favorite bottle of wine on the shelf at a market. As more and more people take advantage of these offerings, the resulting shift in selling and buying habits will make investment in the design of the visitor experience profitable.

KEYWORDS

- **customer loyalty**
- **Cuvaison Estate Wines**
- **direct-to-consumer sales**
- **Lynmar Estate**
- **Paraduxx Winery**
- **winery tourism**

REFERENCE

1. Perkowski, Mateusz. "Direct to Consumer Market Key for Oregon Wine." *Capital Press*. 25 February 2014. Web. 26 February 2014.

APPENDIX

FIGURE A1   Cuvaison Estate Wine – photo #01
Incorporating a dramatic metal awning element at Cuvaison Estate Wines clearly defines entry for arriving guests. Mathew Millman Photography.

FIGURE A2 Cuvaison Estate Wine – photo #02

Sliding glass panels open up the corner of the tasting room providing an indoor/outdoor experience. Mathew Millman Photography.

CHAPTER 10

USING ANNs TO DETERMINE PLACE EVOKED AFFECTIVE CONSUMER REACTIONS IN WINE TOURISM

ALBERT STÖCKL,[1] WOLFRAM RINKE,[2] and ANDREAS EISINGERICH[3]

[1]*Lecturer and Researcher, University of Applied Sciences Burgenland, Austria, E-mail: albert.stoeckl@fh-krems.ac.at*

[2]*University of Applied Sciences Burgenland, Austria*

[3]*Associate Professor of Marketing, Imperial College London, Great Britain*

CONTENTS

10.1   Background 167
10.2   Related Literature 168
10.3   Data Collection 169
10.4   Measures 170
10.5   ANN Model Building 170
10.6   Findings from the First Model 172
10.6   Findings from the Open Form Model and Simulation Results .. 174
10.7   Conclusion 182
Keywords 183
References 183

10.1   BACKGROUND

Tourism experiences in viticultural areas tend to evoke strong positive and affective consumer reactions (Yuan et al., 2008). Ideally they lead to sentiments such as pleasure, satisfaction, nostalgia, or even emotional attachment (Gross and Brown, 2006; Hammitt et al., 2006). Studies show that satisfaction is strongly related to attachment to a certain place (Williams and Huffman, 1986) and pleasure (Orth et al., 2011) and can lead to consumer loyalty (Dodd, 2000; Alexandris et al., 2006) as well as greater spending (Moore and Graefe 1994; Dodd, 2000; Kyle, Absher and Graefe, 2003). In addition, research showed that visitors who are familiar with a region, that is, they have visited the destination before, are more likely to develop strong attachment to that place over time (Williams et al., 1992).

10.2 RELATED LITERATURE

Low and Altman (1992) identified four key elements, which underlie the theory of place attachment: Firstly, that affect, emotion and feeling play a critical role in the concept of place attachment. Secondly, that environments and settings can indeed vary in several important ways with varying degrees of attachment by people. Thirdly, that families and members of communities, and entire cultures collectively can share attachment to a place. Finally, that attachment to a place is influenced by temporal variations.

The specific factors which may or may not lead to attachment such as perceived crowding (Kyle et al., 2004), involvement (Hwang et al., 2005), shared values (Park et al., 2013), or level of specialization (Bricker and Kerstetter, 2000) are numerous and vary from author to author across the different studies in the extant body of literature. Whilst in most of the studies relations among the variables were successfully established, Kyle et al. (2004) propose that further research is necessary in order for researchers to have a better understanding of the development of attachment factors in tourism, its antecedents and behavioral outcomes. Earlier research on this topic particularly investigates short-term effects of affective reactions to a tourism experience. Brakus et al. (2009) point out, however, that the stimulus may extend far beyond short-term impacts such as spending. Therefore, long-term customer relationships i.e. attachment and loyalty have to be investigated more closely, especially with respect to the interrelationships among influencing factors. So far, regression analyses including mediator and/or moderator relationship tests were applied in the majority of studies. There are, however, certain limitations of these techniques that have been noted in the literature. Additionally, artificial neural networks (ANNs) seem to have an advantage over multivariable logistic regression analysis when it comes to the differentiation of influencing factors as well as in the standardization of interrelationships between variables. Specifically, ANN models significantly outperform multivariable logistic regression models in both senses of discrimination and calibration (Eftekhar et al., 2005) and although ANNs lag behind in accuracy (Eftekhar et al., 2005), this modeling technique seems an interesting approach to determine influencing factors in consumer and tourism research. The research goal of this study is hence to identify, and test crucial factors leading to pleasure, satisfaction, consumer emotional attachment, loyalty and spending in a tourism context by applying data mining techniques, that is, ANNs.

In this research we attempted to overcome shortcomings of previous tests in this field by applying data mining techniques, namely, ANNs. ANNs employ nonlinear mathematical models in order to simulate the human brain's own problem-solving process (Eftekhar et al., 2005). Just as humans apply knowledge gained from past experience to current situations, a neural network takes previously solved examples to build a system of "neurons" that makes new decisions, classifications, and forecasts (Terrin et al., 2003). ANNs could be defined as *"an advanced, computer-based method for knowledge discovery from vast and semi-structured databases by building of nonparametric models for decision support. Generally speaking, the neural network model is a hierarchical system of interconnected elements (neurons, nodes, elements) for simultaneous data processing which is analogous to the human data processing and decision-making"* (Marusya, 2008; p. 184). And so, ANNs allow to model nonlinear interdependencies in the response behavior of a sampled population and therefore seem predestined to expand the academic body of knowledge in consumer insight and tourism research.

10.3 DATA COLLECTION

More than 3,200 tourists from 14 tourism destinations in seven countries were interviewed. After an initial explorative factor analysis data mining techniques, namely ANNs were applied in order to detect interdependencies between independent variables. The basis consisted of 36 variables derived from existing literature and including factors such as *service quality, (beauty of) landscape, (high) standard of living, (level of) child-friendliness, possibilities to broaden one's horizon, the perceived price-quality ratio* and *trustworthiness.*

The questionnaire for our empirical study, that was used to collect the data set, consisted of a total of 57 questions including ratings of the wine tourism destinations' characteristics (influencing factors) on 7-point Likert scales. Validated item batteries derived from existing literature and concerning pleasure and emotional attachment were used to assess wine tourists' affections.

10.4 MEASURES

Following Orth et al. (2011), a seven-point six-item Likert scale proposed by Mehrabian and Russell (1974) was applied in order to measure pleasure and a three item seven-point metric developed and validated by Bergami and Bagozzi (2000) assessed emotional attachment. A seven point, three-item semantic differential scale ranging from one (highly satisfactory, very pleasant, and delightful) to seven (highly unsatisfactory, very unpleasant, and terrible) (Sirdeshmukh, Singh, and Sabol, 2002) assessed satisfaction. Thomson, MacInnis and Park's (2005) metrics assessed loyalty (3 items) and spending (2 items).

In an initial exploratory factor analysis and a cut-off at a Cronbach's Alpha value <0.7 seven (of 35) remaining items were identified, automatically grouped (loading on one factor) and taken into further analysis with ANNs. The remaining and therefore most influencing variables are: *familiarity*; *the human factor*; *trustworthiness*; *the offer of leisure activities; relish*; *child-orientation* and *opportunity to broaden one's horizon*.

Dependent variables investigated are: *Pleasure, emotional attachment, satisfaction, loyalty* and *spending*. Both independent variables (regional attachment factors) and dependent variables (affective tourist reactions) as well as referenced questions are shown in Table 10.1.

10.5 ANN MODEL BUILDING

The technology, which is used in this study to establish a model in order to detect relationships between influencing factors, that is, regional attachment factors on the one hand and their influence on affective tourist reactions such as *pleasure, satisfaction, attachment, loyalty* or *spending* on the other hand, are two different kinds of multilayer feed forward perceptron networks, that is, artificial neural networks (Patterson, 1996). This technology is well known and widely used to generate an excellent functional

Using ANNs to Determine Place Evoked Affective Consumer Reactions 171

TABLE 10.1 Model Parameters and Original Questionnaire Numbers

Description	Referenced Questions	Independent Parameter
Regional Attachment Factors	7-point Likert scales	
Familiarity	How well do you know the XY wine region? (This is my first visit – I come here regularly) (v101)	yes
Human factor	Average value of: service staff and tourism personnel take excellent care of their customers (v103); people are friendly and excellent hosts (v116); people are trustworthy and reliable (v118)	yes
Trustworthiness	Concentrating on exploiting tourists rather than on providing true value (v129)	yes
Leisure activity	A wide range of leisure and sport activities are offered (v112)	yes
Relish	Average value of: without peer for fine wining and dining (v123); exactly the place to drink superb wines (v124)	yes
Child-orientation	Ideal for children (v131)	yes
Broaden horizon	An ideal place to broaden one's horizon (v136)	yes
Affective Tourist Reactions	7-point Likert scales except for spending	
Pleasure	Average value of: happy – unhappy (v138); pleased – annoyed (v139)	
Emotional attachment	Average value of: feel strongly attached to the XY region (v152); I am strongly emotionally connected to XY (v153); I do NOT feel any emotional bond towards XY (inverse item) (v154)	
Satisfaction	Average value of: highly satisfactory – highly unsatisfactory (v144); very pleasant – very unpleasant (v145); terrible – delightful (inverse item) (v146)	
Loyalty	Average value of: am willing "to go the extra mile" to get here (v148); I can highly recommend a visit here to relatives and friends (v149); will come back here in the future for holidays (v150)	
Spending	Average value of: Estimated tourist spending to the XY region on average (v155) – own spending (v156)	

mapping between the independent network input and the dependent network output. Although these networks are treated as "black-box" models, several ways exist to learn about relations and dependencies in the underlying data set, by examining the final inner structure of the network or by model simulation (Swingler, 1996). The training of the multilayer network was done with an error back-propagation algorithm following Pao (1989).

In the data preparation phase, which was done before the model-building phase, the original data from the questionnaire needed a careful data inspection and verification. We followed procedures as proposed by Swingler (1996) and Runkler (2010). All questionnaire values were recalculated in such a way, that a low value can be interpreted as a negative or "bad" situation and a higher value as a positive or "good" situation. The value of each model parameter was then calculated as the arithmetic average value of the respective questionnaire answers. In most cases the values were stretched within the whole value range of 1 to 7 except for *satisfaction* (between 3 and 7). An intermediate data set was generated and used for model building. A filter was applied to the intermediate data set to remove outliers. This filter accepted only values within a 2 sigma value range around the arithmetic average value for almost every parameter. Only the parameter to describe *spending* had a broader value range. All data sets, which were incomplete or did not meet the validation rules were removed. From the original data set of more than 3,200 samples only 950 data sets were left as a training data set. Table 10.2 shows the basic statistics for the final training data set.

Subsequently, two kind of models where built. The first model is used to calculate the relationship of independent to dependent parameters. The second model was built as a fully inverted open equation neural network model with the same parameters as the first model. The transformation into an open form allows to better map interrelationships between dependent parameters (Thalhammer, 1993). The second model was used to simulate the *affective tourist reaction* under changing conditions for each model parameter.

10.6 FINDINGS FROM THE FIRST MODEL

For continuous valued mapping functions, the explanation of the network behavior relates to the gradient of each output unit with respect to each input unit. The resultant set of combinations forms a matrix of derivatives known as a Jacobian matrix (Swingler, 1996). To get a comparable insight

Using ANNs to Determine Place Evoked Affective Consumer Reactions 173

TABLE 10.2 Basic Statistics for the Training Data Set

	Minimum	Maximum	Arithm.Avrg.	Std.Dev (N–1)
Familiarity	1	7	3.8	2.2
Human factor	1	7	5.5	1.1
Leisure activity	1	7	4.7	1.4
Relish	1	7	5.1	1.3
Trust	1	7	5.2	1.6
Child-oriented	1	7	4.7	1.6
Broaden horizon	1	7	5.0	1.3
Satisfaction	3	7	5.0	1.6
Loyalty	1	7	5.5	1.1
Emotional attachment	1	7	4.9	1.6
Pleasure	1	7	6.2	0.9
Spending	3.5	4350.0	441.2	556.9

view of the built model with respect to the value ranges, we normalize the values of the resulting Jacobi matrix per dependent output unit. The resulting table tell us how strong a certain independent parameter influences a dependent parameter. The results can be seen in Table 10.3.

The following spider web diagram (Fig. 10.1), visualizes the relationship outlined in Table 10.3 in a graphical form.

Key findings derived from the normalized Jacobi matrix and with regard to the first generated model show that the *human factor* (people) has the highest influence on affective wine tourists' reactions i.e. *pleasure, satisfaction, emotional attachment* as well as *loyalty*. Scale values

TABLE 10.3 Normalized Jacobi Matrix of the Internal Network Weights

Normalized Jacobi Matrix	Satisfaction	Loyalty	Emotional attachment	Pleasure	Spending
Familiarity	0.26	0.33	0.70	0.32	1.00
Human factor	1.00	1.00	1.00	1.00	0.74
Leisure activity	0.16	0.17	0.21	0.19	0.54
Relish	0.33	0.34	0.38	0.34	0.40
Trust	0.36	0.35	0.22	0.37	0.35
Child-oriented	0.23	0.38	0.39	0.32	0.76
Broaden horizon	0.36	0.46	0.48	0.41	0.61

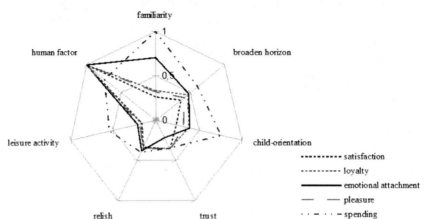

FIGURE 10.1 Spider web diagram of the normalized Jacobi matrix.

in *familiarity* as well as the *human factor* and *child orientation* are highly related to the response behavior regarding *spending*.

10.6 FINDINGS FROM THE OPEN FORM MODEL AND SIMULATION RESULTS

The second model can be interpreted as the open equation form of the previous model. This model is used to simulate the impact of regional factors onto the touristic experiences. The simulation results show the nonlinear characteristics of the relationships between these parameters. Two different sets of model simulations were done. The first set of simulation runs shows how strong dependent parameters are effected by one single independent parameter (Figs. 10.2–10.8) whereas the second set of simulation runs was done to demonstrate which independent parameters do or do not effect one single dependent model parameter (Figs. 10.9–10.13). This way all kind of questions to analyze how far an independent variable must be changed, to have a (significant) positive impact on the *affective tourist reaction* can be analyzed and answered. The findings from the static model calculations can be confirmed and are seen in the simulation runs, although the findings are more detailed and nonlinear. A closer look to some important parameters will be explained more detailed below.

Using ANNs to Determine Place Evoked Affective Consumer Reactions   175

From the simulation results as shown in Fig. 10.2 we can see, that the tourists' ratings of the local people (*human factor*) have a significant impact on *loyalty* and *emotional attachment*. The relationship is close to linear and any improvement of the *human factor* improves *loyalty* to the visited wine tourism region along with *emotional attachment*. The strongest affective reaction can be seen on the parameter *pleasure*. This relationship is non-linear. The strongest improvement can be achieved, when the evaluation of the *human factor* is raised from 0% to 15%. This step leads to an improvement of 25% in *pleasure*. This means that a certain minimum level for the *human factor* is obligatory in order to gain medium a good level of *pleasure*. Further improvement of the *human factor* can improve a wine tourism region's *pleasure* performance by another 10–12% of its value range.

Another important parameter is *familiarity* because it shows a strong positive correlation with the parameter *spending*, which is one of the parameter that describe affective tourist reaction.

In Fig. 10.3 you can see this relationship. A value increase from 2 to 6 can increase the parameter *spending* by about 50% of its value range. In the same time the parameter *satisfaction* can be increased by about 25% and the parameters loyalty and emotional attachment are also increase by about 20% of their value range, respectively.

The parameter broaden horizon is positive correlated with the parameters *loyalty*, *emotional attachment* and *pleasure*. An increase of this

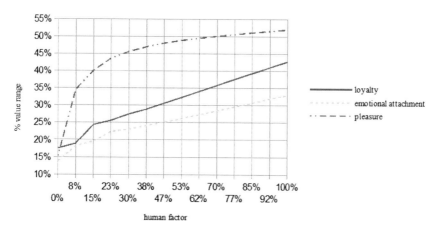

FIGURE 10.2 Influence of human factor on affective tourist reactions.

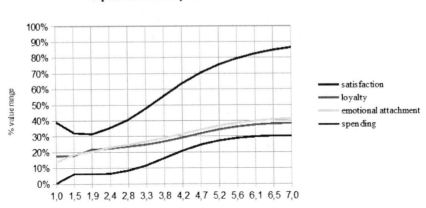

FIGURE 10.3 Influence of familiarity on affective tourist reaction.

parameter from 2 to 7 leads to a increase of about 30% of its value range for the parameter *pleasure* and an increase of about 35% of its value range for the parameters *loyalty* and *emotional attachment*.

The next diagram (Fig. 10.5) shows the influence of the parameter *leisure activity* an *affective tourist reaction*. The parameters *spending* and *satisfaction* are influenced most. As the simulation results show in the diagram an increase

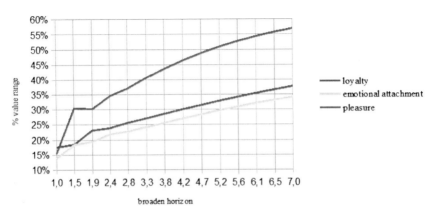

FIGURE 10.4 Influence of broaden horizon on affective tourist reaction.

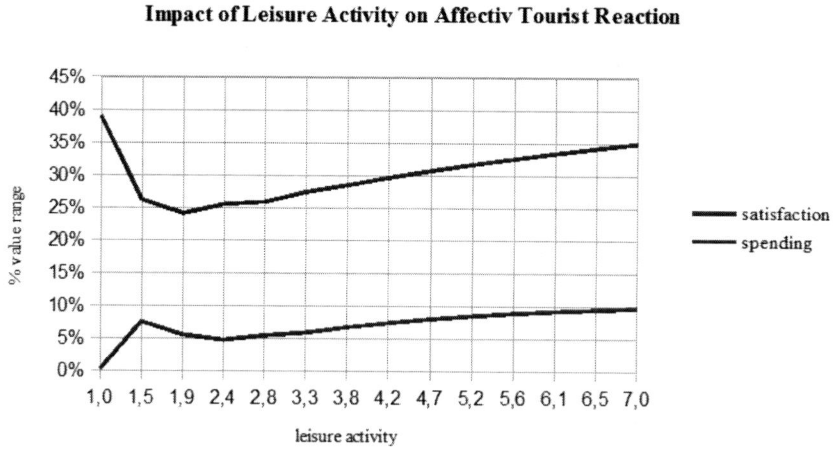

Impact of Leisure Activity on Affectiv Tourist Reaction

FIGURE 10.5 Influence of leisure activity on affective tourist reactions.

in the parameter value of *leisure activity* from 3 to 7 increases the value of *spending* by 10% and the value of *satisfaction* by 5% of the value range.

The next diagram (Fig. 10.6) shows the simulation results from analyzing the parameter *relish* and its influence on the *affective tourist reaction*. The parameter *emotional attachment* shows the strongest effect and a value increase from 3 to 7 leads to a value increase of the parameter *emotional attachment* by about 5% of its value range.

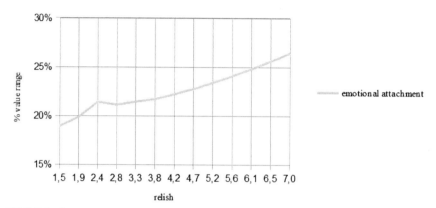

FIGURE 10.6 Influence of relish on affective tourist reactions.

The simulation results from analyzing the parameter *trust* and its influence on the *affective tourist reaction* are shown in the following diagram (Fig. 10.7). The parameters *satisfaction, loyalty and pleasure* shows the strongest effect and a value increase from 2 to 6 on Likert scale leads to an increase of the parameter *pleasure* by 15% of its value range and the parameters *loyalty* and *satisfaction* by over 10% of its value range.

Another interesting simulation result is the analyses of the parameter to what extent a region is *child-oriented*. The results are shown in Fig. 10.8 and the most interesting result is a negative correlated impact to the parameter *pleasure*. Also the positive correlated parameters of *loyalty* and *emotional attachment* are less strong as someone might expect. Our assumption is that we have different tourist profiles, which lead to that different *affective tourist reaction* in this case. We further assume that families with children are positively correlated and others are neutral or negative correlated to this parameter. This assumption needs further investigation and will be part of another research.

The *affective tourist reaction* parameter *pleasure* is influenced by *broaden horizon*, the *human factor, familiarity* and *trust*. The simulation results are shown in the diagram (Fig. 10.9) below.

The strongest positively correlated parameter is *familiarity*, which can improve the parameter *pleasure* by 2 points on the Likert scale. The other influencing parameters as *human factor, relish* and *broaden*

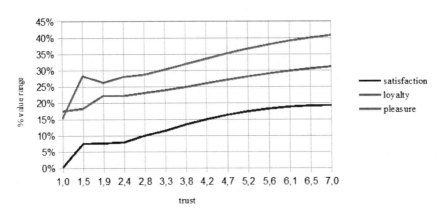

FIGURE 10.7 Influence of trust on affective tourist reactions.

Using ANNs to Determine Place Evoked Affective Consumer Reactions 179

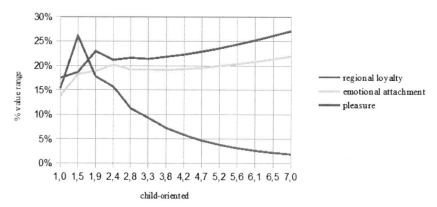

FIGURE 10.8 Influence of child-oriented on affective tourist reactions.

horizon increase the parameter *pleasure* by 1 point on Likert scale. The parameter *emotional attachment* as shown in the following diagram (Fig. 10.10), can be significantly improved by the parameters *familiarity* and *human factor*.

Also *broaden horizon* has a significant impact. An improvement of 30% or more can increase the value of *emotional attachment* by about

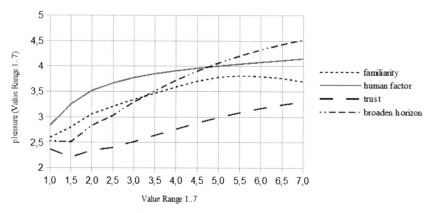

FIGURE 10.9 Parameter "pleasure."

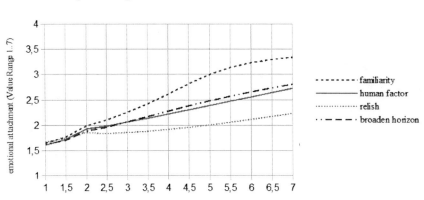

FIGURE 10.10 Parameter "emotional attachment."

15–20%. The parameter f*amiliarity* shows a nonlinear relationship than the other parameters. Improving *familiarity* from 3 to 5 by a step of 2 is more efficient than improving from 5 to 7 on *emotional attachment*.

The parameter *loyalty* as shown in Fig. 10.11 is significantly influenced by *human factor*, *familiarity, broaden horizon* and *trust*. The strongest impact has the *human factor*, where a 10% improvement leads to a 2%

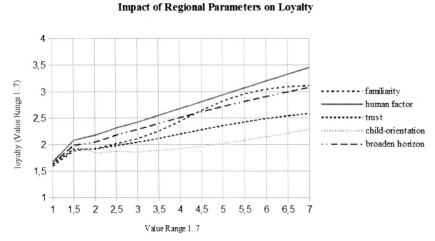

FIGURE 10.11 Parameter "loyalty."

increase in *loyalty*. This is similar with other factors like *broaden horizon* and *trust*. This parameter shows an explicit linear correlation. The *human factor* has a nonlinear impact on the parameter *loyalty*, where an increase by from 2 to 5 (as a given answer to related questions on Likert scale), which is about 50% increase, improves the value for the parameter *loyalty* by about 25% of its value range.

The parameter *satisfaction, as shown in* Fig. 10.12, is significantly influenced by two parameters *familiarity* and *trust*.

The simulation results show that the parameter *satisfaction* has the strongest effect in its value range between 3 and 5. Which means that to increase the value for the parameter *satisfaction* up to a level of 4 on Likert scale, the parameter *familiarity* should be between 4 and 5. Above a value of 5 the effect is minor and not noticeable on the Likert scale.

The parameter *trust* is most effective in the range of 2 to 6 and increase the value for the parameter *satisfaction* by about 10% of its value range.

Looking at the parameter *spending* as shown in Fig. 10.13 above, the parameter *familiarity* has the biggest impact. Another result is that the parameter leisure activity is has an increasing effect on the parameter spending, which can be seen from the simulation.

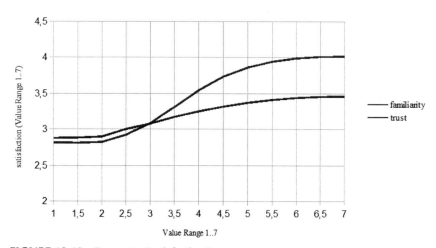

FIGURE 10.12 Parameter "satisfaction."

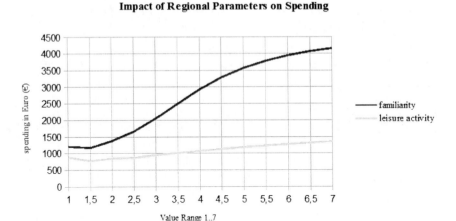

FIGURE 10.13 Parameter "spending."

10.7 CONCLUSION

Artificial neural network (ANN) analysis has been argued to overcome some of the shortcomings of general and widely applied regression analyses. Despite its noted strengths numerous researchers are still hesitant to employ artificial neural network analyses. In our research, we therefore aimed to use artificial neural network to demonstrate the critical role it can play in informing research and marketing practice, particularly in the context of regional tourism and attachment to a certain place. We acknowledge that this research is only a first step and we invite future research to use artificial neural network analyses as part of their research efforts.

Comparing simple regression analyses with the methodology of artificial neural networks you have to look how both techniques are used. Regression analyses try to fit well known linear or nonlinear functions to a data set, by minimizing a certain cost function. Multilayer feed forward artificial neural networks are universal approximators and the type of function you try to fit to your data set is a priori unknown. The only thing you know about your observed system are the input data and related output data. Cybenko (1989) and Hornik et al. (1989) proved that any continuous mapping over a compact domain can be approximated as accurately as necessary by a feed forward neural network with one hidden layer (Omidvar, 1997). This is impossible with traditional regression methods. Based on the theoretical findings, multilayer ANN allows to build robust observation models and to use them for system identification for almost any kind of observable systems. Artificial neural networks can efficiently approximate and interpolate multivariate data and are well accepted for nonlinear statistical fitting and prediction ("ridge regression") (Omidvar, 1997). Consumer emotions, feelings and affections as well as regional aspects can be considered as typical nonlinear. The mathematical relationship between all the different observed parameters and its values, that have been collected for the observed system "touristic region and customer" are unknown. Therefore, we considered to use the proper technology – artificial neural networks – to identify the unknown relationships between regional parameters and consumer affections.

KEYWORDS

- artificial neural networks
- data mining techniques
- loyalty
- open form model
- pleasure
- ridge regression
- satisfaction
- wine tourism

REFERENCES

1. Alexandris, K., Kouthouris, C., Meligdis, A. (2006). Increasing customers' loyalty in a skiing resort: the contribution of place attachment and service quality. International Journal of Contemporary Hospitality Management, 18 (5), 414–425
2. Bergami, M., Bagozzi, R. Self-categorization, affective commitment, and group self-esteem as distinct aspects of social identity in the organization. British Journal of Social Psychology 2000, 39: 555–77.

3. Brakus, J. J., Schmitt, B. H., Zarantonello, L. (2009) Brand experience: what is it? How is it measured? Does it affect loyalty? Journal of Marketing, 73(3), 52–68.
4. Bricker, K. and Kerstetter, D. (2000). "Level of specialization and place attachment," Leisure Sciences, Vol. 22, pp. 233–57.
5. Cybenko, G. (1989). "Approximation by super-positions of a sigmoidal function." Mathematics of Control, Signal and Systems, 2: 303–314
6. Dodd, T. (2000). Influences on cellar door sales and determinants of wine tourism success: Results for Texas wineries. In Hall, C.M., Sharples, L., Cambourne, B. and Macionis, N. (eds.). Wine Tourism Around the World: Development, management and markets. Butterworth-Heinemann: Boston. p. 136.
7. Eftekhar, B., Mohammad, K., Ardebili, H. E., Ghodsi, M., Ketabchi E (2005). Comparison of artificial neural network and logistic regression models for prediction of mortality in head trauma based on initial clinical data. BMC Med Inform Decis Mak, 5: 3. PubMed Abstract
8. Giuliani, M. V., Feldman, R. (1993). Place attachment in a developmental and cultural context. Journal of Environmental Psychology, 13: 267–74.
9. Gross, M. J., Brown, G. (2006). Tourism experiences in a lifestyle destination setting: the roles of involvement and place attachment. Journal of Business Research, 59: 696–700.
10. Hammitt, W. E., Backlund, E. A., Bixler, R. D. (2006). Place bonding for recreation places: conceptual and empirical development. Leisure Studies, 25(1), 17–41.
11. Hidalgo, C., Hernandez, B. (2001) Place attachment: conceptual and empirical questions. Journal of Environmental Psychology, 21: 273–81.
12. Hornig, K., Stinchcombe, M., White, H. (1989). "Multilayer feed forward networks are universal approximators." Neural Networks, 2: 359–366
13. Hwang, S. N., Lee, C., Chen, H. J. (2005). "The relationship among tourists' involvement, place attachment and interpretation satisfaction in Taiwan's national parks," Tourism Management, Vol. 26, pp. 143–56.
14. Ivanova, Marusya (2008). An Analysis of Brand Interdependencies Using Artificial Neural Networks, Conference Proceedings of the 2008 Scientific Conference at the Alexandru Ioan Cuza University in Iai, Romania
15. Kyle, G., Absher, J., Graefe, A. (2003). "The moderating role of place attachment on the relationship between attitudes toward fees and spending preferences," Leisure Sciences, Vol. 25, pp. 33–50.
16. Kyle, G., Graefe, A., Manning, R., Bacon, J. (2003). "An examination of the relationship between leisure activity involvement and place attachment among hikers along the Appalachian Trail," Journal of Leisure Research, Vol. 35 No. 3, pp. 249–73.
17. Kyle, G., Graefe, A., Manning, R., Bacon, J. (2004). "Effect of activity involvement and place attachment on recreationists' perceptions of setting density," Journal of Leisure Research, Vol. 26, pp. 209–31.
18. Mehrabian, A., Russell, J. A. An approach to environmental psychology. Cambridge: MIT Press, 1974.
19. Moore, R. L., Graefe, A. R. (1994). Attachments to Recreation Settings: The Case of Rail-Trail Users. Leisure Sciences, 16, 17–31
20. Omidvar, O., Elliott, D. L. (1997). Neural Systems for Control, Academic Press, ISBN 0-12-526430-5.

21. Orth, U. R., Limon, Y., Rose, G. (2010). Store-evoked affect, personalities, and consumer emotional attachments to brands. Journal of Business Research, 63(11), 1202–8.
22. Orth, U. R., Stöckl, A., Veale, R., Brouard, J., Cavicchi, A., Faraoni, M., Larreina, M., Lecat, B., Olsen, J., Rodriguez-Santos, C., Santini, C., Wilson, D. (2011). "Using attribution theory to explain tourists' attachments to place-based brands," Journal of Business Research, 65 (9), 1321–1327.
23. Pao, Yoh-Han (1989). Adaptive Pattern Recognition and Neural Networks, Addison-Wesley Publishing Company, ISBN 0-201-12584-6.
24. Park, C. W., Eisingerich, A. B., Park, J. W. (2013). "Attachment-aversion (AA) model of customer-brand relationships," Journal of Consumer Psychology, 23 (2), 229–48.
25. Patterson, Dan, W. (1996). Artificial Neural Networks: Theory and Applications, Prentice Hall Simon & Schuster, ISBN 0–13–295353–6
26. Runkler, Thomas, A. (2010). Data Mining, Vieweg+Teubner Fachverlag, Wiesbaden 2010, ISBN 978–3-8348–0858–5
27. Sirdeshmukh, D., Singh, J., Sabol, B. (2002). Consumer trust, value and loyalty in relational exchanges. Journal of Marketing, 66(1), 15–37.
28. Swingler, Kevin (1996). Applying Neural Networks, Academic Press Harcourt Brace & Company Publishers, ISBN 0–12–679170–8
29. Terrin, N., Schmid, C. H., Griffith, J. L., D'Agostino, R. B., Selker HP (2003). External validity of predictive models: A comparison of logistic regression, classification trees, and neural networks.
30. Thalhammer, Manfred (1993). "Neue Reglerstruktur auf Basis Neuronaler Netzwerke," PhD Thesis, Technical University of Vienna 1993
31. Thomson, M., MacInnis, D. J., Park, C. W. The ties that bind: measuring the strength of consumers' emotional attachments to brands. Journal of Consumer Psychology 2005, 15(1), 77–91.
32. Williams, D. R., & Huffman, M. (1986). Recreation specialization as a factor in backcountry trail choice, IN Proceedings of the National Wilderness Research Conference: Current Research. (pp. 31–45), Ogden, UT: Intermountain Research Station, USDA Forest Service
33. Williams, D. R., Patterson, M. E., Roggenbuck, J. W., & Watson, A. E. (1992). Beyond the Commodity Metaphor: Examining Emotional and Symbolic Attachment to Place. Leisure Science, 14, 29–46
34. Yuan, J., Morrison, A. M., Cai, L. A. and Linton, S. (2008). A model of wine tourist behaviour: A festival approach. Int. J. Tourism Res., 10, 207–219. doi: 10.1002/jtr.651

CHAPTER 11

EFFECTIVE WINERY TASTING ROOM MANAGEMENT

STEPHANIE FRIEDMAN

Direct Sales Manager, Gary Farrell Vineyards and Winery, 10701 Westside Rd, Healdsburg, CA 95448, United States

CONTENTS

11.1 Introduction 187
11.2 Importance of the Tasting Room 188
11.3 Strategic Operations 190
11.4 Qualities of an Effective Tasting Room Manager 196
11.5 Measuring Tasting Room Effectiveness 199
11.6 Conclusion 203
Keywords 203
References 203

11.1 INTRODUCTION

Winery tourism has become a global business and the number of winery tasting rooms increases every year. A tasting room serves not only as the main venue for visitation among wineries large and small, but it has also evolved into a key source of revenue with its ability to deliver high profit margins. As a critical component of the direct-to-consumer sales channel, the ability to maximize results from the tasting room is growing

188 Strategic Winery Tourism and Management

in importance, and wineries are investing in top-performing managers to oversee this effort.

With this in mind, this chapter provides an overview of the key components of effective tasting room management. First, it explains the importance of the tasting room and the guest experience. Next, it describes the strategic operations on which the winery must focus to position the tasting room for success. Then, it describes the core competencies that an effective tasting room manager should possess, including considerations pertinent to building and managing the tasting room team. Finally, it identifies the key metrics used to measure the effectiveness of the tasting room manager and team in achieving winery goals.

11.2 IMPORTANCE OF THE TASTING ROOM

The tasting room is a venue where visitors may sample the winery's products, namely wine. They are often attached to the winery's production or administration facilities, but stand-alone tasting rooms are becoming more common in metropolitan areas. Tasting rooms were once established with marketing and public relations in mind, offering complimentary samples of wine to guests to build brand awareness that would foster sales in the broad market. With the growth of winery tourism, tasting rooms have become their own profit centers, delivering immediate revenue from wine, merchandise, tasting fees and events, as well as contributing to the winery's long-term revenue potential by the recruitment of new wine club members.

Winery visitation plays a strong role in the overall customer experience. The effects on customer loyalty are significant, and the tasting room experience can make or break the relationship a guest has with a brand over its lifetime. The tasting room gives the brand an identity in the guest's mind and creates long-lasting memories, for better or for worse. When a guest has a positive experience at the winery, she is likely to make a purchase, join the wine club or recommend the winery to friends. These are positive outcomes for the winery, and positive for the customer as they have developed an emotional connection to the brand. When the experience fails to meet the guest's expectations, however, very little good is done for the winery and the results can sometimes be

Effective Winery Tasting Room Management

devastating. In a saturated market such as the wine industry, consumers can easily find a plethora of substitutes without having to search far. Wineries are advised to pay great attention to the guest experience and quickly resolve any negative interactions, for the visitors may take their business elsewhere; or worse, they might let the world know about their dissatisfaction via user-generated review websites such as Yelp and TripAdvisor.

In order to deliver a positive, memorable experience, wineries must exceed the guest's expectations, and this is usually easier said than done. Winery visitors will have varied motivations for visiting, as well as varied levels of wine knowledge, ranging from the curious wine novice to the well-educated expert. Each will have different expectations, and it is advantageous to the winery to deliver a somewhat tailored experience to each type of guest—one size does not fit all in the wine industry. It is imperative that wineries understand what types of guests will be visiting and then develop their tasting room strategy accordingly (Fig. 11.1).

FIGURE 11.1 Gary Farrell Vineyards and Winery, Russian River Valley.

11.3 STRATEGIC OPERATIONS

Tasting room management is not simply about the process of greeting guests and pouring wine. Standard operations include everything from marketing, hospitality and sales to inventory management, point-of-sale systems and even landscaping in some cases. A winery must strategically consider its tasting room operations to create opportunities for success. The following are fundamental questions around which all tasting room decision-making and activities should revolve.

11.3.1 HOW DO WE DRIVE VISITORS TO THE TASTING ROOM?

Marketing can affect the success of the tasting room and it is often the responsibility of the tasting room manager to develop and execute certain marketing initiatives. One part of marketing is the creation and promotion of interesting guest experiences that are attractive to visitors, which will be remembered and recommended to others. These might include tours, specialty tastings of limited wines, wine and food pairings, or a tasting with the winemaker or owner. Whatever the setting, the experience needs to match the personality of the winery and fit with the overall brand essence. For example, a biodynamic winery might offer a tour of their vineyards and gardens in addition to a tasting of wine and small bites prepared from the produce grown on-site. A winery owned and developed by three generations of family might offer a seated wine and food pairing, with dishes created from secret family recipes passed down over the years. Additionally, it is important for wineries in mature wine regions to continually push the envelope and keep the experiences fresh so that jaded visitors who have "already done that" can be lured back (Thach, 2013).

One of the most significant marketing efforts for which a tasting room manager must be responsible is outreach to local industry partners. Regional associations representing the viticultural area, city or county can offer marketing support through detailed maps, printed publications and website listings. Neighboring wineries, lodgings and other local businesses can drive a substantial amount of traffic to the tasting room since most visitors are not just visiting one winery while on a trip to wine country.

Making friends with other tasting room teams and partnering to generate referrals can often result in a large amount of visitors who arrive by recommendation. In some cases, wineries create formal programs to incentivize their referral partners to send guests their way. Rewards in the form of bottles of wine and complimentary, or discounted, experiences at the winery are common. Whether or not a formal referral program is developed, thorough visitation records (i.e., the referral source and notation of any dollar purchase or wine club sign-up) should be kept as this information will help the manager better understand which channels are working well, which relationships can be nurtured to achieve better results, and what ties can be cut loose to allow for more focus on the other networks. The quality of guests must be considered as much as the quantity of guests since an increase in visitors does not necessarily equate to an increase in buyers or revenue. This concept will be further discussed later in the chapter.

User-generated review websites, including Yelp and TripAdvisor, have become a prevalent marketing component for wineries, presenting both opportunities and challenges. With the popularity of these types of web-based referrals, wineries have direct and indirect opportunities to reach consumers that may not otherwise know about the brand. Wineries that have generated many positive reviews can more easily become highly ranked and highly promoted attractions within the site, thus appealing to visitors who utilize the site for trusted peer recommendations. These reviews may come organically from guests without any encouragement from the winery, or tasting room staff may actively encourage guests to write positive reviews in an effort to build the winery's online reputation. Additionally, a winery might use these sites for advertising, offering web-based coupons that allow consumers to receive free or discounted tastings, savings on a purchase, or other types of perks when they visit the winery. While user-generated review sites can offer fantastic support in promoting tasting room visitation, they also present a very concerning challenge. A winery that has failed to meet the expectations of its guests may find that the negative reviews on these websites are a strong deterrent for potential visitors. While it is possible to know the number of guests that have visited because of such websites, it is impossible to know how many are *not* coming. Surely there is an opportunity cost when these potential guests choose not to visit, and, in some cases, tasting rooms could see a decrease in visitor traffic if the reputation has been deeply tarnished. Warren Buffet once said, "It takes 20 years to build a reputation and five minutes to ruin it. If you think about that, you'll do things differently" (Tuttle, 2010). Tasting room managers are advised to monitor to these websites and manage the reputation of the winery by responding to negative reviews humbly and apologetically. However, it is much more effective to prevent negative reviews in the first place by offering a world-class tasting room experience to all guests.

11.3.2 HOW DO WE PROVIDE A WORLD-CLASS TASTING ROOM EXPERIENCE?

After a winery has developed and marketed its guest experiences to drive tasting room visitation, the tasting room manager and team must fulfill the winery's promise and deliver world-class hospitality to the guests. *World-class* can often connote a sense of high caliber or ranking as judged by others, much in the way high-end restaurants receive Michelin stars. In this case, however, the concept relates to setting and striving for a standard of excellence. Effective tasting room management is about striving for excellence in all areas, particularly hospitality; it means knowing the customer, what they are seeking, where else they might be visiting, and working purposefully to exceed their expectations. It also means accommodating guests with patience and grace when unreasonable expectations have been set.

Knowing the customer and their reasons for visiting is critical to delivering a world-class tasting room experience. Consumers, wine club members, media and trade are all potential visitors, and the level of knowledge about wine and tasting etiquette will vary among them. One step a manager can take to prepare to host any type of customer is to hire team members with a variety of backgrounds and knowledge. A team composed entirely of formally trained, highly sophisticated wine experts will not be effective if the guests walking through the door are mostly novice wine consumers looking to have a good time with friends. Conversely, a team of hospitality-oriented servers will not be effective in catering to the serious oenophiles who want to ask questions about malolactic fermentation and barrel coopers. Having a balanced team – one that can speak knowledgably about wine and the winery while also being able to make friendly small talk – is essential to effectively interact with anyone who enters the tasting room.

Different types of customers will have a variety of expectations for the tasting room, many of which may have been drawn from their experiences at other wineries. From the types of wines and prices to the ability to picnic on-site, customers often expect that all wineries operate in the same manner. One of the most notable challenges a tasting room manager will face is the expectation of consumers regarding the wine tasting fee. While tasting fees were once unheard of, they have become common enough now that consumers expect wineries to charge for wine tasting. However, it also generally expected that the winery will waive the fee with a purchase of wine because so many wineries offer this concession. It is at the discretion of every winery if and how much to charge their customers, as well as whether or not to waive any of those charges, but customers have a difficult time understanding this and may become irritated if they expect the fee to be waived and it is not. The winery must weigh the financial effects of waiving tasting fees against the hospitality and marketing effects of not doing so; it is not surprising that many of the negative winery reviews on Yelp, for example, make reference to a winery's policy on waiving tasting fees. With regard to monetary issues such as tasting fees and wine discounts, tasting room managers are advised to develop a framework of operations with formal policies, but set parameters for the team to bend those policies to accommodate guests when the situation warrants a customer resolution.

The setting and ambiance are additional considerations when striving to deliver a world-class tasting room experience, and facilities management is a fundamental part of the tasting room manager's role–despite often being listed toward the bottom of the job description. The initial things the guest sees when she arrives at the tasting room create a first impression. If the parking lot is not paved, the landscaping is unkempt, or signage is small and illegible, the guest could be turned off before even setting foot in the tasting room. Housekeeping is also an area where attention must be paid; tens or hundreds of visitors may be seen in a given day and the tasting room, restrooms, and other facilities should look fresh each morning and throughout the day. Some wineries hire professional cleaning services to come daily or weekly, but it is often the responsibility of the tasting room staff to maintain cleanliness. More important than the first impression is the last impression left on a guest. Tasting room managers need to manage the physical use of the space to ensure all guests have an enjoyable time and leave with positive feelings about their experience. Large groups, for example, take up a lot of space in the tasting room and make it difficult for the team to serve other guests. They can also be very loud and create a party-like atmosphere, diminishing the experience for other guests trying to enjoy a calm and intimate tasting. Similarly, wine club members can create difficulty for the team when they arrive unannounced on a busy day and expect to receive VIP treatment. It might be difficult for a host to accommodate them immediately or offer a deep level of engagement while tending to multiple tasting groups. Tasting room managers can tackle some of these challenges by having multiple tasting areas or utilizing the given space to its fullest potential, and by encouraging guests to make an appointment ahead of time.

Exceeding expectations requires preparedness and the more a manager can do to know the customers, what they are looking for and where they have been, the better the tasting room will be positioned to deliver a world-class experience resulting in happy customers and financial gains for the winery.

11.3.3 HOW DO WE SELL WINE TO THESE GUESTS NOW AND IN THE FUTURE?

Tasting room managers and their team often view hospitality as the main purpose of their jobs, as if giving the guests a unique, memorable experience is what the tasting room is all about. While it has been identified that world-class hospitality is extremely important, this should be considered a means to an end, with the end being a sale to the customer that generates revenue for the winery. Tasting room revenue generally comes from the sale of wine, merchandise, and tasting fees, but it is important to remember that wineries are in the business of selling wine first and foremost, and tasting rooms can be a very lucrative channel if managed in this context.

The tasting menu can be a strong tool in selling wine and should be developed strategically by the tasting room manager. The wines that are featured, the order in which they are tasted, their relative price points and other technical information can lead to customer preferences and purchase decisions. Some wineries have found it beneficial to include accolades from prestigious wine critics on the tasting menu to give credibility to the wines and offer a sense of support or validation to guests who are insecure about their own wine knowledge or palate. Other terms that indicate a wine's status or uniqueness within the winery's portfolio, such as *reserve*, *limited*, *library*, or *club-only*, may also be helpful indicators to the guest and point toward a decision to buy, or at least to spark further conversation between the guest and the host.

Tasting room employees should aim to achieve the most they possibly can from the customer on their visit, presenting the best and most costly opportunities to the guest first, and then working down from there. In other words, it is a lot easier to ask a guest to buy a case of wine and then settle on a bottle or two if they cannot commit to the higher spend, versus asking the guest to buy a bottle and trying to convince them after they have agreed why they should buy twelve bottles. The experience with the guest in the tasting room could be the only interaction the winery ever has with this person, so it is imperative that the employee utilize the time and seize the opportunity to make a sale. The most important thing that can be done to capitalize on the time spent with the guest is to convert the guest to a wine club member, assuming the winery has a wine club. Wine clubs are the bread and butter of the direct-to-consumer channel as they act as a long-term financial annuity for the winery. Wine club membership entails the customer committing to an expected purchase arrangement on an annual or ongoing basis in exchange for benefits often including wine discounts and complimentary future tastings in the tasting room. By converting the guest to a club member, the tasting room employee has ensured that the guest will be more than a one-time customer and the winery will reap financial rewards for some time to come.

Sometimes guests choose not to make a purchase for various reasons outside of the control of the winery or employee. Perhaps they already have too much wine at home, have spent more money on their vacation than they were planning to, or are just out wine tasting for the sake of having something to do on a Saturday. This is not ideal for the winery in terms of revenue, but this is where world-class hospitality can lead to a sale in the future. It is the responsibility of the tasting room employee, at the very least, to ensure each guest has had a good experience, knows where and how she can make a purchase in the future, and invite her to leave some form of contact information to be added to the winery's mailing list. In this way, the winery can connect with the customer again in the future and repeat the sales process, hopefully garnering a new wine club member, or a wine sale, at a later date.

There are many other considerations the winery must make to be able to be able to accomplish the activities previously described. Point-of-sale software, cash registers, printed materials, signage, inventory, shipping logistics and compliance are all factors that will affect the ability of the tasting room team to be successful, and fall under the administration of the tasting room manager. It is important to keep in mind that the nature of the day-to-day business will vary somewhat by the type of tasting room the winery has established. A traditional tasting room that is open to the public for approximately 6–8 hours each day will face different opportunities and challenges than the three variations to the traditional tasting room: the By-Appointment-Only, the Co-op, and the Virtual Tasting Room (Wagner, 2010). Tasting room managers are advised to consider the nature of their tasting room setting when making decisions about marketing, hospitality and sales goals and objectives.

11.4   QUALITIES OF AN EFFECTIVE TASTING ROOM MANAGER

Tasting room managers are the leaders of the tasting room space and are generally responsible for the overall functionality of this department within the winery. Most job descriptions for this role highlight important responsibilities including customer service and sales, team leadership, and, in some cases, event planning and execution. General qualifications might include the ability to work in a fast-paced environment, moderate to extensive wine knowledge and computer literacy. These responsibilities and qualifications are undoubtedly part of the position; however, this is by no means a comprehensive list or even the most important way to view the role of the tasting room manager. With numerous facets to the job, an effective tasting room manager views the role as if he is General Manager of that space, operating the tasting room its own business entity. Thus, an effective tasting room manager must be an attentive *business* manager. Business management is about strategic planning, budgeting and forecasting, marketing, and operations; an effective tasting room manager should have skills and abilities that support most, if not all of these areas. There are several core competencies that will position a tasting room manager to be able to think like a business manager and deliver on the goals and objectives for the tasting room (Fig. 11.2).

Time management is, above all else, the most important skill a tasting room manager must master because without this skill, it is extremely difficult to balance the competing priorities this position faces. A tasting room manager's responsibilities fall into two categories – *urgent* and *important* – though sometimes a task can fall into both simultaneously. Urgent tasks tend to take up most of the workday and put the manager in a reactive state; customer service, point-of-sale transactions and team management, for example, are all tasks that must be handled in a timely manner and cannot be scheduled for a later date or time. Important tasks are those on which the manager must focus to proactively plan for the future; for example, inventory management, team training and development, sales forecasting and expense budgeting. An effective tasting room manager can multi-task and will schedule time wisely, blocking out periods where he can perform the important activities off-the-floor without distraction of the urgent on-the-floor environment. He must also manage the time of the tasting room team, scheduling weekly shifts, ensuring proper rest and meal breaks are taken, and monitoring the flow of visitors so that individual team members are not overwhelmed.

✓ Time management

✓ Problem solving

✓ Relationship-building proclivity

✓ Team development

✓ Sales leadership

FIGURE 11.2 The core competencies of an effective tasting room manager.

Problem solving is a skill that is helpful in just about every aspect of the tasting room. What appropriate resolution can I offer to the customer who is dissatisfied? Two employees called in sick – how will I manage being understaffed on this busy Saturday? How will we sell more wine so that we may achieve our goal this month? What tools can I offer my team to support their ability to be successful? An effective manager possesses the ability to be calm and rational under pressure, to manage chaos or distress in the urgent environment, as well as the ability to logically plan and prepare for the important long-term financial needs of the business. Skilled problem solvers must also be effective communicators and handle confrontation professionally, so these are valuable traits that position the manager to be successful in people and project management.

Relationship-building proclivity refers to the innate ability and interest to create meaningful relationships with people. Tasting room managers must quickly build relationships with customers to ensure they depart with positive feelings about their winery experience and, hopefully, some wine in hand. Managers must build strong relationships with colleagues including other managers and subordinates. It is important that the manager get along with other winery departments to be able to work collaboratively on the execution of ideas and utilization of winery space outside the tasting room walls. Industry partners, such as employees at other wineries and local regional organizations, offer valuable referral networks, and long-term partnerships can position the tasting room for great success.

Team development refers to the ability to effectively manage, lead and inspire a tasting room staff, offering education and training to position them for success. An effective manager will earn the respect of his team by leading by example, participating in the daily tasting room activities and occasionally doing some of the same monotonous tasks that the team must perform in the course of business. Working side-by-side with the team allows the manager to witness the competencies of each individual team member, further enabling him to utilize their strengths and coach effectively to improve weaknesses. An essential part of team development is education and training, both upon hire of new staff and periodically throughout the year for even the most seasoned employees. The possibilities for learning are endless, but common practices include tastings with the winemaker to learn more about the wines and winemaking process, field trips to other

Effective Winery Tasting Room Management 199

wineries to understand similarities or differences in wines and even hospitality. Sometimes more formal classroom training may be offered pertaining to sales, hospitality or wine knowledge. Another important part of the manager's job is to continually motivate the team and coach them in areas that could be improved. Incentive programs are not only a part of tasting room staff compensation, but they create fun ways for staff to engage in friendly competition and for the manager to monitor in which areas a team member excels or fails to keep up. Playing to the team's strengths while also encouraging improvement will effectively create a cohesive team where members support one another to succeed.

Sales leadership is last, but certainly not least, among the core competencies a tasting room manager must possess. After all, if the tasting room is not selling wine, the manager is not being effective at delivering on the department's fundamental goal. However, it is important to distinguish sales leadership from being a salesperson. While the manager may engage with customers and conduct sales as a regular part of his day, the emphasis of sales leadership is on the ability to strategize and support the team in their sales efforts. As a leader, providing a vision to the team is important to set the tone for how the staff should approach the customer and view the focus of their position. Coaching the team is essential, as a manager who is a successful seller will not create a successful team if he does not build the team's capabilities; one super salesperson cannot effectively deliver on the financial goals of the entire tasting room. The central component of sales leadership is the use of financial metrics. Identifying benchmarks against which to measure success is the most important thing a manager can do to lead his team. The tasting room staff can be better motivated and work as a team when progress and achievements are monitored and rewarded.

11.5 MEASURING TASTING ROOM EFFECTIVENESS

It has been said, "What gets measured, gets managed, "and this is especially true in the direct-to-consumer channel of the wine business. Without appropriate measurements, it is difficult to budget and manage the investment of time and resources, and to know whether one is succeeding by strategy or by chance. With regard to sales leadership, it is vital that the tasting room manager have a set of key performance indicators or metrics to monitor progress and manage toward the achievement of goals. There is an endless set of measurements one could monitor, and not all metrics provide valuable information for decision-making. Managers need to distinguish information as *interesting* or *actionable*; interesting information in the form of anecdotal observations can help identify cursory opportunities or challenges, but the valuable information that will allow a manager to make sound, actionable decisions is best gleaned from quantifiable metrics. There are five key metrics that are critical to effective tasting room management and may be calculated from net revenue (gross revenue less discounts) including wine and/or non-wine revenue (Fig. 11.3). Some wineries include non-wine revenue as a core part of their finances, so it is up to each winery and tasting room manager to determine how best to consider the information relative to their business model.

Conversion to purchase is calculated by the number of transactions divided by the number of visitors. This metric is an important indicator of how well the staff is managing visitation and turning those guest experiences into sales. Doing the appropriate marketing to drive visitation is important, but simply increasing the number of bodies that walk into the room does not have any effect on revenue if these guests are not making a purchase. Most tasting room managers include visitor counts in regular reporting to upper management, and while this is a key source of data that affects marketing decisions and budgeting, it is not a metric that leads to an actionable decision for the tasting room team. If, for example, a winery has 100 people visit on a given day and its conversion to purchase rate is 60%, then 60 people will have made a purchase. If the winery always has a 60%

1. **Conversion to purchase:** the percentage of visitors who make a purchase

2. **Average order value:** the average dollar amount per transaction

3. **Wine club conversion:** the percentage of visitors that join the wine club

4. **Labor percent of net revenue:** the labor costs as a percentage of net revenue

5. **Sales per labor hour:** the net revenue generated by staff per hour of work

FIGURE 11.3   Five key tasting room metrics.

Effective Winery Tasting Room Management

conversion rate it will have to drive greater numbers of visitors to achieve increases in sales. However, if the tasting room manager can offer the right training, coaching and tools to the staff to be able to increase the conversion rate to 70–80%, the need for more visitors is reduced as the winery can better capitalize on its current guests. This metric is centered on the question, "How do we influence more guests to make a purchase?" and enables the tasting room manager to understand the sales ability of his team, affecting future decisions for hospitality, staff training and incentive programs.

Average order value provides another actionable sales leadership opportunity and is calculated by dividing total net revenue by the number of transactions. This metric is an important indicator of customer value, as well as offering an understanding of what is considered a "normal" purchase among the products and price points. If a winery's bottle of wine is, on average, $50 and the average order value is $75, this tells the tasting room manager that most customers are purchasing fewer than two bottles each. This metric is centered on the question, "How do we sell more to the guests who are making a purchase?" and enables the tasting room manager to make decisions regarding the product mix and sales promotions offered, as well as staff training to effectively sell more to each customer. Or, it could lead to a more strategic decision about winery visitation as it is possible that the visitors are not able to afford the price points and may not be the winery's target demographic. (On a side note, point-of-sale and customer relationship management systems can be problematic and may not offer the level of detail needed to be able to calculate this metric easily. A similar metric that will afford the same managerial opportunities is *average sale per visitor*, calculated by dividing total net revenue by the number of visitors. This is a common way of assessing the same type of information but is not as desirable as average order value since the number of visitors is not a direct factor on sales, as mentioned earlier.) By knowing the number of visitors, the percentage of those that purchase and the average dollar amount spent, a tasting room manager has a variety of actionable options to lead toward achieving revenue goals and can effectively forecast future sales.

Wine club conversion is calculated by the number of tasting room guests who join the wine club divided by the number of visitors. While this metric does not directly impact the short-term revenue goal of the tasting room, it addresses another major goal – to convert visitors to long-term club members, increasing future revenue for the wine club channel. Understanding and managing this conversion rate is vital to annual planning and sales forecasting because the wine club is the engine that drives the direct-to-consumer channel. Wine club members are a key source of revenue and customer acquisition via referrals and the tasting room is often the sole, but is certainly the main, vehicle for recruitment.

Labor percentage of net revenue is calculated by the total labor costs (including wages, commissions and benefits) divided by total net revenue. This is a common metric in the food and beverage industry but is underutilized by the wine industry. Tasting room managers can benefit from understanding this ratio as it is constructive to annual budgeting and staff scheduling. If the winery demands an increase in revenue for the next fiscal year, a tasting room manager who knows his historical labor percentage of revenue can make a case for the budgeting of an increased labor expense to achieve the revenue goal. Additionally, the tasting room manager can better phase annual revenue projections and labor hours over the months of the year, based on historical data, to ensure realistic goals are set.

Sales per labor hour is calculated by dividing total net revenue by the number of labor hours incurred to achieve that revenue. This metric may be evaluated in terms of a team average, or individually by team member. For example, John Smith worked 8 hours and achieved net revenue of $1,000 in that time period, so he achieves, on average, $125 in sales per hour that he works. Measuring sales per labor hour is an appropriate way for a manager to identify super stars, or those who need coaching, based on a true benchmark. It would not be accurate to say that someone who has total sales of $10,000 is a higher contributor or more effective salesperson than someone who has total sales of $5,000. The former employee may work twice as much as the latter, and thus has more opportunity to convert guests to purchasers and incur revenue. Sales per labor hour offers a fair and balanced way of benchmarking staff against each other, as well as against a team average or target goal.

Information output is only as good as data input, so it is important to remember that all metrics must be analyzed with an understanding that variances and skewed data may occur. Winery software systems have limitations and tasting room managers are advised to receive thorough training on the winery's systems, and create procedures and protocols for their teams that foster consistency in data entry.

11.6 CONCLUSION

The tasting room is a vital profit center for wineries and the ability to maximize results is the core focus for managers of this department. Engaging in quality marketing activities and delivering a world-class guest experience will bring consumers to the winery door and then it is up to the team to convert these guests into purchasers and wine club members. The tasting room manager who is a strong business manager can best position his team for success by focusing on the appropriate metrics that support revenue and expense management, enabling him to be an effective sales leader and the team to achieve fiscal goals.

KEYWORDS

- **problem solving**
- **relationship-building proclivity**
- **sales leadership**
- **tasting room**
- **team development**
- **time management**
- **wine club conversion**
- **winery tourism**

REFERENCES

1. Thach, L. (2013, October 21). Sonoma county wineries push the envelope on innovative wine tourism experiences. *Wine Business Magazine*. Retrieved October 25, 2013, from http://www.winebusiness.com.
2. Tuttle, B. (2010, March 1). Warren buffett's boring, brilliant wisdom. *Time Magazine*. Retrieved October 26, 2013, from http://business.time.com.
3. Wagner, P., Olsen, J., & Thach, L. (2010). *Wine marketing and sales: Success strategies for a saturated market* (2nd ed.). San Francisco, CA: The Wine Appreciation Guild.

CHAPTER 12

SERVICE QUALITY, BRAND LOYALTY, AND WINE TOURISM

MELISSA A. VAN HYFTE

Program Director, Assistant Professor, Hospitality and Event Management, Lasell College, 1844 Commonwealth Avenue, Auburndale, MA 02466, United States

CONTENTS

12.1	Introduction	206
12.2	Chapter Significance	207
12.3	Tourism	208
12.4	Global Tourism	209
12.5	Tourism in the United States	210
12.6	Trends in Tourism	210
12.7	Sectors of Tourism	211
12.8	Wine Tourism	212
12.9	Critical Success Factors in Wine Tourism	213
12.10	Service Quality	214
12.11	Unique Nature of Services	215
12.12	Servicescape	217
12.13	Servicescape in Wine Tourism	217
12.14	Core Service and Employee Service	218
12.15	Continuous Quality Improvement and Total Quality Management	218

12.16	Satisfaction	219
12.17	Zones of Tolerance	220
12.18	Satisfaction and Service Measurement	221
12.19	Trust and Commitment	225
12.20	Future Behavioral Intentions and Loyalty	226
12.21	Wine Tourism and Building Brand Loyalty	230
Keywords		231
References		231

12.1 INTRODUCTION

The conceptualization of the service quality construct, its relationship to ongoing customer satisfaction, loyalty and spending patterns, and methods of evaluating it, have been a central theme of hospitality literature and research over the past 15 years. Hospitality organizations must now cater to a progressively discerning customer-base, who, are now willing shop around and cut traditional consumer ties due to service-based competitive differentiations. Consequently, a large proportion of marketing effort is now being directed at both getting and keeping customers. Evidence suggests that an organization's ability to consistently satisfy customers with quality service will go a long way toward achieving this core objective. Not surprisingly, a large proportion of organizational effort is now being directed at developing an operational means for improving customer service perceptions. Inherent in any such approach is the need to continually monitor operational performance and create new service opportunities so that energies can be better directed at consistently satisfying customer needs.

Nowhere is this more apparent than in the wine tourism sector. Wine tourism is now acknowledged as a growing area of tourism product development globally, and is an increasingly significant component of the regional and rural tourism product of most wine producing regions. With its wide range of benefits including foreign exchange earnings, the creation of a wide range of both full and part-time jobs and the generation of secondary economic activity, wine tourism is a very lucrative industry with the ability to generate substantial and sustainable wealth and growth. Not surprisingly support for and investment in the wine tourism industry is now regarded as an essential regional economic development strategy by both governments and the wine industry globally.

Research has shown that an organizations ability to provide positive outcomes determines a customers' commitment to a mutual relationship. Trust is defined as a willingness to rely on an exchange partner with whom one has confidence (Moorman et al., 1993). More specifically, Anderson and Narus (1990) defined trust in manufacturer-distributor relationships as a firm's belief that another company will not take unexpected actions that result in negative outcomes for the firm. Perceptions of service/product performance can be viewed as antecedents to relationship satisfaction, which, in turn, affects trust, commitment, and business loyalty (Caceres and Paparoidamis, 2007). Long-term orientation is shown to be affected by the extent to which customers trust their vendors (Ganesan, 1994). It is, therefore, a major determinant of relationship commitment (Morgan and Hunt, 1994). Furthermore, Ganesan (1994) proposed that a key component of trust is the extent to which the customer believes that the vendor has intentions and motives beneficial to the customer and is concerned with creating positive customer outcomes. Organizations that are perceived as being concerned with positive customer outcomes will therefore be trusted to a greater extent than suppliers who appear interested only in their own welfare, thus creating a greater likelihood of long term commitment. The cellar door experience then provides a unique position, in which wineries are given the opportunity to build trust among potentially new customers in a product-based industry.

The increased significance of the wine tourism sector has led to a heightened concern by producers and consumers for the quality of services being offered. Whereas once a winery's success was determined solely by the quality of its output, the development and significance of the cellar door concept (comprising tasting room, education center, food and beverage facilities and merchandising outlets) and the total visitor experience now means that success will, more often than not, also be determined by the level of quality perceived by the wine tourist at the cellar door.

12.2 CHAPTER SIGNIFICANCE

This chapter seeks to define and confirm the cellar door service construct and it's importance to both the service and the wine production industries.

At the heart of this chapter is a clear understanding of those factors that define success during the interaction that occurs between host and guest; whether consumption or education oriented. This chapter attempts to shed light on those factors that comprise the average visitor service experience and how it relates to appropriately targeting the quality improvement efforts of winery operators and explaining and predicting overall visitor satisfaction with the winery visit, their trust in the brand, and their intention to purchase the winery's product into the future.

12.3 TOURISM

One of the key components of this chapter is the subject matter itself, wineries and their visitors, who are often not considered when the broader topic of tourism is discussed. In order to properly present the subject matter, a discussion of the broader terms of tourism must first be conducted in an effort to understand where wine tourism falls within this industry. Tourism is considered to be travel and it's related services for recreation, leisure, religious, family and friend, and business purposes, usually for a limited length of time. The World Tourism Organization (WTO) defines *tourists* as people "traveling to and staying in places outside their usual environment for not more than one consecutive year for leisure, business and other purposes."

One particular sector of the tourism industry that has shown significant growth over the past few decades is *gourmet tourism*. Gourmet tourism is commonly associated with the food and beverage industry and targeted toward travelers with a complex level of understanding or a desire for such levels of understanding related to gastronomy. Key components of this type of tourism include tours, tastings, and product education. Another important piece of the gourmet tourism construct is that it can be just as easily accomplished in a local setting as it would be by traveling long distances for many tourists. Clearly, wine tourism then falls under the general realm of gourmet tourism as it encompasses each of the facets listed above with visitors traveling from both far and near to explore their pallets and to be further educated on the wine industry and it's prize products. The connection between wine tourism and gourmet tourism is a unique one, with many visitors often basing their experience around simply gaining a deeper understanding of a product and it's development processes rather than typical activities and leisure experiences that encompass most of the broader tourism industry.

12.4 GLOBAL TOURISM

Currently, the global tourism market is a hot bed for economic activity. Even in tough economic times, in developed nations such as Australia, Spain, and the United States, tourism is a considerable contributor to each nation's gross domestic product (GDP). According to the World Travel and Tourism Council (WTTC), the total contribution of travel and tourism to the global GDP was USD$ 6,990.3 billion in 2013 and is forecasted to rise by 4.3% in 2014 and to rise by 4.2% pa to USD10,965.1 billion (10.3% of GDP) in 2024. The WTTC also asserts that in 2013, the total contribution of Travel & Tourism to employment, including jobs indirectly supported by the industry, was 8.9% of total employment (265,855,000 jobs). This is expected to rise by 2.5% in 2014 to 272,417,000 jobs and rise by 2.4% pa to 346,901,000 jobs in 2024 (10.2% of total). Because the tourism industry is one of the largest industries in the world, global tourism provides strength to many struggling economies. Moreover, tourism can improve subjugated economies by creating what is known as the *multiplier effect* (Khan et al., 1995). The economic multipliers' effect is composed of two dimensions; direct and indirect impacts. For example, "air lines, travels agents, hotels, shops, restaurants, and other tourist facilities, "(Khan et al., 1995, p. 65) are known as direct multipliers. On the other hand, "hotels purchase raw food for their restaurants and detergents for their house keeping departments, " (Khan et al., 1995, p. 65) these are known as indirect multipliers. On the other hand, global tourism does have its challenges. From terrorism to the resurgence of developed nations' domestic tourism, managers must continuously improve and reevaluate their service delivery systems in order to increase customer satisfaction and encourage future return visits. Furthermore, in order for companies to remain competitive, they must focus on issues such as safety, quality, service, and recovery. In other words, companies must invest in total quality management systems in order to face the new public mind-set. It is a well accepted fact that tourism professionals now have to serve a more skeptical customer base, who are more eager than ever before to complain and transfer their allegiances to perceived providers of quality tourism services (O'Neill and Palmer, 2004).

12.5 TOURISM IN THE UNITED STATES

Tourism in the United States remains strong. The Office of Travel and Tourism Industries (OTTI) found that the U.S. travel and tourism industry supported 7.6 million jobs in 2013 and that U.S. travel and tourism industry-related spending increased by 4.1% in 2013 from the previous year, totaling nearly $1.5 trillion. Further, the current U.S. Commerce Secretary, Penny Pritzker, recently announced that the United States can expect a 4% average annual growth in tourism during the next 5 years, and that a record 72.2 million foreign travelers are projected to visit the United States in 2014 alone. The Spring 2014 Forecast for International Travel, released semi-annually by the U.S. Commerce Department's International Trade Administration, predicts continued strong growth through 2018 following consecutive 4 years of record visitor volume (United States Department of Commerce, 2014).

With varied climates and regions throughout the U.S., tourists can visit mountains, beaches, lush forests, and even deserts. It is home to many of the world's largest cities and spectacular, natural beauty. Not surprisingly, practitioners have chosen to build a tourism infrastructure around these natural environments that can both attract and retain visitors over the longer term.

12.6 TRENDS IN TOURISM

To stay current in the field of tourism and continue to grow in a positive manner, one must consider the current trends and their implications. First and foremost, it is important to look at the current economic state. Tourism is an industry that is built around discretionary income, therefore a likely one to suffer in tough economic times and to flourish in times of economic prosperity. It is therefore reasonable to presume that in an economic decline, tourists are likely to travel less, stay closer to home, and spend less money, thus creating room for recent phenomena such as "staycations"

Service Quality, Brand Loyalty, and Wine Tourism 211

and "daycations," both new urban terminology used describe tourism of an extremely short nature and that happens close to home.

Another popular topic today is that of sustainability. Many people are paying much more attention to the welfare of their natural environment and it's products and feeling the need to protect the natural resources that we have left. In an effort to do that, tourists are often finding more ways to commune with these natural environments, experience more local, natural, and organic production processes and thus consider destinations and activities that fit this lifestyle. Similarly, healthy lifestyle is another area that has continued to flourish in the tourism industry. Travelers are no longer just seeking a beach to lie on, but considering options that lend to a healthier lifestyle, such as hiking and biking or enjoying healthier culinary and beverage options. In recent years, health and wellness tourism has become a popular alternative to the traditional.

Another important trend that the industry is seeing is the search for rural engagement. According to the United Nations 2007 Revision of World Urbanization Prospects, for the first time in the world's history, there are now more people living in cities than in rural areas. Because of this many travelers are seeking to get out of their current urban lifestyle and get back in touch with their more natural environment.

In looking at these trends, it is an obvious connection that in order to stay competitive, regions must pay close attention to their natural environment and it's products that are bringing in these tourism dollars and understand how to both protect and grow them and keep them as desirable options for potential tourists.

12.7 SECTORS OF TOURISM

There is no definitive list of all sectors of tourism. This is because many types of tourism are arguable as is the fact that many fit in to sub-categories of other sectors. A brief Internet search of tourism sectors indicates an overwhelming amount of categories and subcategories that each of these "types" of tourism could fall under. The popular Wikipedia site, on any given day, shows over 70 different categories of tourism. For example, some of the more popular sectors often found are rural tourism, space tourism, medical tourism, health and wellness tourism, archeological tourism, religious tourism, cultural tourism, disaster tourism, heritage tourism, literary tourism, music tourism, poverty tourism (or poorism), sex tourism, ecotourism, gourmet tourism and wine tourism. For this chapter, the focus will be on the latter of topics mentioned, gourmet and wine tourism. Eadington and Smith (1992) suggest that disillusionment with traditional mass tourism forms and the many problems it has triggered have forced an "alternative tourism" agenda over recent decades. These authors define alternative tourism as tourism that is consistent with "natural, social and community values and which allows both hosts and guests to enjoy positive and worthwhile interaction and shared experiences." Many of the afore-mentioned types of tourism could obviously fall under this category. And one particular alternative tourist activity that has grown in terms of economic significance globally is gourmet tourism and in particular, wine tourism as a sector of gourmet tourism.

12.8 WINE TOURISM

Originally wine tourism was something that industry professionals were just "playing around with." After launching further tourism initiatives, wineries quickly realized that this type of tourism could have a huge impact on overall revenue. Wine tourism is now also noted as "an opportunity for wineries to develop long term relationships with their customers" (O'Neill, Palmer, and Charters, 2002). It generates millions of dollars throughout the world on a yearly basis. Thus, this chapter is meant to justify the time, money, and effort put in to increasing the service quality for these experiences. This type of tourism is typically comprised of a combination of merchandise sales, food, beverage, tastings, education, and related tourism activities.

Previously, the wine industry has primarily been interested in production and agriculture. It is only in recent years that tourism has become a notable factor. Because of this, industry professionals are not necessarily well versed in service, one of the main ingredients to a successful tourism program. In 2003, Beames found that there is a lack of inter-industry cooperation between the wine and tourism industries and a definite need to create an overall experience for guests. In spite of this, Dodd and Bigotte (1997) found that "in addition to sales revenue, winery tourism offers benefits such as opportunities for market intelligence, increased margins above other retail outlets, and the chance to encourage brand loyalty toward a winery."

Specific benefits of wine tourism to a community include: employment, recognition of the region, focus on the sustainability of the region's natural resources, taxation benefits, economic impact, direct spending, and the development and overall growth in tourism. For wineries, there are even further benefits such as potential profits for wine and merchandise sales and the potential for delighting consumers with service experiences who could then, in turn, choose to continue purchasing said brand of wine based on their tourist experiences. When regarded as a key, profitable segment of the tourism industry, it is no wonder that issues such as service and visitor satisfaction have begun to be recognized.

12.9 CRITICAL SUCCESS FACTORS IN WINE TOURISM

In order to better serve the needs of this growing breed of tourist we must first understand what factors play a role in their satisfaction levels. In addition we need to understand how exactly these satisfaction levels will affect the bottom line. We know, for example, that delivering high quality service is important because it costs about five times as much money, time and resources to attract new customers as it does to retain existing ones (Pizam and Ellis, 1999, p. 326) and levels of service relate directly to customer retention. One clear way to increase revenue is by developing long-term relationships with these customers. Research has shown that quality, value, and satisfaction can directly influence future behavioral intentions, even when the effects of each of these constructs are considered simultaneously (Cronin, Brady and Hult, 2000). It is therefore imperative for wine tourism professionals to understand what they can do at the cellar door to increase guest satisfaction levels and ultimately the customers' willingness to return or repurchase their product.

One study conducted in 1999 examined the level and characteristics of demand for long-distance wine tourism among wine consumers located far from wine regions. In this study specific attention was given to the importance attached by wine consumers to various destination and trip attributes when deciding upon a wine tourism experience. It was determined that highly motivated, long-distance wine tourists prefer destinations offering a wide range of cultural and outdoor attractions, thus illustrating that cellar door operators need to not only focus on service, facilities, and merchandise, but on the leisure and experiential component of the wine tourist experience as well (Getz et al., 1999).

In 2003, a study looked at the challenges facing the further development of the wine tourism industry in Australia. Some problems identified in the study included the product focus of the wine industry, a lack of inter-industry cooperation between the wine industry and the tourism industry, and the need to create an overall experience, all clearly illustrating a further need for more in-depth research on both local and global scales, and cooperation and operational planning amongst the players in the wine tourism industry (Beames, 2003).

12.10   SERVICE QUALITY

Inherent to the service component of the hospitality industry is service quality. Service quality has been defined as the consumer's judgment of the overall excellence (Zeithaml, 1988) and even more descript as the customer's perception of the goods and services to a specification that satisfies their needs (O'Neill and Palmer, 2001). Studies have found that there are two forms of service quality – technical and functional. This suggests that quality is determined by both "what is delivered" and "how it is delivered" (Gronroos, 2001) to consumers. Additionally, research has suggested that there is a direct link between service quality and customer satisfaction (Cronin and Taylor, 1992; Gabbot and Hogg, 1997; and Gwynne et al., 1998).

Service can be defined as an intangible good. It is both produced and consumed simultaneously. It is characterized as perishable and labor intensive. Given this intensively laborious characteristic, employees must be trained in company established systems and procedures in order to deliver a specific product. Bearing in mind that a product can be delivered by different individuals, variability in the way the product is perceived and/or received becomes a challenge. When dealing with service delivery systems, Bell and Winters (1993) state that "there is no better place to implement specific solutions, however, than in the hospitality industry, where customer service is inseparable from employee performance" (p. 93).

Customer service, and service quality, is now a focus for many corporate or marketing strategies and high levels of service are typically seen as a means for an organization to achieve a competitive advantage. Langer (1997, p. 7) states that "most industries continue to face dramatic changes in their environment, ranging from the increasingly global nature of the marketplace to the growing importance of services as a tool of competitive differentiation." Delivering exceptional service, especially in the hospitality industry, creates a plethora of opportunities for companies to surpass the competition and become recognized leaders in their industries. As mentioned above, service quality can be broken down into two dimensions: technical quality and functional quality. Technical quality refers to what is being delivered while functional quality is concerned with how the service is delivered. It takes both of these elements to create a superior service quality experience yet it is difficult due to a unique characteristic of service; the simultaneous production and consumption of services. Hospitality services also suffer from a high level of heterogeneity.

Services vary in standard and quality over time because they are delivered by people to people and are a function of human performance. Each service experience is different because it varies from producer to producer and from customer to customer. The customer's overall evaluation of a service encounter does not rest solely on the processing of tangible attributes or the intangible elements from the service provider but instead on a combination of the above, paired with the customer's mood, emotions and attitudes (Mantel and Kardes, 1999).

12.11 UNIQUE NATURE OF SERVICES

Services in general are unique unto themselves when compared to more traditional goods. It is often understood that tourism and hospitality services have a host of attributes that differentiate them from tangible goods (Berry, et al., 1985). These attributes only contribute to the complexity of providing and maintaining a high level of service quality, retaining customers and increasing profits and loyalty. Below are the list of these attributes.

- Intangibility. When a service is purchased, there is often not a tangible object to show for it. "Because they are performances and experiences rather than objects, precise manufacturing specifications concerning uniform quality can rarely be set" (Zeithaml et al., 1990). Although the performance of most services is supported by tangibles, the essence of what is being bought is a performance provided by one party, for another. They cannot be displayed, sampled, tested or evaluated before purchase (Bagozzi et al., 1999).

- Inseparability of Production and Consumption. Service Inseparability implies that production takes place simultaneously with consumption. Generally, goods are first produced, sold, and then consumed. Services on the other hand are usually sold first, and then produced and consumed simultaneously. Further complicating the issue is the fact that service is very laborious. Getting every employee of a hotel or restaurant to do the right thing is often an enormous challenge (Reisinger, 1992; Berry et al., 1985).
- Heterogeneity. Services by nature are heterogeneous, meaning they are less standardized and uniform than goods because they are delivered by people to people and are a function of human performance. Because the customers buying services meet face-to-face with service employees, service outputs can hardly be standardized as products are. Also, an important aspect to note when discussing heterogeneity is that customers differ in both their needs and expectations (Reisinger, 1992).
- Consistency. It is difficult to provide the same level of service time after time. Employee performance varies depending on a multitude factors including the employee's mood, motivation, training, personality, and even factors related to the customer receiving the service. Additionally, this is affected by whether or not the customers communicate their wants and needs to said employee. Also there is a shortage of uniform, objective standards according to which tourism service performance and quality can be assessed (Wiele et al., 2005).
- Perishability. Service perishability notes that linked to the notion of heterogeneity or simultaneity is the idea that services must be provided and utilized at the point of consumption, during the service encounter. Services cannot be stored. If they are not consumed then they are lost forever. A guest room that is not occupied for a night is lost revenue in much the same way that an unsold seat at a concert is also potential profit lost. Tourism services must be consumed at the same time that they are produced (not purchased) or they are perpetually lost (Wiele et al., 2005). These are each important factors

to bear in mind when considering service as a source for customer satisfaction. Another important factor to consider is the atmosphere in which the service is being delivered, or servicescape.

12.12 SERVICESCAPE

Because of the unique nature of service, including intangibility and heterogeneity, it has often been hypothesized that consumers turn to more tangible aspects of their service encounter when judging their experience (Jamal and Naser, 2001; Wakefield and Blodgett, 1994). Support for this idea comes from empirical evidence suggesting that the tangible and physical surroundings of the service environment can have a significant impact on customers' perceptions of service quality (Wakefield and Blodgett, 1994; Jamal and Naser, 2001). Often referred to as servicescape, these tangible items are the physical environment in which the actual service is being provided. Items such as the overall appearance of vineyards and wineries, cleanliness of restroom facilities, and availability of merchandise are evaluated by the customer. The evaluation of these factors (and others) will then, in part, help to evaluate the overall determination of satisfaction. For example, young parents who are entertaining their children on a cruise ship might place more emphasis on the availability of recreation facilities than would an elderly couple celebrating their 50th wedding anniversary.

12.13 SERVICESCAPE IN WINE TOURISM

Research on servicescape has been previously conducted in wine tourism settings. It has been found to be a crucial component in the formation of customer satisfaction in wine tourism. George (2006) investigated the relationship between the type of wine tourist motivation and how much they were motivated by each piece of the wine servicescape (or *winescape*). George found that wine customers driven by the secondary motivators like socialization and entertainment consider servicescape as more important to their satisfaction than their counterparts, driven by the primary motivators like wine tasting and wine buying.

12.14 CORE SERVICE AND EMPLOYEE SERVICE

The interaction between service quality and the different types of leisure tourism have been broken down in to two realms, one being the physical plant as discussed previously (servicescape) and the other being the interaction between the consumer and the service provider. Key to this personal contact is the role of the core service and the employee. The core service has been defined as the processes by which the service is delivered, whereas the employee service refers to the behaviors or performances of the employees in the delivery of the service (Grace and O'Cass, 2004). These authors further contend that where there is consensus in the literature that both the core service and employee service influence the customers' perception of value and their level of satisfaction with the service, some advocate that increasing emphasis should be placed on the interpersonal dimensions of the service offering (Grace and O'Cass, 2004, p. 453). Clearly, core service is an important component; however employee service is also a key factor. Due to the intangible disposition of services, consumers tend to look at the behavior of employees as a means for evaluating their overall satisfaction level (Jamal and Naser, 2001; Stauss, 2002). This personal contact can also be seen as being affected by the service recovery process.

When there is a service failure, consumers become inherently more dependent on the services that they receive. The ability of the service provider to overcome the initial service failure and rectify the situation is crucial.

12.15 CONTINUOUS QUALITY IMPROVEMENT AND TOTAL QUALITY MANAGEMENT

In focusing on the different factors in service that ultimately lead to customer satisfaction, one must not overlook Continuous Quality Improvement (CQI). CQI is a managerial process in which organizations identify, plan, and implement ongoing improvements in service delivery. CQI provides a critical way to assess and monitor the delivery of services to ensure that they are consistent with an organization's best practice principles. It is regarded as a critical component for an increasing number of hospitality organizations. This is the basis for what is often referred to as Total Quality Management, or TQM. TQM is best described by Beich as a quality centered, customer-driven, management-led process to achieve an organization's strategic mission through continuous service improvement (1994). The customer perceives the quality of a service depending on the competence of the staff; therefore management depends on the competence of other staff members to provide customers with a continually excellent service experience. Once customer satisfaction has been reached, it must then be continually upheld. TQM is often used as a way to maintain customer satisfaction. People by nature have limitless desires, which are never permanently satisfied (Walsh et al., 2002). "Therefore, TQM initiatives must include an in-built culture of continuous improvement which can help an organization satisfy the needs of its customers on an ongoing basis" (p. 300). Hellsten and Klefsjo (2000) describe TQM as, "some form of 'management philosophy' based on a number of core values, such as customer focus, continuous improvement, process orientation, everybody's commitment, fast response, result orientation and learn from others" (p. 239). Babbar and Aspelin (1994) state that TQM is often a misunderstood concept because many companies believe it is something that can easily be purchased and implemented like some form of package deal. Some companies buy into TQM as some sort of quick fix program instead of realizing it is a complicated process that needs the commitment of the entire company with the understanding it is a long-term course of action. Sashkin and Kiser (1993) describe TQM as the development of an organizational culture, which is defined by, and supports, the constant attainment of customer satisfaction through an integrated system of tools, techniques and training.

12.16 SATISFACTION

Currently, the most widely used definition of satisfaction states that satisfaction is "the consumer's fulfillment response. It is a judgment that a product or service feature, or the product or service itself, provided (or is providing) a pleasurable level of consumption-related fulfillment, including levels of under-or-over fulfillment" (Oliver, 1997, p. 13). Within this definition there are a couple of noteworthy details. One important point to note is that the evaluation of a consumer's satisfaction generally occurs at the end of the processing activity, this allows for both hasty judgments of products and services that are consumed relatively quickly, as well as judgments of satisfaction resulting from products or services with lengthy consumption periods. This does not mean, however, that consumers cannot make some form of evaluation during any part of the consumption process. In reality, evaluation of satisfaction starts from the moment consumption begins; therefore some form of evaluation can be given while the overall assessment of satisfaction is being developed. Another factor to consider is that satisfaction can be regarded in terms of singular events leading up to a consumption outcome and as a collective impression of these events. Furthermore, customers can be either satisfied or dissatisfied with the level of satisfaction received. The idea that a guest could be satisfied but still unhappy with the end result leads to a theory that expectations play a major role in the evaluation of satisfaction. For example, if an avid traveler visits stays at a hotel that he has heard has exemplary guest accommodations, he may expect an extreme level of quality of his guest room. Because this traveler has been given such a high impression by others, the expectations that he has would be very high. While the traveler may experience a decent level of satisfaction with the guest room, when compared with the expectations of other exemplary properties, the end evaluation may be one of dissatisfaction. If this level of satisfaction had been received during any other overnight stay, the end result may have been positive, but because the expectation of phenomenal accommodations was present, the adequate guest room was found to be disappointing. Because each of our consumers come with a variety of expectations, there is a clear need to assess the expectations of the consumer, their predispositions, and the perceptions of reality that he or she may bring to the service delivery equation. Put simply, customers' perceptions are their reality, therefore, due to the competitive nature of the wine industry, wineries have to provide 'added value' elements to attract customers (O'Neill, et. al., 2002) and further, exceed their expectations once given. Service quality is proven to be a vital antecedent of satisfaction and research shows that satisfaction plays a mediating role between service quality and future behavioral intentions.

12.17 ZONES OF TOLERANCE

One important component of satisfaction to consider is consumers' zones of tolerance. This theory suggests that customers hold several different expectations about service. The first of these expectations, desired service is essentially the level of service that a customer hopes to receive. This is a combination of what the customer believes can be and should be provided in the context of customer service and service quality. The second expectation is referred to as acceptable service, or the level of service that a customer will accept (Zeithaml and Bitner, 2000). If conceptualized as points on a line, the space between the two points (acceptable service and desired service) can be thought of as the zone of tolerance. If service drops below the acceptable service point customers will be discouraged and their satisfaction with the company challenged. If service performance surpasses the desired service point then customers will be delighted and probably quite surprised as well (Zeithaml and Bitner, 2000). Just as services can all be different, so can consumers. Different customers will have different zones of tolerance. Some customers will have wide zones of tolerance, leaving a large range of service from providers and others will have much more restricted zones, requiring a tighter range of service. There are many factors that play in to customers' zones of tolerance, like time that a customer has or the price of the service. It has been found that higher prices do not necessarily drive up expectations, however the acceptable service point may increase, thus causing the overall zone of tolerance to become smaller (Hoyer and MacInnis, 2001; Zeithaml and Bitner, 2000). The more important a factor is to an individual customer, the narrower the zone of tolerance is likely to be. Naturally, it is the customer that determines which parts of the service provided are the most important and which ones are secondary. In recognizing that consumers each have their own zones of tolerance, which are dictated by different factors for each, specific drivers of satisfaction should also be investigated.

12.18 SATISFACTION AND SERVICE MEASUREMENT

With a consumer market very willing to complain, businesses within the services industry are scrambling to gain a competitive edge. With the multitude of challenges, models are needed to take factual, qualitative data, and quantify those measures. To do this, companies should assess its consumers' profiles. Simply put, what are the characteristics or behaviors of the services, which the company provides to keep guests coming back?

There are several proven methods for assessing consumer profiles. Each of these methods have advantages and disadvantages. Here are a few examples. Comment cards are regularly used and play an important part of continuous quality improvement. The primary reasons this method is used are inexpensiveness and administration requirements. This kind of survey gives a firsthand account of a guest's experience. However, there are noticeable complications with comment cards. More times than not, consumers feel inconvenienced. Furthermore, the surveys tend to be utilized in the event of major negative or positive experiences. In addition, "a major disadvantage is low return rate" (O'Neill and Palmer, 2004). Focus groups present another venue to measure service reliability. There are mass amounts of information, which can be gathered in focus groups. In particular, information which frontline employees bring forth can be most enlightening. To be more effective, focus groups should, and most times do involve guests. "Once again, expense is a problem, especially for the small-to medium-sized enterprise" (O'Neill and Palmer 2004).

A third and very qualitatively rich form of measurement is a mystery shop program. Mystery shops are consistent and specifically measurable. Most programs are created with qualitative data, which is previously established. In most cases, they are unobtrusive and most employees cannot tell when, where, or what time the shops will take place. It is most important to note, mystery shopper programs are expensive. In addition, analyzing the data is very time consuming and laborious.

Another important related concept is the Disconfirmation Paradigm, which is the knowledge of customer expectations and requirements and is essential for two reasons – it provides understanding of how the customer defines quality of service and products, and facilitates the development of a customer satisfaction questionnaire (Pizam and Ellis, 1999). One main problem with this is that the perception of quality lies within the customer. Groth and Dye (1999) state that "the total perceived value of a service comes from two sources. First, customers perceive value that originates from the service act itself. Second, customers perceive value that originates from the quality of the service act" (p. 277). Perceptions can change with customers' moods and emotions and may not accurately reflect the quality of the service. Moreover, customers' perceptions of quality service may differ drastically from the actual quality of the events that created the service (Groth and Dye, 1999). This thinking is the basis for the disconfirmation paradigm, which is described by Pizam and Ellis (1999) as when customers purchase goods and services with pre-purchase expectations about anticipated performance. Once the product or service has been purchased and used, outcomes are compared against expectations. When outcome matches expectations, confirmation occurs. Disconfirmation occurs when there are differences between expectations and outcomes. Negative disconfirmation occurs when the product or service performance is less than expected. Positive disconfirmation occurs when the product or service performance is better than expected (p. 328). The Disconfirmation Model has three outcome states on a variable scale. According to Robert Johnston (1995), the three states are "dissatisfaction," resulting from poor perceived quality (negative disconfirmation), "delight" from high quality (positive disconfirmation) and "satisfaction" from adequate quality (confirmation). When expectations exceed the actual outcome of an interaction, negative disconfirmation occurs and the customer is often left dissatisfied. The events that created this disconfirmation are considered to be service failures (Johnston, 1995). It is the responsibility of the service organization to resolve these situations.

There are multiple ways to measure quality but while doing this, we should first look at the different types of measures. In the service industry, two types of research methods are typically used, and often together. According to Leddy and Ormrod (2005), quantitative research is used to answer questions about relationships among measured variables with the purpose of explaining, predicting and controlling phenomena. On the contrary, qualitative research is typically used to answer questions about the complex nature of phenomena, often with the purpose of describing and understanding the phenomena from the participants' point of view (Leddy and Ormrod, 2005). Additionally, qualitative measurement is regularly used for gathering data by means of comment cards, mystery shoppers and even management observation. This information is typically then used to formulate objective measures to quantitatively evaluate customer feedback. Quantitative measurement generally takes the form of surveys and questionnaires.

One of the most widely used instruments to measure service quality is the SERVQUAL scale developed by Parasuraman, Zeithaml, and Berry in 1985. The model was created based on the disconfirmation paradigm. "The model on which SERVQUAL is based proposes that customers evaluate the quality of a service on five distinct dimensions: reliability, responsiveness, assurance, empathy, and tangibles; and that service quality is the difference between a customer's expectations and perceptions of the quality of a service" (Wong et al., 1999, p. 137). The SERVQUAL model identifies specific criteria by which customers evaluate service quality. Measurements are taken using surveys and questionnaires and are weighted by importance, usually on a five-point *Likert scale*. The questionnaire consists of two sections: a section to measure customers' service expectations of organizations within a specific sector and a corresponding section to measure customers' perceptions of a particular organization in that sector. According to Parasuraman et al. (1985), service quality should be measured by subtracting customer perception scores from customer expectation scores ($Q = P - E$). The gap may exist between the customers' expected and perceived service is not only a measure of the quality of the service, but also a determinant of customer satisfaction/dissatisfaction. This is important because it shows the connection between the expectations and perceptions of customers and can show companies where they need to improve. The SERVQUAL instrument is one of the most commonly used constructs when attempting to measure service quality and satisfaction. In essence the five elements of the RATER model are:

- Reliability – The ability to perform the promised service dependably and accurately.
- Assurance – The knowledge and courtesy of employees and their ability to inspire trust and confidence.
- Tangibles – The physical facilities, equipment, and appearance of the location.
- Empathy – Caring, individualized attention, and appearance of personnel.
- Responsiveness – Willingness to help customers and provide prompt service.

Berry et al. (1985) believe that these five dimensions are a concise representation of the core criteria that customers employ in evaluating service quality (O'Neill, et. al. 1992).

This scale is considered to be an indirect or disconfirmation measure of service quality and satisfaction (Yuksel and Rimmington, 1998).

Service Quality, Brand Loyalty, and Wine Tourism 225

The model contends that service quality can be conceptualized as the difference between what a consumer expects to receive and his or her perceptions of actual delivery. It suggests that product and service performance exceeding some form of standard leads to satisfaction while performance falling below this standard results in dissatisfaction (Oliver, 1997).

On the other hand, there is a perception model called SERVPERF, which is based only on perceptions of performance. SERVPERF and SERVQUAL share the same concept of perceived quality; however, Llusar and Zornoza (2000, p. 901) explain, that "The main difference between these models lies in the formulation adopted for their calculation, and more concretely, in the convenience in the utilization of expectations and the type of expectations that should be used." Robledo (2001) contends, "Supporters of this paradigm maintain that expectations are irrelevant and even misleading information for a model intended to evaluate perceived service quality. They maintain that the perception of the customer is the only measure required" (p. 23). Once service quality is measured, companies must find a way to continually improve their quality and continue to keep customers satisfied.

12.19 TRUST AND COMMITMENT

Trust has been defined as a willingness to rely on an exchange partner in whom one has confidence (Moorman et al., 1993). Additionally it has been described as a firm's belief that another company will perform actions that will result in positive outcomes, and that the other company will not take unexpected actions that result in negative outcomes for the firm (Anderson and Narus, 1990). Garbarino and Johnson found trust to be a precursor to commitment (1999) and is generally viewed as an essential ingredient for successful relationships (Berry 1995; Dwyer et al., 1987; Moorman et al., 1993; Morgan and Hunt 1994). Further, Caceres and Paparoidamis found both trust and commitment to be mediators between satisfaction and loyalty (2007).

We also know that benefits, trust, switching costs, and perceptions of value lead directly to relationship commitment. Benefits and trust are shown to be the most important antecedents of said commitment by the consumer. Research also indicates that this commitment to a relationship results in increased product use by the customer (Bowen and

226   Strategic Winery Tourism and Management

Shoemaker, 1998), thus illustrating the importance of gaining a consumers trust through available service opportunities.

Similar to trust, commitment is recognized as an essential ingredient for successful long-term relationships (Dwyer et al., 1987; Morgan and Hunt, 1994). It has been defined as "an enduring desire to maintain a valued relationship" (Moorman et al., 1992).

Research shows us that commitment has three main components:

- an instrumental component of some form of investment by the consumer,
- an attitudinal component that may be described as affective commitment or psychological attachment, and
- a temporal dimension indicating that the relationship exists over time (Gundlach et al., 1995).

Each of these components offer practitioners opportunity to delight our consumers in ways that trust and commitment can be potentially build over time.

12.20 FUTURE BEHAVIORAL INTENTIONS AND LOYALTY

As part of an organization commitment to relationship marketing and quality, measurements of loyalty and future behavioral intentions (FBI) have become a priority. It seems intuitive that there should be a contributory link between quality of service, level of customer satisfaction, and the organization's success. Higher quality of performance and levels of satisfaction are perceived to result in increased loyalty and future visitation, greater tolerance of price increases, and an enhanced reputation (Baker and Crompton, 2000). Each of these are critical in regard to increasing revenue, namely through intent to return and to positively recommend. These actions are generally a result of customer loyalty. Edvardsson et al. (2000, p. 918) define loyalty as "a customer's predisposition to repurchase from the same firm again." Oliver (1997, p. 392) elaborates by stating that "customer loyalty is a deeply held commitment to re-buy or re-patronize a preferred product or service consistently in the future, despite situational influence and marketing efforts having the potential to cause switching behavior." Importantly, Reichheld (1996) found that loyal customers impact organizations by generating more income, allowing for less marketing dollars to be spent in keeping a customer (rather than recruiting one) and becoming desensitized to price. Customer's progress through four different phases of loyalty are discussed below.

- Cognitive – The information base to the consumer compellingly points to one brand over another. This phase consists of loyalty based on cognition alone. This one factor, however, does not make a customer loyal.
- Affective – Affect is connected to satisfaction through both cognition and attitude.
  As a part of this phase, a consumer has either a positive or negative feeling or attitude toward a specific brand or product. This phase must be based on some type of prior interaction or experience (i.e., cognitive loyalty).
- Conative – The behavioral intention dimension of loyalty that is influenced by changes in affect toward the brand. This phase implies an intention or commitment to behave toward a goal in a particular manner. It is a loyalty state containing the deeply held commitment to buy.
- Action – The motivation intention in the previous phase is converted into readiness to act. This is also accompanied by a desire to overcome obstacles that might prevent the act. If this is repeated, action inertia develops, which facilitates repurchase. Readiness to act is related to the deeply held commitment to re-buy or re-patronize a preferred product or service consistently in the future, whereas overcoming obstacles is related to re-buying despite situational influences and marketing efforts having the potential to causes witching behavior (Oliver, 1999).

In the tourism industry, customer satisfaction and service quality do not always lead directly to loyalty. Because of the afore-mentioned benefits or retaining existing customers, the development of customer loyalty has become an important focus for marketing strategy research in recent years (Gwinner et al., 1998; Hagen-Danbury and Matthews, 2001; McMullan, 2005). According to Olorunniwo, Hsu and Udo, loyal customers impact the profitability and overall success of the organization in three ways. First, a customer's repeat business generates income for the company. Second, due to the cost of marketing and advertising, an organization makes less of

228   Strategic Winery Tourism and Management

a financial commitment in retaining customers compared to recruiting new customers. And third, loyal and satisfied customers often spread the word and recommend the services to others (2006).

Researchers argue that much of the effect on satisfaction on profits and sales growth is mediated by increased customer loyalty (Edvardsonn et al., 2000, p. 917). They further contend that consumer costs generally occur early in an organization's relationship with that consumer, while profits tend to accumulate only after a customer has been loyal for some time. Research shows that there are 6 factors that affect overall costs, revenues and resulting cash flows, as listed below:

- Acquisition costs – These costs transpire early in an organizations relationship with a new customer. Incentive programs, awareness advertising, and prospecting costs are all examples of acquisition costs. These tactics, designed to recruit and retain new customers often entail considerable costs to before any revenue is generated by the consumer.
- Base revenues – Throughout each time period that a consumer remains loyal to an organization, said organization will receive base revenues. This revenue is more evenly distributed as the re-purchase cycle continues. For example, a revolving bill such as magazine subscription would fit into this category.
- Revenue growth – As a customer becomes increasingly satisfied and consequently, more loyal with an organization they will generally find more opportunity to reward the organizations "good behavior" and consequently gain trust in the quality of the output. In doing so, the revenue gained in this step generally comes from two sources, the cross-selling of additional products and services and an increase in purchase volume.
- Operating costs – As the purchase-consumption-repurchase cycle continues, operational costs will likely decrease. The more an organization forms a relationship with its customers, the easier it should be to understand their preferences and therefore be less costly to cater to them.
- Customer referrals or word of mouth – Organizations that continually generate high levels of satisfaction, and therefore loyalty, will ultimately generate customer referrals and positive word of mouth advertising which, in turn, will generate additional sales revenue.

- Price premiums – Finally, when customers reach this stage of loyalty, they are more willing to pay a price premium than newer consumers would likely be willing to give. Also, loyal customers are more likely to be in a repeat purchase mode as opposed to a mercenary mode. Because of this, they are less likely to take advantage of price discounts or other offers for switching to a competitor (2000).

With all of this evidence of increased revenue and decreased costs, organizations cannot afford NOT to pay attention to loyalty generating systems and practices in order to have continuous improvement. Further, hospitality and service based organizations in particular should be concentrating heavily on operational methods of generating said customer loyalty through use of their face to face and service interactions.

Edvardsson et al. (2000, p. 919) follow up their discussion by illustrating this theory in the Loyalty Profit Chain diagram (Fig. 12.1). The authors further maintain the value of the model by stating that "The overall result is a per customer profit stream that increases over time. The more loyal the customer and the longer the customer is retained, the more sales and profits the customer generates." As a result, the impact that satisfaction and its part in the configuration of loyal consumers plays a critical role in the continued success of tourism organizations. Because of the unique disposition of wine tourism in particular, it is critical that there be a measurement in place that can decipher exactly what factors lead to satisfaction and ultimately visitor loyalty. After all, we now know that the higher the level of customer satisfaction in the relationship-not just the product or service-the greater the likelihood that the customer will be loyal to the company providing that service or product (Payne et al., 1999).

In 2006, a study was completed in order to establish whether or not positive affect, in combination with product quality, fair pricing, and customer-focused operations leads to higher levels of customer satisfaction and repurchase intentions in a winery setting. This study found product quality, positive emotions experienced, preference for wine, customer commitment, and fair pricing all to be significant predictors of repurchase intentions. The results supported the evidence that through positive tasting room experiences, wineries can cultivate relationships with customers that build both commitment and loyalty.

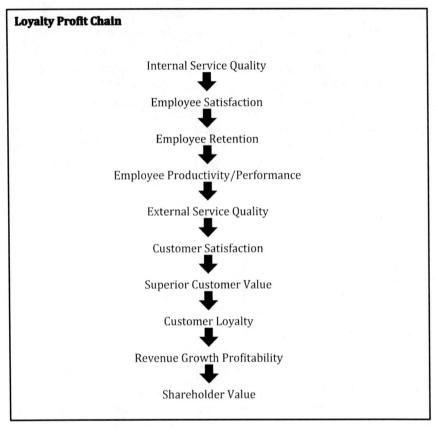

FIGURE 12.1 Loyalty Profit Chain.

12.21 WINE TOURISM AND BUILDING BRAND LOYALTY

We now know that it has become crucial for the wine and subsequent wine tourism industries to fully understand the impact tourism has on post-tour purchasing behavior. Putting the pieces together for the very unique blend of service and product that is the wine tourism industry, we know that levels of satisfaction with a quality service experience directly effect our consumer's future behavioral intentions, more specifically, their likelihood to purchase our products in the future and potentially become brand loyal. This means that a consumer who is 'delighted' or even just satisfied with a cellar door experience could actually become brand loyal to a product simply because of a positive experience with a service. We have a new breed of tourist, who are experiencing what we offer at the cellar door and transferring their satisfaction, and hopefully, subsequent brand loyalty, to the wine brand itself, thus making this type of service experience a vital component to capturing and retaining new customer bases and contributing to the future financial success of the wine brand. As such, wineries should be taking an in depth look at their procedure(s) at the cellar door in order to evaluate their effectiveness in and increase their likelihood in attaining brand loyal customers.

KEYWORDS

- **brand loyalty**
- **continuous quality improvement**
- **gourmet tourism**
- **gross domestic product**
- **multiplier effect**
- **service quality**
- **servicescape**
- **tourism sectors**
- **tourism trends**
- **wine tourism**

REFERENCES

1. Anderson, E. and Narus, J. (1990). A Model of Distributer Firm and Manufacturer Firm Working Partnerships. *Journal of Marketing,* 54 (January), 42–58.
2. Babbar, S., & Aspelin, D. J. (1994). TQM? It's as easy as abc. The TQM Magazine, 6–3.
3. Baker, D. and Crompton, J. (2000). Quality, satisfaction and behavioral intentions. *Annals of Tourism Research.* 27 (3), 785–804.
4. Bagozzi, R. P., Gopinath, M. & Nyer, P. U. (1999). The role of emotions in marketing. *Journal of the Academy of Marketing Science*, 27 (2), 184–206.
5. Beames, G. (2003). The Rock, the reef and the grape: The challenges of developing wine tourism in regional Australia. *Journal of Vacation Marketing,* 9(3), 205–212.
6. Beich, E. (1994). TQM for training. New York: McGraw-Hill.

7. Bell, R. A & Winters, L. C. (1993). Using marketing tools to improve employee relations. *Cornell Hotel and Restaurant Administration Quarterly.* Dec 1993; 34, (6), 38–42.

8. Berry, L. L. (1995). On great service: a framework for action, New York: Free Press.

9. Berry, L. L., Zeithaml, V. A., & Parasuraman, A. (1985). Quality Counts In Services, Too. Business Horizons, May-June, 44–52.

10. Bowen, J. T. & Shoemaker, S. 1998). Loyalty: A Strategic Commitment. *Cornell Hotel and Restaurant Administration Quarterly*, 39(1), 12–14.

11. Caceres, R. and Paparoidamis, N. (2007). Service quality, relationship satisfaction, trust, commitment and business–to–business loyalty. *European Journal of Marketing*, 41 (7/8), 836–867.

12. Cronin, J. J., Brady, M. K., & Holt, G. T. (2000). Assessing the effect of quality, value and customer satisfaction on consumer behavioral intentions in service environments. *Journal of Retailing*, 76(2), 193–218.

13. Cronin, J. J., & Taylor, S. A. (1992). Measuring service quality: A reexamination and extension. *Journal of Marketing*, 56(7), 55–68.

14. Dodd T., and Bigotte V. (1997) Perceptual Differences Among Visitor Groups to Wineries." *Journal of Travel Research* 35 (3), 46–51.

15. Dwyer, F., Schurr, P. and Oh, S. (1987). Developing Buyer-Seller Relationships. *Journal of Marketing,* 51 (2) 11–27.

16. Eadington, W., and Valene L. Introduction: The emergence of alternative forms of tourism. *Tourism alternatives: Potentials and problems in the development of tourism* (1992): 1–12.

17. Edvardsson B., Johnson M. D., Gustafsson, A., & Strandvik, T. (2000). The effects of satisfaction and loyalty on profits and growth: Products versus services. *Total Quality Management*, 11(7), 917–927.

18. Gabbot, M. and Hogg, G. (1997). Contemporary services marketing management: a reader. London: The Dryden Press.

19. Garbarino E., and Mark S. Johnson. The different roles of satisfaction, trust, and commitment in customer relationships. *The Journal of Marketing* (1999): 70–87.

20. Ganesan, Shankar. Determinants of long-term orientation in buyer-seller relationships. *The Journal of Marketing* (1994) 1–19.

21. George, B. (2006). Wine tourist motivation and the perceived importance of servicescape: A study conducted in Goa, India. *Tourism Review*, 61 (3), 15–19.

22. Getz, D., Dowling, R., Carlsen, J., & Anderson, D. (1999). Critical success factors for wine tourism. *International Journal of Wine Marketing, 11*(3), 20–43.

23. Grace & O'Cass, A. (2004). Examining service experiences and post-consumption evaluations. *Journal of Services Marketing*, 18 (3).

24. Gronroos, C. (2001). A service quality model and its marketing implications. *European Journal of Marketing*, 18(4), 36–44.

25. Groth, J. C., & Dye, R. T. (1999). Service quality: perceived value, expectations, shortfalls, and bonuses. *Managing Service Quality.* 9(4), 274–285.

26. Gundlach, Gregory T., Ravi S. Achrol, and John T. Mentzer. "The structure of commitment in exchange." *The Journal of Marketing* (1995): 78–92.

Service Quality, Brand Loyalty, and Wine Tourism 233

27. Gwinner, K., Gremler, D., & Bitner, M. J. (1998). Relational benefits in services industries: The customer's perspective. *Journal of the Academy of Marketing Science,* 26 (Spring).
28. Gwynne, A.; Devlin, J.; Ennew, C. T. (1998). Service quality and customer satisfaction: A longitudinal analysis," at The British Academy of Marketing Annual Conference, Sheffield Hallam University, 8–10 July 1998, 186–191.
29. Hagen-Danbury, A., Matthews, B. (2001). The impact of store image and shopping involvement on store loyalty in a clothes purchasing context. Proceedings of the Annual Academy of Marketing Conference, Cardiff University.
30. Hellsten, U., & Klefsjo, B. (2000). TQM as a management system consisting of values, techniques and tools. The TQM Magazine. 12–4, 238–244.
31. Hoyer & MacInnis. (2001). Consumer behavior. Houghton Mifflin Company, New York, NY.
32. ITA Office of Travel and Tourism Industries (2014). *An information service from the National Travel & Tourism Office (NTTO), Retrieved from: http://travel.trade.gov/tinews/archive/tinews2014/20140827.html, August 27 2014.*
33. Jamal & Naser. (2001). Customer satisfaction and retail banking: An assessment of some of the key antecedents of customer satisfaction in retail banking. *The International Journal of Bank Marketing,* 20 (7), 335–354.
34. Johnston, R., The zone of tolerance: exploring the relationship between service transactions and satisfaction with the overall service. *International Journal of Service Industry Management* 6.2 (1995): 46–61.
35. Khan, H., Phang, S., & Toh, R. S. (1995). The multiplier effect: Singapore's hospitality industry. *Cornell Hotel and Restaurant Administration Quarterly.* 36(1), 64–70.
36. Langer, M (1997). Service quality in tourism: Measurement and empirical analysis. New York, New York: Frankfurt am Main, 7–10.
37. Leddy, P. D. & Ormrod, J. E. (2005). Practical research: planning and design. Columbus, OH: Merrill Prentice Hall.
38. Llusar, J. C. B., & Zornoza, C. C. (2000). Validity and reliability in perceived quality measurement models. *International Journal of Quality and Reliability Management,* 17–8, 899–918.
39. Mantel, S. P. & Kardes, F. R. (1999). The role of direction of comparison, attitude-based processing, and attitude-based processing in consumer preference. *Journal of Consumer Research,* 25(3), 335–352.
40. McMullan, R. (2005). A multiple-item scale for measuring customer loyalty development., *Journal of Services Marketing,* 19(7), 470–481.
41. Moorman C., Deshpande R., and Zaltman, G. (1993) Factors affecting trust in market research relationships. *The Journal of Marketing,* 81–101.
42. Moorman C., Zaltman G., and Deshpande, R. (1992). Relationships between providers and users of market research: The dynamics of trust. *Journal of Marketing Research* 29 (3), 314–328.
43. Morgan, R., and Hunt, S. (1994) The commitment-trust theory of relationship marketing. *The Journal of Marketing,* 20–38.
44. Oliver, R. L. (1997). Satisfaction: A behavioral perspective on the consumer. London: McGraw Hill, 12–397.

45. Olorunniwo, F., Hsu, M. K., & Udo, G. J.(2006). Service quality, customer satisfaction, and behavioral intentions in the service factory. *Journal of Services Marketing*, 20 (1).
46. O'Neill, M. A., and Palmer A. (2001) Survey timing and consumer perceptions of service quality: an overview of empirical evidence. *Managing Service Quality* 11(3), 182–190.
47. O'Neill, M. A. and Palmer A. (2004) Importance-performance analysis: a useful tool for directing continuous quality improvement in higher education. *Quality assurance in education* 12(1), 39–52.
48. O'Neill, M. A., Palmer, A., & Charters, S. (2002). Wine production as a service experience-the effects of service quality on wine sales. *Journal of Service Marketing*, 16(4), 342–362.
49. Parasuraman, A., Zeithaml, V. A., & Berry, L. L. (1985). A conceptual model of service quality and its implications for future research., *Journal of Marketing*, 49 (Fall), 41–50.
50. Parasuraman, A. Zeithaml, V. A. & Berry, L. L. (1988). SERVQUAL: A multiple item scale for measuring consumer perceptions of service quality. *Journal of Retailing*, 64, 12–37.
51. Parasuraman, A., Zeithaml, Valerie A., Berry, Leonard L. (1988). SERVQUAL: A Multiple Item Scale for Measuring Consumer Perceptions of Service Quality. *Journal of Retailing, 64,1.*
52. Payne, A., Christopher, M., Peck, H., & Clark, M. (1999). Relationship marketing. *Handbook of Relationship Marketing*, 39.
53. Pizam, A. and Ellis, T. (1999). Customer satisfaction and its measurement in hospitality enterprises. *International Journal of Contemporary Hospitality Management*, 11 (7), 326–339.
54. Reichheld, F. F., & Teal, T. (1996). The loyalty effect., Boston: Harvard Business School Press.
55. Reisinger, Y. (1992). Unique characteristics of tourism, hospitality and leisure services, service quality management in hospitality, tourism and leisure. The Haworth Hospitality Press, New York.
56. Robledo, M. A. (2001). Measuring and managing service quality: integrating customer expectations. *Managing Service Quality*, 11, 22–31.
57. Sashkin, M., and Kiser, K. J. (1993). Total Quality Management, San Francisco: Berrett Koehler.
58. Stauss, B. (2002). The dimensions of complaint satisfaction: Process and outcome complaint satisfaction versus cold fact and warm act complaint satisfaction., *Managing Service Quality*, 12 (5), 397–415.
59. United Nations New York. (2007) The World Urbanization Prospects – The 2007 Revision, Retrieved from: http://www.un.org/esa/population/publications/wup2007/2007WUP_Highlights_web.pdf, February 2008.
60. Wakefield, K. L. & Blodgett, J. G. (1994). The Importance of Servicescapes in Leisure Service Settings, *Journal of Services Marketing*, 8 (3), 66–76.
61. Walsh, A., Hughes, H., & Maddox, D. P. (2002). Total quality management continuous improvement: Is the philosophy a reality? *Journal of European Industrial Training*. 26–6, 299–307.

Service Quality, Brand Loyalty, and Wine Tourism

62. Wiele, T., Van Iwaarden, J., Williams, R., and Dale, B. "Perceptions about the ISO 9000 (2000) quality system standard revision and its value: the Dutch experience." *International Journal of Quality & Reliability Management* 22, no. 2 (2005): 101–119.

63. Wong, A., Mei, O., Dean, A. M., & White, C. J. (1999). Analyzing service quality in the hospitality industry. *Managing Service Quality*, 9(2), 136–143.

64. World Travel and Tourism Council. (2014). Travel and Tourism Economic Impact Report 2014.

65. Yuksel, A., & Rimmington, M. (1998). Customer-satisfaction measurement. *Cornell Hotel and Restaurant Administration Quarterly*, 39 (6).

66. Zeithaml V. (1988) Consumer perceptions of price, quality, and value: a means-end model and synthesis of evidence. *The Journal of Marketing*, 2–22.

67. Zeithaml, V. A. & Bitner. (2000). Services marketing: Integrating customer focus across the firm. Irwin McGraw-Hill Publishing, New York, New York.

68. Zeithaml, V. A., Parasuraman, A. & Berry, L. (1990). Delivering quality service: Balancing customer perceptions and expectations, New York: The Free Press.

CHAPTER 13

EXPLORING AN EFFECTIVE WINERY REVENUE MANAGEMENT STRATEGY

KYUHO LEE

Assistant Professor of Marketing, Sonoma State University, Rohnert Park, CA, USA

CONTENTS

13.1	Introduction	237
13.2	Theoretical Foundations of Winery Revenue Management and Winery Service Quality	238
13.3	Revenue Management	241
13.4	Yield Management	242
13.5	Standardized Service System	242
13.6	Technology	243
13.7	Conclusion	244
Keywords		244
References		244

13.1 INTRODUCTION

A growing number of US wineries are placing importance on cellar door sales, due to the high profit margin they generate (Holman and Hunter, 2012; Getz and Brown, 2006). Although direct to customer sales represent only 3% of US wine sales, direct to customer sales through cellar door sales have become essential to small US wineries, which account for about 98% of US wineries (Stonebridge, 2011). In particular, direct sales generated $1.55 billion for wineries in 2006 (Stonebridge, 2011).

The traditional three-tier wine distribution system in the US has led wineries to go through a number of wine distribution channels that can hamper the profit margins of wine sales (Wagner et al., 2010). On the other hand, cellar door sales have a number of benefits for wineries, including increased customer brand loyalty, higher profit margins, and reduced perceived customer risks (Carlsen, 2011; Dodd, 1995). In addition, Dodd et al. (2005) posit that those wine consumers who visit wineries and participate in wine tastings feel confident about their wine knowledge compared to wine consumers who do not visit wineries or participate in wine tastings. Furthermore, wine consumers who have built their wine knowledge through winery visits and the wine tasting experience tend to drink more wine due to confidence in their wine knowledge (Dodd et al., 2005).

Although there are a number of advantages to selling wine through the cellar door, winery operators need to consider a variety of issues to increase these sales. Compared to selling wines through third party distribution channels, selling wines through the winery tasting room requires many different approaches for wineries. Importantly, winery operators need to create a holistic experience for winery visitors rather than emphasizing selling wine products them. In other words, winery operators need to maximize the visitor experience by utilizing all aspects of the winery, such as the tasting room, garden and wine production.

Thus, this study is designed to answer the following questions.

1. How can a winery operator develop a competitive winery revenue management strategy to increase a winery's cellar door sales?
2. How can a winery provide impeccable customer service to winery visitors?

13.2 THEORETICAL FOUNDATIONS OF WINERY REVENUE MANAGEMENT AND WINERY SERVICE QUALITY

Hojman and Jones (2012) contend that providing excellent winery service is critical to building a long-term relationship with winery visitors.

According to Hojman and Jones (2012), winery visitors visit a wine region or wineries not only to taste wines but also to enjoy leisure activities. Due to the hedonic nature of the wine product, winery visitors tend to be attracted to a winery's landscape, and a wine region's scenery (Bruwer and Alant, 2009).

Dodd (1999) discusses the importance of building a long-term relationship with winery visitors. According to Dodd (1999), repeat winery visitors spend almost 50% more money than do first time visitors. Dodd (1999) also suggests that the quality of wine is less important to first time visitors than to repeat visitors who are more concerned about the quality of wine. First time visitors also tend to value a winery's scenery and surroundings, such as the winery garden (Bruwer and Alant, 2009; Dodd, 1999).

Sparks (2007) asserts that winery tourists look for the multi-dimensional aspects of a winery when choosing a winery destination. According to Sparks (2007), winery visitors prefer to select a winery and region where they can experience and learn about a new culture through winery visits. Charters and Ali-Knight (2002) segment winery tourists as wine lovers, wine connoisseurs, wine interested, and wine novices based on each group's involvement in wine.

Wine lovers are those who are interested in obtaining more wine knowledge and education whereas wine novices are those who are more interested in the diverse activities at a winery, such as dining and vineyard tours (Charters and Ali-Kinight, 2002). Therefore, winery operators need to tailor their products and services to meet each segment of winery tourists.

Also, a number of researchers (Bruwer and Alant, 2009; Carlsen, 2011; Dodd and Bigotte, 1997; Gets and Brown, 2006) discusses the importance of service quality at wineries in order to attract and retain winery tourists. For example, Carlsen (2011) develops a winery service-mapping framework. Carlsen (2011) also analyzes all the tangible and intangible aspects of service that a winery can offer to visitors. According to Carlsen (2011), there are major five types of experience that winery visitors can experience during a visit. They are sight, smell, sound, taste, and touch. Sight includes the design and theme of a winery whereas touch includes the surfaces of the winery floor and the quality of winery merchandise.

Dodd and Bigotte (1997) postulate that friendliness, courtesy, and employee knowledge are the key attributes of winery service. Williams and Dossa (2003) claim that non-local winery visitors' look for multiple activities during their visits. For example, non-resident tourists want to participate in a variety of local events more than do non-local winery visitors.

Getz and Brown (2006) identify the major factors what winery tourists consider important in a wine region. The results of the study reveal that there are four major factors that influence winery tourists' selection of a wine region. They include a core wine product category that represents the local wineries, wine festivals, knowledgeable winery staff, and visitor friendly wineries. Other important factors that encompass a wine region's core destination appeal include climate, reasonable accommodation, and availability of fine restaurants, in a wine region.

Consistent with prior studies, Marzo-Navarro and Pedraja-Iglesias (2012) found that one of the major factors that motivates winery tourists to visit a winery is the quality of the winery's service. In particular, winery visitors' value wine tasting room facilities, extra services such as children's activities, and the ability to participate in wine production as important criteria in measuring the service quality of a winery.

Bruwer and Alant (2009) assert that most winery tourists would like to experience the terroir and landscaping of wineries. Experiencing a winery's terroir, including its soils, slope, and natural surroundings, has become an important activity for winery tourists. Furthermore, the authors argue that winery visitors value hedonic experiences over utility purposes. Yuan and Jang (2008) investigate how the quality of a wine festival influences visitors' loyalty to a wine region and its wineries. The results of the study indicate that the quality of wine festivals is positively correlated with winery visitors' loyalty. In other words, the more winery tourists are satisfied with a region's wine festivals the more likely they are return to the region and its wineries and purchase wine.

Overall, researchers argue that winery operators need to focus on the quality of their service to attract and retain winery visitors. Specifically, winery visitors tend to value staff friendliness, and an attractive winery landscape, and garden. In conclusion, winery visits have become an essential part of leisure activities among a growing number of tourists.

13.3 REVENUE MANAGEMENT

A number of researchers (Kimes et al., 1999; Kimes, 2004) contends that service companies can optimize their profits by developing competitive revenue management. One of the characteristics of service is when service production and consumption occur at the same time. Due to the nature of the services offered, operators are not able to maintain an inventory of their service products. This creates a challenge for winery operators since a large number of visitors tends to visit wineries on weekends and Fridays. During the peak times and days for winery visits, such as Fridays and weekends at lunch time, winery operators often suffer from a lack of staff and limited facilities, such as seats in the winery tasting room, which may hamper the service quality of winery operations. More importantly, poor service quality at a winery can negatively influence the loyalty of the winery's visitors Winery operators may lose an opportunity to generate more income since they cannot accommodate more visitors during peak times.

Kimes (2004) suggests that restaurant operators can develop a number of strategies to serve more customers during the peak times and days of restaurant operation. Restaurant operators can increase low seat occupancy by diversifying the table mix, pre-bussing, systematic payment procedures, and effective communication between host and servers (Kimes, 2004). For example, restaurant operators can serve more customers by minimizing times between new table settings through pre-bussing (Kimes, 2004). In addition, Kimes (2004) contends that restaurant operators can save time by presenting checks to customers before customers ask for their checks, which helps restaurant operators turn tables over faster.

Furthermore, Kimes and Robson (2004) investigate how the type of table and the configuration of tables can influence customers' meal duration. The results of the study found that restaurant patrons tend to stay longer and spend more per minute when they dine in booth tables compared to other types of tables, such banquette and half wall. Booth tables help restaurant patrons maintain their privacy more than other types of restaurant tables (Kimes and Robson, 2004). Lin (2004) suggests that music plays an important role in customer satisfaction. Specifically, slow music can reduce consumers' stress level and may increase customers' time and spending in a restaurant, whereas fast music can speed up a customer's meal duration.

In sum, winery operators need to develop a competitive revenue management strategy that allows them to serve more winery visitors efficiently during the peak visitor times and days while offering great service. Below I summarize key revenue management strategies for winery operators to increase cellar door sales.

13.4 YIELD MANAGEMENT

Winery operators might consider developing yield management. Winery operators should review their demand analysis carefully and \ develop related pricing strategies (Jones and Hailliton, 1992). For example, during the days of the week when there is weak visitor demand, a winery operator can develop different pricing strategies to draw more winery visitors. Lowering the price of the wine tasting room or wines can be an incentive for winery tourists to visit wineries on the lower demand days, such as Monday, Tuesday and Wednesday. At the same time, operators may increase the prices of wine tastings on Saturdays and Sundays when demand is high. Furthermore, analyzing the historical demand data of the number of winery visitors might help in developing a competitive yield management system (Sill and Decker, 1999). On the basis of a winery's historical demand data, its operators may create a variety of events to bolster the number of visitors during the low season.

13.5 STANDARDIZED SERVICE SYSTEM

Developing a standardized service system is important to increasing efficiency in winery service operations. Operators can develop a winery service process map or a blueprint to analyze each process in a winery's service delivery and improve and standardize all of the winery's processes (Sill and Decker, 1999).

In general, there are three major stages to service delivery, which a winery operator should follow. They are the visitor's arrival, the wine tasting, and the after wine tasting stages. During the visitor's arrival stage, specific

Exploring an Effective Winery Revenue Management Strategy 243

service standards reflecting the visitor's expectations can be established. For example, a winery can establish that each visitor will be greeted by a staff member within two minutes of their arrival. Or, for the wine tasting stage, tasting room staff may be trained to spend up a certain amount of time with each visitor.

In conclusion, standardizing a winery's service procedures through a service blueprint can help increase the efficiency of a winery's service delivery system and help it provide consistent service to winery visitors. In addition, standardized service procedure will help in training employees.

13.6 TECHNOLOGY

Winery operators may consider using a number of technologies to effectively serve more winery visitors. Many service organizations have already adopted this approach. For example, Panera Bread has adopted online ordering and ordering kiosks to speed up its customer service (Horovitz, 2014). Elsewhere in the restaurant industry, such as Applebee's and Olive Garden, tabletop ordering devices have appealed to millennial customers (Ruggless, 2014) who are more open to new technologies.

Winery operators have many technology options to provide a better customer service. For example, winery operators may use beepers for those who need to wait for their wine tastings during peak times. Beepers allow visitors to walk around the vineyard and explore the winery while they wait. Thus, customer waiting time is an opportunity to show off their wineries to visitors.

Wineries might also use tablets to introduce their wines to those waiting for certain services or activities. Specifically, installing or developing a virtual winery tour that highlights the winery's main features may be effective. In addition, winery operators might promote gift cards to increase winery sales. The sales of gift cards in many service organizations have been growing. For example, Starbucks generated 25% of the firm's revenue from Starbucks cards (Gonzalez, 2014). Also, Gonzalez (2014) claims that customers who possess a Starbucks gift card tend to be more loyal as compared to those who do not use a Starbucks card. Similarly, winery gift cards may increase not only revenue but also customer loyalty.

13.7 CONCLUSION

This chapter suggests a number of strategies for a winery operator to increase cellar door sales. In response to fierce competition in the wine industry, it has become more important for winery operators to provide competitive customer service and develop effective winery revenue management to increase cellar door sales.

All the facilities of a winery, ranging from the cellar tasting room to the garden, can be a place where winery visitors experience great hospitality and service. Providing great customer service becomes more salient as winery visitors look for hedonic experiences rather than a utility goal. Furthermore, although wine consumption in the US has increased, 88% of US adults have never bought wine through a winery's direct sales. Thus, winery operators need to provide a competitive winery experiences to increase winery cellar door sales (Stonebridge, 2011).

KEYWORDS

- **revenue management**
- **service quality**
- **technology**
- **traditional three-tier wine distribution system**
- **yield management fractal analysis of macromolecules**
- **heredity theory**
- **highly cross-linked epoxy-amine polymers**
- **modeling**

REFERENCES

1. Brown, G. P., Havitz, M. E., & Getz, D. (2006). Relationship between wine involvement and wine-related travel, Journal of Travel and Tourism Marketing, 21(1), 31–46.
2. Bruwer, J., & Alant, K. (2009). The hedonic nature of wine tourism consumption: an experiential view, International Journal of Wine Business Research, 21(3), 235–257.

3. Carlsen, J. (2004). A review of global wine tourism research, *Journal of Wine Research,* 15(1), 5–13.

4. Carlsen, J. (2011). Assessing service quality at wineries and cellar doors through service mapping, International Journal of Wine Business Research, 23(3), 271–290.

5. Charters, S., & Ali-Knight, J. (2002). Who is the wine tourist, Tourism Management, 23(3), 311–319.

6. Charters, S., Fountain, J., & Fish, N. (2009). Experiencing real service at the winery tasting room, Journal of Travel Research, 48(1), 122–134.

7. Dodd, T. (1995). Opportunities and pitfalls of tourism in a developing wine industry, International Journal of Wine Business Research, 7(1), 5–16.

8. Dodd, T. (1999). Attracting repeat customers to wineries, International Journal of Wine Marketing, 11(2), 18–28.

9. Dodd, T., & Bigotte, V. (1997). Perceptual differences among visitors groups to wineries, *Journal of Travel Research*, 35(Winter), 46–51.

10. Dodd, T., Laverie, D., Wilcox, J., & Duhan, D. (2005). Differential effects of experience, subjective knowledge, and objective knowledge on source of information used in consumer wine purchasing, *Journal of Hospitality and Tourism Research, 29*(1), 3–19.

11. Galloway, G., Mitchell, R., Getz, D., & Crouch, G., & Ong, B. (2008). Sensation seeking and the prediction of attitudes and behaviors of wine tourists, Tourism Management, 29, 950–966.

12. Getz, D., & Brown, G. (2006a). Critical success factors for wine tourism regions: a demand analysis, Tourism Management, 27, 146–158.

13. Getz, D., & Brown, G. (2006). Benchmarking wine tourism development: The case of the Okanagan Valley, British Columbia, Canada, *International Journal of Wine Marketing,* 18(2), 78–97.

14. Gonzalez, A. (2014). Starbucks prepaid cards hit a record $1.3B in holiday quarter, Retrieved on May 14, 2014 from http://seattletimes.com/html/businesstechnology/2022616275_starbuckscardsxml.html.

15. Hojman, D. E., & Jones, P. H. (2012). Wine tourism: Chilean wine regions and routes, *Journal of Business Research*, 65, 13–21.

16. Horovitz, B. (2014). Panera goes to high-tech ordering, Retrieved on May 15, 2014 from http://www.usatoday.com/story/money/business/2014/05/13/panera-bread-fast-food-restaurants/9036545/.

17. Jones, P., & Hamilton, D. (1992). Yield Management: Putting people in the big picture, Cornell Hotel and Restaurant Administration Quarterly, 23(1), 89–95.

18. Lin, I. Y. (2004). Evaluating a servicescape: The effect of cognition and emotion, *International Journal of Hospitality Management*, 23, 163–178.

19. Kimes, S. E. (2004). Restaurant revenue management: Implementation at Chevys Arrowhead, Cornell Hospitality Quarterly, 45(1), 52–67.

20. Kimes, S. E., Barrash, D. I., & Alexander, J. E. (1999). Developing a restaurant revenue-management strategy. *Cornell Hotel and Restaurant Administration Quarterly*, *40*(5), 18–29.

21. Kimes, S. E., & Robson, S. K. A. (2004). The impact of restaurant table characteristics onmeal duration and spending. *Cornell Hotel and Restaurant Administration Quarterly*, *45*(4), 333–346.

22. Marzo-Navarro, M., & Pedraja-Inglesias, M. (2012). Critical factors of wine tourism: incentives and barriers from the potential tourist's perspective, International Journal of Contemporary Hospitality Management , 24(2), 312–334.
23. Parasuraman, A., Zeithmal, V. A., & Berry, L. L. (1985). A conceptual model of service quality and its implications for future research. *Journal of Marketing, 49*, 41–50.
24. Ruggless, R. (2014). Survey: Younger diners embrace tabletop ordering, Retrieved on August 12, 2014 from http://nrn.com/technology/survey-younger-diners-embrace-tabletop-ordering.
25. Sill, B., & Decker, R. (1999). Applying capacity management science, Cornell Hotel and Restaurant Administration Quarterly, 40(3), 22–30.
26. Sparks, B. (2007). Planning a wine tourism vacation? Factors that help to predict tourist behavioral intentions, Tourism Management, 28, 1180–1192.
27. Stobridge, Yuan, J., & Jang, S. (2008). The effects of quality and satisfaction on awareness and behavioral intentions: Exploring the role of a wine festival, Journal of Travel Research, 46(2), 279–288.
28. Wagner, P., Thach, L., & Olsen, J. (2010). Wine Marketing & Sales, Wine Appreciation Guild, CA.
29. Williams, P. W., & Dossa, K. B. (2003). Non-resident wine tourist markets: Implications for British Columbia's emerging wine tourism industry. *Journal of Travel and Tourism Marketing, 14* (3/4), 1–34.

CHAPTER 14

FINANCIAL RATIO AND VALUATION ANALYSES OF CONSTELLATION BRANDS INC.: A CASE STUDY

MICHAEL R. SANTOS and VINCENT RICHMAN

Professor, School of Business and Economics, Sonoma State University, California, USA

CONTENTS

Abstract 247
14.1 Constellations Brands in the Wineries and
    Distillers Industry 248
14.2 Financial Ratios 251
14.3 Valuation Methods 257
14.4 Conclusion 265
Keywords 265
References 266

ABSTRACT

This chapter provides a case study for Constellation Brands Inc. operating in the Wineries & Distillers Industry with a portfolio of products that includes well-known premium brands of wine, beer and distilled spirits. Two competing firms in the industry; Diageo plc and Brown-Forman Corporation, have similar products, and therefore the financial ratio-averages for these two firms are calculated to represent industry benchmarks. First, we compare Constellation's financial ratios to the industry benchmarks and find that Constellation has relatively high debt service combined with low profitability ratios, perhaps making the common stocks of Constellation less attractive to the investors. Second, we apply four valuation techniques: dividend growth, free cash flow, earnings, and relative value (multiples) models for Constellation's common stock (STZ), and find that it is undervalued in 2013. This finding is consistent with the analyst recommendations of mostly "buy" and some "hold" decisions for STZ.

14.1 CONSTELLATIONS BRANDS IN THE WINERIES AND DISTILLERS INDUSTRY

Constellations Brands Inc. is a leading wine company in the U.S., Canada, and New Zealand employing about 4,500 full-time staff. It is headquartered in Victor, New York and its common shares are traded at the NYSE. Recently in 2011, the firm sold most of its holdings in Australia and the U.K. to improve its profit margins. While divesting these holdings, Constellations Brands also heavily invested $4.5 billion to acquire a significant share in Crown Imports and Modelo Brands of Piedras Negras in Mexico boosting its beer sales in the U.S. In addition, the company completed the acquisitions of The Ruffino and Mark West in the higher-margin premium wine brands (from 2013 10-K Report). Potentially, these acquisitions and divestitures can make Constellation more diversified and competitive in the wineries and distillers of beverages industry.

Table 14.1 presents that Constellation has a product portfolio made up with premium wine and beer, and distilled spirits such as brandy and whisky. On the financial side, while the firm's bonds have BB ratings of non-investment grade (high-yield) from Fitch Ratings, 84% of its common stocks is owned by institutional investors. In the wine and distillers industry, Constellation compete with well-known firms such as E&J Gallo Winery, The Wine Group, Treasury Wine Estates, W.J. Deutsch & Sons, Ste. Michelle Wine Estates and Kendall-Jackson, Diageo plc, Pernod Picard, Brown Forman Inc. and Beam Inc. Also, from the operational perspective, Constellation Brands organizes business operations in four segments; Constellation Wines North America, Constellation Wines Australia and

Financial Ratio and Valuation Analyses of Constellation Brands Inc 249

TABLE 14.1 Constellations Brands Inc. Firm Information

Variables	Information	Source
Industry	Beverages – Wineries & Distillers	Finance.yahoo.com
Sector	Consumer Goods	Finance.yahoo.com
Major Products	**Wine**: Robert Mondavi Brands, Clos du Bois, Estancia, Black Box, Arbor Mist, Blackstone, Rex Goliath, Simi, Toasted Head, Mark West, Ravenswood, Franciscan Estate, Ruffino, Wild Horse, Kim Crawford, Mount Veeder, Nobilo, Inniskillin and Jackson-Triggs.	Finance.yahoo.com
	Beer: Modelo Brands; Corona Extra, Corona Light, Modelo Especial, Pacifico, Negra Modelo and Victoria.	
	Premium spirit brands: SVEDKA Vodka, Black Velvet Canadian Whisky and Paul Masson Grande Amber Brandy.	
Number of Employees	4,500 full-time in August 2003	Finance.google.com
Exchange	NYSE	Finance.yahoo.com
Percentage of Shares Held by Institutional Investors	84%	Finance.yahoo.com
Bond Rating	BB	Fitch Ratings
Competitors	E&J Gallo Winery, The Wine Group, Treasury Wine Estates, W.J. Deutsch & Sons, Ste. Michelle Wine Estates and Kendall-Jackson in the U.S.; Andrew Peller, E&J Gallo Winery, Treasury Wine Estates and Kruger in Canada; and Pernod Ricard, Lion Nathan and Treasury Wine Estates in New Zealand. Constellation Wines and Spirits' principal distilled spirits competitors include: Diageo (DEO), Beam, Pernod Ricard, Bacardi and Brown-Forman (BF-B).	Finance.yahoo.com

TABLE 14.1   (Contined)

Market Capitalization	$13.27 billion. The average capitalization of DEO and BF-B was $49.20 on December 29, 2013.	Finance.yahoo.com
Annual Cash Interest Payments (average)	$220.33 million. The industry average for DEO and BF-B was $295.63 for the period of 2010–2013.	Finance.yahoo.com
Analyst's recommendation	1.8 where (Strong Buy) 1.0 – 5.0 (Sell) on October 11, 2013	Finance.yahoo.com

Europe, Constellation Wines New Zealand, and Crown Imports. Further, for its marketing network in North America, the company uses wholesale distributors and state and provincial alcoholic beverage control agencies to reach consumer markets. There is significant segmentation in the wine industry with many small to large size firms competing in the same market despite increasing trend towards more consolidations through mergers and acquisitions. In 2013, the 10-K Report filed by Constellation lists several industry trends as the main factors for the company's recent divesting and acquisition decisions:

- Consolidation of suppliers, wholesalers and retailers;
- An increase in global wine consumption, with premium wines growing faster than value-priced wines;
- Premium spirits growing faster than value-priced spirits; and
- High-end beer (imports and crafts) growing faster than domestic beer in the U.S.

As a result, Constellation is focusing its production and distribution efforts to away from the value-priced (cheaper) products to more of the premium products (expensive) of premium wine, beer, and distilled spirits, because of the higher consumer demand and growth observed in the premium brands.

This chapter first analyzes the financial ratios to determine financial health of Constellation. Also, it provides several methods to value Constellation's common stock.

14.2 FINANCIAL RATIOS

The industry benchmark financial ratios for the wineries and distilleries industry were not readily available for the analysis of Constellation, and therefore the financial ratio-averages of two major competitors, Diageo plc and Brown Forman Inc., are calculated as approximations for the industry benchmarks. Table 14.2 provides several firm-size measures for Constellations, Diageo, and Brown Forman respectively. By all measures, Constellations is about the same size as Brown Forman and smaller than Diageo.

All firms, Constellations, Diageo, and Brown Forman are is large-capitalization firms with values over $10 billion. Diageo plc and Brown Forman Inc. are chosen to represent the wineries and distillers industry due to their diverse portfolios with products similar to Constellation's.

Table 14.3 presents financial ratios in five performance categories; short-term solvency, long-term solvency, efficiency, profitability, and market value for the 2010–2013 period.

14.2.1 SHORT-TERM SOLVENCY

The current ratios of Constellation are similar to the industry benchmarks and do not raise any flag. The quick ratio of Constellation for the 2010–2013 period is slightly lower than the industry averages for the 2010–2012 but it reaches to the industry levels in 2013, 1.46 and 1.45, respectively, as it is shown at Fig. 14.1(a). Additionally, we compare these findings to the results of a Silicon Valley Bank (SVB) study that analyzes the financial

TABLE 14.2 Size Comparison of Constellations to Its Industry Benchmark Firms; Diageo and Brown Forman (in billions of dollars)

Measures of Firm-Size	STZ	DEO	BF-B
Revenues	$3.60	$18.38	$2.93
Market Capitalization	$13.27	$82.32	$16.08
Total Assets	$14.12	$38.25	$3.88
Number of Employees	4,500	28,470	4,000

*Source: Finance.yahoo.com and finance.google.com, 29 December 2013.

252 Strategic Winery Tourism and Management

TABLE 14.3   Financial Ratios of Constellations Brands Inc. and the Industry Ratios

Financial Ratios*	Constellations (Stz)				Industry** (Bf-B And Deo)			
Years	2013	2012	2011	2010	2013	2012	2011	2010
1. Short-Term Solvency								
Current Ratio	3.65	1.70	3.14	1.89	2.70	2.92	2.13	2.28
Quick Ratio	1.46	0.55	1.08	0.52	1.45	1.63	1.32	1.27
2. Long-Term Solvency Ratios								
Total Debt Ratio	0.63	0.62	0.64	0.68	0.64	0.58	0.59	0.62
Times Interest Earned	2.59	2.81	2.47	1.01	17.11	14.82	18.92	13.20
3. Efficiency Ratios (in days)								
Accounts Receivable Period	62	68	67	56	72	65	68	66
Inventory Period	320	315	234	314	341	309	295	285
Accounts Payable Period	45	30	22	45	72	70	72	58
Operating Cycle	382	383	301	369	413	374	363	350
Cash Cycle	337	353	279	325	341	304	292	292
4. Profitability Ratios								
Gross Profit Margin	0.40	0.40	0.36	0.35	0.65	0.63	0.63	0.62
EBITDA Margin	0.22	0.22	0.19	0.14	0.33	0.32	0.32	0.31
Net Profit Margin	0.14	0.17	0.17	0.03	0.21	0.18	0.21	0.17
Return on Equity	0.14	0.17	0.22	0.04	0.36	0.30	0.32	0.32
Return on Assets	0.05	0.06	0.08	0.01	0.13	0.12	0.13	0.11
5. Market Value Ratios								
Earnings Per Share (EPS, trailing)	2.10	2.29	2.65	0.45	4.33	3.58	3.64	2.83
Book Value Per Share (BPS)	15.48	13.77	12.09	11.59	12.16	11.68	11.15	8.75
Sales Per Share (SPS)	15.13	13.66	15.78	15.14	20.20	19.53	18.09	16.47
P/E (Price/EPS, trailing)	23.51	9.43	8.45	40.89	23.64	30.82	27.36	35.46
P/B (Price/BPS)	3.19	1.57	1.85	1.58	8.48	8.92	8.71	11.26
P/S (Price/SPS)	3.26	1.58	1.42	1.21	5.00	5.70	5.66	6.19

Financial Ratio and Valuation Analyses of Constellation Brands Inc 253

TABLE 14.3 (Continued)

*Definition of Financial Ratios: Current Ratio = Current Assets/Current Liabilities, Quick Ratio = (Current Assets − Inventory)/Current Liabilities, Total Debt Ratio = Total Liabilities/Total Assets, Times Interest Earned = EBIT/Interest Expense, Accounts Receivable Period (also called Days in Account Receivables or Collection Period) = 365/(Revenues/Receivables), Inventory Period (Days in Inventories) = 365/(Costs of Goods Sold/Inventory), Accounts Payables Period (Days in Payables) = 365/(Costs of Good Sold/Accounts Payables), Operating Cycle = Inventory Periods + Accounts Receivables Period, Cash Cycle = Operating Cycle − Accounts Payable Period, Gross Profit Margin = Gross Profits/Revenues, Net Profit Margin = Net Income/Revenues, Return on Equity (ROE) = Net Income/Total Equity, Return on Assets (ROA) = Net Income/Total Assets, Earnings Per Share (EPS) = Net Income/Outstanding Shares, Book Value Per Share (BPS) = Total Equity/Outstanding Shares, Sales Per Share (SPS) = Revenues/Outstanding Shares, P/E = Price/EPS, P/B = Price/BPS, P/S = Price/SPS.

**Industry benchmarks are calculated from the averages of the two firm's ratios: Brown-Forman Corporation (BF-B) and Diageo plc.

***Price corresponds to the closing price on April 30th of each year from 2010 to 2013. This period matches the financial statements information (income statements, balance sheets, and statement of cash flows) for Constellations.

****Appendix I shows financial ratios of DEO and BF-B.

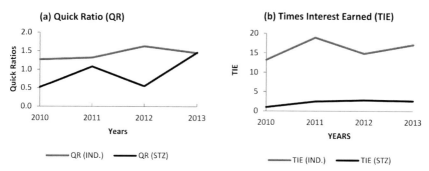

FIGURE 14.1 Quick ratios and times interest earned ratios for Constellations and its industry.

ratios of 90 small wineries located in Northern California, California's Central Coast, Oregon and Washington for the 2007–2008 period (Douglas et al., 2010). The current ratios of Constellations is similar to that of the SVB study, but the quick ratios for Constellation Brands are much higher than those of the SVB study, perhaps indicating larger inventory holdings at the small SVB wineries. Additionally, the difference in the quick ratios could be due to product portfolio of Constellation that includes premium beer and distilled spirits in addition to its wine inventories.

14.2.2 LONG-TERM SOLVENCY (DEBT) RATIOS

The total debt ratios of Constellation Brands and industry are between 0.62 and 0.68 in comparison to its industry having ratios between 0.58 and 0.64 for the 2010–2013 period. These are relatively high debt ratios placing the wineries and distilleries industry to next to the highest indebted industries such as air transport, power and utilities, maritime transportation, oil and gas distribution, and tobacco (Damodaran, 2013). Also, the high total debt ratio for Constellation may be the result of its latest acquisitions totaling to $4.5 billion, implying relatively large interest payments for the company.

Another long-term solvency measure, Times Interest Earned (TIE) as shown above at Fig. 14.1(b), for Constellations for the 2010–2013 period is alarmingly low compared to the industry benchmarks. Since covering interest payments many times with operating income is desirable, the larger the TIE, better it becomes. This implies either Constellation has to increase its operating revenues or reduce its debt and interest payments. Another suggestion may be changing capital structure to become more equity and less debt by raising funds through new common stock sales and paying of its debt. The ratio of interest payments to debt for Constellations for 2013 is 9.4% as opposed to 6.9% and 4.8% for Diageo and Brown Forman respectively as it is shown on Table 14.4. This result indicates that the current debt service for Constellation Brands is relatively higher than its competitors in the industry.

14.2.3 EFFICIENCY RATIOS

The next performance category includes accounts receivable, inventory period, and accounts payable periods. The accounts receivable period for Constellations varies from 52 to 68 days in comparison to its industry having 64 to 72 days. The accounts receivable period from the SVB study is 44 days lower than both Constellation and the industry. Also, while the inventory period for Constellations varies between 234 and 320 days in comparison to its industry varying between 285 to 341 days for the period of 2010–2013. The SVB study indicates a much longer inventory period for the small wineries, about 1,028 days. Again, the difference of small wineries having longer inventory periods may be related to two factors; (a) wine production and distribution on

Financial Ratio and Valuation Analyses of Constellation Brands Inc   255

TABLE 14.4   Interest Payments and Debt for STZ and Industry

Years	2013	2012	2011	2010
Constellations				
Interest payments	307.70	203.30	173.30	197.00
Total debt	3,277.10	3,136.70	2,421.40	3,277.80
Percentage (interest/debt)	9.4%	6.5%	7.2%	6.0%
Diageo				
Interest payments	937.64	856.49	878.26	852.20
Total debt	13,511.57	13,512.59	14,135.34	15,835.37
Percentage (interest/debt)	6.9%	6.3%	6.2%	5.4%
Brown forman				
Interest payments	32.00	26.00	33.00	32.00
Total debt	699.00	759.00	510.00	1,002.00
Percentage (interest/debt)	4.6%	3.4%	6.5%	3.2%

Source: Obtained from the financial statements of STZ, DEO, and BFB at finance.google.com.

the average may require longer inventory periods than beer and other distilled products, and (b) large firms such as Constellation has more efficient distribution networks through wholesale distributors and state and provincial alcoholic beverage control agencies to reach consumer markets. Further, accounts payable period for Constellation is shorter than that of the industry, between 22 to 45 days versus 58 to 72 days. However, this difference is not concerning because it is expected the firms to use different trade credit policies. The difference may be related to the lower market power and credit scoring of Constellation than the other firms in the industry. However, having slightly longer accounts receivables period for Constellation does not affect its cash cycle to be too different than its industry; 279 to 353 for Constellations and 292 to 341 for the industry. The length of operating cycles for both STZ and the industry are also similar.

14.2.4   PROFITABILITY RATIOS

In the next category for the average profitability ratios for all four measurements; gross profit margin, EBITDA margin, net profit margin, and return on equity (0.38, 0.19, 0.13, and 0.14), are all significantly lower for Constellation than the average of the industry benchmarks (0.63, 0.32, 0.19, and 0.32) for the 2010–2013 period respectively. Similarly, Gross Profit Margin for Constellations varies between 0.35 to 0.40 while the industry ratios are between 0.62 and 0.65 as shown at Fig. 14.2(a) below. In addition, Return on Assets (ROA) ratios are also shown on Fig. 14.2(b) indicating a low range of 0.01 to 0.08 for Constellations and a relatively higher range for the industry between 0.11 and 0.13.

14.2.5 MARKET VALUE RATIOS

Finally, the market value ratios show that especially Constellation multiples of Price/EPS, Price/BPS and Price/SPS are all lower than those of its industry ratios. This is consistent with the earlier finding that Constellation's common stock value is most likely depressed in the stock markets. Again, it is likely that this result is due to having proportionally high interest payments on Constellation's debt with its low profitability causing investors to be cautious about Constellation's common stocks. Even though the profit margins and return on equity are lower than the industry averages, those ratios are still higher than the average ratios of small wineries from the SVB study. This could also indicate that profit margins of wine industry may be lower than the premium beer and distilled spirits businesses.

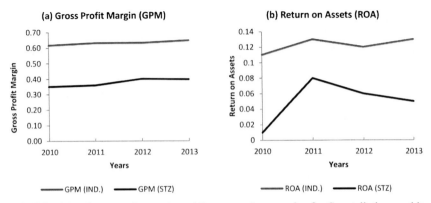

FIGURE 14.2 Gross profit margin and Return on Assets ratios for Constellations and its industry.

Financial Ratio and Valuation Analyses of Constellation Brands Inc   257

Overall financial ratio analysis indicates that Constellation's relatively high debt service together with low profitability margins may be responsible for the company's depressed stock prices. The Company's 2013 10-K report explains that to divestment decision to sell its operations in the U.K. and Australia in 2011 was due to the company's desire to increase its profit margins. As a result, Constellation's additional spending of 4.5 billion increasing the company stake to 50% in Modelo Brands of Mexico and the increased share in premium wine brands can be seen as opportunity as well as risk depending on the future success in the integration of these new units to the company's overall strategic planning. However, outside investors may continue to be cautious about the Constellation stocks until better profitability margins from the company emerge in the future.

14.3   VALUATION METHODS

Four valuation methods are used to assess the value of the Constellation common stock (STZ); dividend growth model, free cash flow, earnings, and relative value (multiples) models. The goal is to find the intrinsic value of STZ from the average of intrinsic prices found from the application of these four methods.

14.3.1   DIVIDEND GROWTH MODEL (DGM)

The DGM is the most common valuation methodology but the application can be challenging if the firm in question does not pay dividends or when the growth rate of dividends is greater than the firm's required return. In the case of Constellation, we face the first issue: Constellation Brands (STZ) does not pay dividends. We overcome this problem by substituting the industry's average dividend payments at time 0 for Constellation. Additionally, we use the average dividend growth rate of the industry as a substitution for Constellation's dividend growth. These substitutions will yield reliable results only if the firms in the industry are similar in their operations. We believe that Diageo, and Brown-Forman has portfolio of products (premium wine, beer, and distilled spirits) similar to those of Constellation, and therefore these substitutions can be justified.

258   Strategic Winery Tourism and Management

Table 14.5 exhibits the details of the DDM application. First, the average of quarterly dividend payments is calculated as $D_0 = \$1.97$ for Diageo (DEO) and Brown-Forman (BF-B) companies during 2013. Then,

TABLE 14.5   Dividend Growth Model (DGM): $P_0 = \dfrac{D_0(1+g)}{k-g} \, or \, P_0 = \dfrac{D_1}{k-g}$

Variable	Values	Information
D_0	$1.97	Dividend Payment at time 0 (Last Dividend Payment). It is calculated from the industry average as the last 4 quarterly dividends of BF-B and DEO firms.
1-b	40.00%	Dividend Payout Ratio. It is the industry average calculated from the average dividend payout ratios of BF-B and DEO firms.
b	60.00%	Retention Ratio (Industry) = 1 – Payout Ratio.
g	13.83%	Growth Rate of Industry. The average is obtained from two methods; Method 1: the average dividend growth rate (8.07%) for BF-B (6.11%), and DEO (10.03%). Method 2. g = Retention Rate × ROE, 34.78% and 30.99%, respectively).
Beta	1.16	Calculated from monthly stock data of STZ from 1/1/2010 to October 11, 2013.
Beta (average)	1.14	Confirmation with the average of betas for STZ obtained from three sources: Finance.yahoo.com, Finance.google.com, and Money.msn.com, respectively, 1.19, 1.11, and 1.11 on Oct. 1, 2013.
R_M	13.09%	Required rate of return for Market. It is calculated as the geometric average of monthly return of S&P500 index and converted into annual geometric average return: Annual Geometric Average Return = (1+Monthly Geometric Average Return)^{12}– 1. Data for S&P500 index is from January 4, 2010 to October 11, 2013 consistent with the period used for the Financial Ratios.
R_{RF}	3.74%	Risk-Free rate of return from the 30-Year Treasury bond rate on October 11, 2013.
k	15.23%	Required return for Constellations Brands Inc. (STZ) by using CAPM where $k_{STZ} = R_{RF} + \beta_{STZ} \times (R_M - R_{RF})$.
P_0	**$160.33**	Intrinsic (fundamental) Price.
Market P_0	**$62.99**	UNDERVALUED on October 11, 2013.

*We used 30-year Treasury bond yield rather than the 3-month T-bill rates because the expected common stock return is based on long term cash flows since common stock has infinite maturity.

Financial Ratio and Valuation Analyses of Constellation Brands Inc   259

we calculated growth rate of the industry, g = 13.83%, as the arithmetic average of the results from the following two methods:

Method 1: $g_{INDUSTRY} = (g_{DEO} + g_{BF-B})/2 = (10.03\% + 6.11\%)/2 = 8.07\%$ where $g_{DEO} = 10.03\%$ and $g_{BF-B} = 6.11\%$. The g_{DEO} and g_{BF-B} are found as geometric averages of quarterly growth rates from the historical dividend data for the 3/3/2008 – 9/3/2013 period. Subsequently, the quarterly geometric average growth rates are converted to annual geometric average growth rates by using: $g_{ANNUAL} = (1 + g_{QUARTERLY})^4 - 1 = g_{DEO\,(ANNUAL)} = (1 + 0.0242)^4 - 1 = 10.04\%$ where $g_{BF-B\,(ANNUAL)} = (1 + 0.0149)^4 - 1 = 6.10\%$.

Method 2: $g_{INDUSTRY} = (g_{DEO} + g_{BF-B})/2 = (0.1843 + 0.2076)/2 = 19.60\%$ where $g_{DEO} = $ Retention Rate$_{DEO} \times ROE_{DEO} = (53.00\% \times 34.78\%) = 18.43\%$ and $g_{FB-B} = $ Retention Rate$_{BF-B} \times ROE_{BF-B} = (67.00\% \times 30.99\%) = 20.76\%$. Thus, the average of two method provides $g_{AVE} = (g_{METHOD1} + g_{METHOD2})/2 = (8.07\% + 19.60\%)/2 = 13.83\%$.

Next, the required return for Constellations is calculated, k_{STZ}, by using the Capital Asset Pricing Model (CAPM): $k_{STZ} = R_{RF} + Beta_{STZ} (R_M - R_{RF}) = 3.74\% + 1.16 (13.09\% - 3.74\%) = 15.23\%$ where R_{RF} corresponds to the 30-year Treasury Bond yield on Oct. 11, 2013, Beta$_{STZ}$ is found from monthly common data for STZ and S&P500 index from the 1/4/2010 –10/1/2013 period, and R_M is calculated from the same data by finding monthly geometric returns first, and converting to annual geometric returns later as: $R_{M,(ANNUAL)} = (1 + R_{M(MONTHLY)})^{12} - 1 = (1 + 0.0103)^{12} - 1 = 13.09\%$.

Finally, the DGM is applied:

$$P_0 = \frac{D_0(1+g)}{k-g} => \$160.33 = \frac{\$1.97\,(1+0.1383)}{0.1523 - 0.1383}$$

where $P_0 = \$160.33$ is higher than the market price of $62.99 on October 11, 2003 and therefore, it can be concluded that Constellation's stock (STZ) is undervalued.

14.3.2 FREE CASH FLOW MODEL (FCF)

Table 14.6 presents the application of the free cash flow model. We calculated free cash flow at time 0, FCF$_0$, by using the following equations:

Free Cash Flow (FCF) = Operating Cash Flow (OCF) – Changes in NWC (ΔNWC) – Net Capital Spending (NCS) where:

OCF = EBIT – Taxes + (Depreciation + Amortization),

ΔNWC = (Current Assets – Current Liabilities)(t) – (Current Assets – Current Liabilities)(t – 1), and

NCS = Net Fixed Assets (t) – Net Fixed Assets (t–1) + (Depreciation + Amortization)(t).

TABLE 14.6 Free Cash Flow (FCF) Model: $V_0 = \dfrac{FCF_0(1+g)}{WACC - g}$ or $V_0 = \dfrac{FCF_1}{WACC - g}$

Variables	Values	Information
FCF_0	$287.10	Free Cash Flow at time 0 in millions of dollars.
g	13.83%	Growth Rate of Industry. It is the average of growth rates calculated from Method 1: Dividend growth rates, and Method 2. g = Retention Rate × ROE, respectively 8.07% and 19.60%. The industry average is based on BF-B and DEO firms.
k_E	15.23%	Adopted from the DGM model.
k_D	3.507%	Yield to Maturity (YTM) from one of the bonds with the longest maturity obtained from Finance.yahoo. com for Constellation. The specification of the bond: 4.625% semi-annual coupon, premium bond with maturity date set at 1-Mar-2023 currently priced at $109.5 and its yield to maturity is 3.507%.
FCF_1	$326.82	In millions of dollars. Last Dividend. The industry average is used from the summation of last 4 quarterly dividends for BF-B and DEO firms.
D + E	$18,469.29	V_0 = D + E = $6,830.00 + 11,639.29 = $18,469.29
$w_D + w_E$	1	$w_D + w_E$ = 36.98% + 63.02% = 1.
T	25.43%	Average tax rate for STZ for the period of 2010–2013.
Q	184.78	Number of Outstanding Shares in millions on October 11, 2013.
P_0	N/A	Intrinsic (fundamental) price. Not Available since WACC < g.
Market P_0	**$62.99**	October 11, 2013.

Financial Ratio and Valuation Analyses of Constellation Brands Inc. 261

Table 14.6 provides the variables used in the FCF model and brief explanations to each variable. In order to apply the model, first the financial statements (income, balance sheet, and cash flows recorded on 02/28 of each year) for Constellation are obtained from Finance. google.com for the period of 2010–2013. The calculated FCFs for 2011, 2012, and 2013 are averaged to eliminate the large fluctuations in FCFs due to annual investment decisions, and FCF_0 is calculated as $287.10. The growth rate for the industry is adopted from the DGM as g = 13.83%.

Next, the Weighted Average Cost of Capital (WACC) for Constellations is calculated from the following formula:

$$WACC = k_{WACC} = w_D k_D (1-T) + w_E k_E = \left(\frac{D}{D+E}\right) k_D (1-T) + \left(\frac{E}{D+E}\right) k_E$$

where w_D and w_E are the weights of debt and equity components respectively. Additionally, the market capitalization and enterprise values are obtained as $11,639.29 and $18,469.29 respectively, and used to calculate w_D and w_E as the following:

Enterprise Value = Market Capitalization + Market Value of Debt.

Or, V = E + D where D = V – E = $6,830.00 = $18,469.29 – $11,639.29. And, therefore w_D = ($6,830.00/$18,469.29) = 36.98% and w_E = ($11,639.29/$18,469.29) = 63.02%.

Further, the constraint of $w_D + w_E$ = 1 holds as 36.98% + 63.02% = 1. The average corporate tax rate, T = 25.43%, is obtained from the income statements of Constellation for the 2010–2013 period as: Tax rate = (Taxes Paid/Taxable Income).

The required return for equity, k_E, is adopted from the previous section as k_E = 15.23%. Thus, the weighted average cost of capital, k_{WACC} = (36.98%)(3.507%)(1–25.43%) + (63.02%)(15.23%) = 10.56%. Since, it is required that k_{WACC} > g to apply FCF model, and we have k_{WACC} < g as 10.56% < 13.83%, and therefore, the application of FCF model is not appropriate.

14.3.3 RELATIVE VALUE (MULTIPLES) MODEL

Relative value models are easy to use since the firm and benchmark industry firms' multiples are easily available. Also, it is believed that each multiple such as P/E, P/B, and P/S captures slightly different price dynamics and fundamentals reflected in earnings, book value, and sales respectively. Therefore, by using several multiples, we can estimate more reliable intrinsic values. However, the easiness of this application comes at a cost when financial markets are said to be in an asset bubble (Penman, 2013). However, the current financial markets after 2008 crisis have experienced a significant downturn adjustment to eliminate any overvaluations of the common stocks. And, thus the concerns of market bubbles can be overlooked in 2013.

Table 14.7 presents multiples for P/E, P/S, and P/B in the second column for BF-B and third column for DEO. The fourth column shows the averages of these multiples. The fourth column presents EPS, SPS, and BPS respectively for STZ. All the numbers are obtained from Table 14.7 showing the financial ratios. By multiplying the fourth and fifth columns, the stock prices from each category can be obtained as:

$$P_0 = 28.99 \times \$2.10 = \$60.84, \ P_0 = 6.17 \times \$15.13 = \$93.31,$$
$$and \ P_0 = 10.37 \times 15.48 = \$160.90$$

And the arithmetic average of three prices provides us the intrinsic price as $164.53. Since the market price of $62.99 is less than the average intrinsic

TABLE 14.7 Relative Value (Multiples) Model:

$$P_0 = \frac{P_0}{EPS} EPS, P_0 = \frac{P_0}{SPS} SPS, P_0 = \frac{P_0}{BPS} BPS$$

Multiples	Bf-B	Deo	Average Multiples	Stz	Stock Price
Price/EPS	25.82	19.95	22.89	9.37	214.43
Price/Sales	5.20	4.22	4.71	19.08	89.87
Price/Book	8.96	6.86	7.91	23.93	189.29
Intrinsic P_0					$164.53
Market P_0	**$62.99**	Undervalued on October 11, 2013.			

Financial Ratio and Valuation Analyses of Constellation Brands Inc

price of \$164.53, it can be said that Constellation's stock is undervalued in 2013 based on the relative value model.

14.3.4 EARNINGS MODEL

Earnings model is another approach to a firm's valuation that emphasizes EPS and the difference between ROE and the required return on equity. After capitalizing next period's EPS with the required return on equity, the incremental value comes from the difference: ROE − k from the retained earnings being invested into the firm's operations as $RE_1(ROE − k)$. ROE can be perceived as how much return a firm generates for its invested funds that costs k. Also, the firm can generate incremental value only if ROE > k for the retained earnings are invested in the firm's operations.

TABLE 14.8 Earnings Model (EM): $P_0 = \left(\dfrac{1}{k}\right)\left(EPS_1 + \dfrac{RE_1 * (ROE - k)}{k - g} \right)$

Variable	Values	Information
k	15.23%	Required return for STZ.
EPS_0	2.10	Earnings Per Share at time 0 in 2013 for Constellations Brands Inc.
EPS_1	2.39	Earnings Per Share at time 1: forecasted one-period ahead as $EPS_1 = (1+g)*EPS_0$.
ROE	34%	Return on Equity, from the quarterly financial statements on August 31, 2013.
b	60.00%	Retention Ratio (industry average from BF-B and DEO).
1-b	40.00%	Dividend Payout Ratio (industry average from BF-B and DEO).
g	13.83%	Growth Rate of Industry (as the average of growth rates calculated from 1. DGM and 2. g = Retention Rate × ROE, respectively 8.07% and 19.60%)
RE_1	1.43	Reinvested (Retained) Funds Per Share at time 1.
P_0	**\$166.00**	Intrinsic (fundamental) Price.
Market P_0	**\$62.99**	Undervalued on October 11, 2013.

Table 14.8 presents the earnings model application. The incremental gain on the retained earnings for Constellation is $ROE - k = 34\% - 15.23 = 18.77\%$ and it is obtained from the quarterly financial statements on August 31, 2013. The following formula shows the application details:

$$P_0 = \$166.00 = \left(\frac{1}{0.1523}\right)\left(2.39 + \frac{1.43 * (0.34 - 0.1523)}{0.1523 - .1383}\right)$$

The intrinsic value of $166.00 found and it is greater than $62.99 of market price. Therefore, the Constellation's common stock is undervalued.

14.3.5 AVERAGE OF THE INTRINSIC PRICES FROM VALUATION MODELS

Table 14.9 collects and summarizes all the results from the valuation models used: Dividend Growth Model, Free Cash Flow Model, Relative Value Model (Multiples), and Earnings Model to find the intrinsic value of the Constellation stock (STZ). Three out of four models had been applied and FCF model could not be applied since $k_{WACC} < g$. However, the average intrinsic value from three other models (DGM, multiples, and EM) is $163.62 and greater than the market price of $62.99 on Oct. 11, 2013, and therefore, the Constellation stock is undervalued.

TABLE 14.9 Valuation Methods for Constellations Brands Inc.

Methods	Price	Quantity	Equity	Debt	Total Value
1. DGM	$160.33	184.78	$29,625.78	4,777.80	$34,403.58
2. FCF	N/A	184.78	N/A	N/A	N/A
3. Multiples	$164.53	184.78	$30,401.85	4,777.80	$35,179.65
4. EM	$166.00	184.78	$30,673.48	4,777.80	$35,451.28
Average Intrinsic Price	$163.62	184.78	$30,233.70	$4,777.80	$35,011.50
Market P_0	$62.99 on Oct. 11, 2013, Undervalued	184.78	11,639.29	6,830.00	18,469.29

*Equity, Debt, and Value numbers are in millions of dollars.

14.4 CONCLUSION

Constellation firm's financial ratios are similar to those of two other publicly traded firms in the Wineries & Distillers Industry except in the debt and profitability categories. The financial ratio analysis indicates that annual interest payments for Constellation are relatively high in comparison to the other firms in the industry; Diageo plc and Brown-Forman Corporation. In addition, profitability ratios are significantly lower than the industry benchmarks. Therefore, these results may make stock market investors to be cautious about buying the Constellation's common stocks.

Additionally, the valuation analysis for Constellation Brands shows that the firm's common stock is significantly undervalued in 2013.

The managerial implications of this case study is two-fold: (i) even though Constellation's strategic decision to reorient firm by leaving (divesting) low margin products and markets and investing (acquisitions) into high margin products and markets may be sound, the financial market participants are concerned about firm's debt levels and ability to integrate new products into overall firm's objectives. (ii) The higher debt and interest payments may require Constellation to orient its capital structure by issuing more equity and using the proceeds to reduce its debt. However, this adjustment may not be beneficial if the firm's stock price stays depressed in the financial markets.

KEYWORDS

- **Constellation Brands Inc.**
- **dividend growth**
- **earnings**
- **efficiency ratios**
- **free cash flow**
- **long-term solvency**
- **profitability ratios**
- **relative value**
- **short-term solvency**

REFERENCES

1. 2013 10-K Report, Constellation Brands Inc., filed at SEC at: http://www.sec.gov/edgar/searchedgar/companysearch.html.
2. Damodaran, A. (2013). Debt fundamentals by sector. Retrieved from http://pages.stern.nyu.edu/~percent20adamodar/New_Home_Page/datafile/dbtfund.htm.
3. Douglas J. J., Aguilar D. & Gilinsky, A. (2010) Benchmarking winery financial performance, Wine Business Monthly, 60–67.
4. Penman, S. H. (2013), Financial statement analysis and security valuation (5th ed.). New York: McGraw-Hill.

APPENDIX I: Financial Ratios of Constellations Brands Inc. and the Industry Ratios

Financial Ratios*	Diageo (Deo)				Brown-Forman (BF-B)			
YEARS	**2013**	**2012**	**2011**	**2010**	**2013**	**2012**	**2011**	**2010**
1. Short-Term Solvency								
Current Ratio	1.55	1.52	1.46	1.76	3.85	4.33	2.79	2.80
Quick Ratio	0.79	0.69	0.75	0.93	2.10	2.57	1.88	1.60
2. Long-Term Solvency Ratios								
Total Debt Ratio	0.72	0.75	0.73	0.79	0.55	0.40	0.45	0.44
Times Interest Earned	6.16	5.75	4.95	4.21	28.06	23.88	32.88	22.19
3. Efficiency Ratios (in days)								
Accounts Receivable Period	73.97	65.56	66.71	69.34	70.21	63.67	70.01	61.79
Inventory Period	344.75	338.95	316.12	292.16	337.65	280.04	273.96	276.94
Accounts Payable Period	89.74	92.39	89.75	75.07	54.30	47.20	53.35	41.26
Operating Cycle	418.72	404.51	382.83	361.50	407.85	343.71	343.97	338.73
Cash Cycle	328.98	312.12	293.08	286.44	353.55	296.52	290.62	297.47

Financial Ratio and Valuation Analyses of Constellation Brands Inc 267

APPENDIX I: (Continued)

Financial Ratios*	Diageo (Deo)				Brown-Forman (BF-B)			
YEARS	2013	2012	2011	2010	2013	2012	2011	2010
4. Profitability Ratios								
Gross Profit Margin	0.61	0.60	0.60	0.58	0.69	0.66	0.67	0.65
EBITDA Margin	0.34	0.33	0.30	0.30	0.33	0.31	0.35	0.31
Net Profit Margin	0.22	0.18	0.19	0.17	0.21	0.19	0.22	0.18
Return on Equity (ROE)	0.35	0.35	0.36	0.41	0.36	0.25	0.28	0.24
Return on Assets (ROA)	0.10	0.09	0.10	0.08	0.16	0.15	0.15	0.13
5. Market Value Ratios								
Earnings Per Share (EPS)	6.06	4.74	4.64	3.62	2.60	2.41	2.63	2.04
Book Value Per Share (BPS)	17.15	13.65	12.82	8.90	7.16	9.71	9.47	8.60
Sales Per Share (SPS)	27.87	26.29	24.29	21.73	12.53	12.78	11.89	11.20
P/E = Price/EPS	20.17	25.76	26.31	33.76	27.12	35.87	28.40	37.16
P/B = Price/BPS	7.12	8.95	9.53	13.72	9.84	8.89	7.89	8.80
P/S = Price/SPS	4.38	4.65	5.03	5.62	5.62	6.76	6.28	6.76

*Definition of Financial Ratios: Current Ratio = Current Assets/Current Liabilities, Quick Ratio = (Current Assets – Inventory)/Current Liabilities, Total Debt Ratio = Total Liabilities/Total Assets, Times Interest Earned = EBIT/Interest Expense, Accounts Receivable Period (also called Days in Account Receivables or Collection Period) = 365/(Revenues/Receivables), Inventory Period (Days in Inventories) = 365/(Costs of Goods Sold/Inventory), Accounts Payables Period (Days in Payables) = 365/(Costs of Good Sold/Accounts Payables), Operating Cycle = Inventory Periods + Accounts Receivables Period, Cash Cycle = Operating Cycle – Accounts Payable Period, Gross Profit Margin = Gross Profits/Revenues, Net Profit Margin = Net Income/Revenues, Return on Equity (ROE) = Net Income/Total Equity, Return on Assets (ROA) = Net Income/Total Assets, Earnings Per Share (EPS) = Net Income/Outstanding Shares, Book Value Per Share (BPS) = Total Equity/Outstanding Shares, Sales Per Share (SPS) = Revenues/Outstanding Shares, P/E = Price/EPS, P/B = Price/BPS, P/S = Price/SPS.

CHAPTER 15

THE RISE OF WINE EDUCATION IN MAINLAND CHINA: A FIRST-HAND ACCOUNT AND ANALYSIS

EDWARD RAGG

Co-founder, Dragon Phoenix Wine Consulting, Associate Professor, Department of Foreign Languages and Literatures, Tsinghua University, Beijing 100084, China

CONTENTS

15.1 Constellations Brands in the Wineries and Distillers Industry.. 270

15.2 The Dynamics of the Mainland Chinese Market: Imported vs. Domestic Wine... 270

15.3 Paths to Wine Education in Mainland China 277

15.4 Who Is Studying? Motivations for Wine Education (Trade and the New Consumers)................................. 282

15.5 Challenges Encountered in Wine Education............................ 283

15.6 Impacts on Wine Tourism 286

15.7 Conclusion: The Present and Future of Wine Education in Mainland China.. 287

Keywords 288

References... 288

15.1 INTRODUCTION

This chapter provides a first-hand and analytical account of the growth in wine education in Mainland China over the 2008–2013 period. It investigates the characteristics and dynamics of the overall mainland Chinese wine markets, contrasting imported and domestic sectors – including the latest and most reliable data concerning imports (for the January–September 2013 period).[1] It traces the origins and current performance of the imported sector – especially in light of President Xi Jinping's "anti-extravagance measures"– and compares this overall growth with the general rise in wine education in the Chinese mainland. The chapter explains how the demand for wine education has grown and how the UK's *Wine & Spirit Education Trust* (WSET) has dominated the education market, observing the latest WSET figures for the academic year 2012–2013 and comparing these with earlier data, not least with respect to uptake of the WSET's courses and examinations in Mandarin Chinese.

The chapter also explores the allied roles of wine trade body visits, the development of professional wine challenges (with international and local Chinese judges), the all-important influence of Chinese social media (especially the micro-blogging platform Weibo) and the development of the wine media in impacting on wine education and overall awareness of wine. Discussion is also given over to the demographics of who is studying wine, what the motivations for study are and what challenges arise in wine education and communicating about wine in Mainland China. Throughout, given the overall subject-matter of this book, attempts are made to suggest the impacts on winery tourism and strategies for marketing wine to mainland Chinese tourists/consumers that have arisen from the general rise in wine education and interest in "wine culture" in the PRC.

15.2 THE DYNAMICS OF THE MAINLAND CHINESE MARKET: IMPORTED VS. DOMESTIC WINE

In order to understand the contemporary challenges facing the wine business in Mainland China as well as the very real increase in wine education

---

[1]Data supplied to the author by the official body known in English as the China Association of Importers & Exporters of Wine & Spirits.

the country has witnessed especially during the last two years, it is important to appreciate the comparative youth of the imported wine market as well as the significant changes that have occurred in the overall 2008–2013 period, both within China and internationally. Clearly, reviewing such developments has a bearing also on the wider issue of international wine tourism, in the sense that increasingly knowledgeable mainland Chinese consumers are visiting international wine regions in increasing numbers, at least those regions better equipped to receive international guests: for example, the US West Coast, western Canada, South Africa, Australia and New Zealand, and certain parts of Europe, notwithstanding the cultural and linguistic challenges that present themselves for Chinese visitors encountering, in particular, certain Old World-producing countries (those where English, the preferred second language, and, obviously, Mandarin Chinese are seldom spoken).

The market for imported wine in Mainland China can trace its origins to the early-to-mid-1990s and the foundation of such import companies as Montrose Fine Wines, ASC Fine Wines and Aussino Fine Wines, not forgetting also the early (or earlier) involvement of French companies such as Pernod Ricard (see Pernod Ricard China) or the operations of the Chinese government itself with respect to imported wine (precisely when COFCO, the government's agricultural arm, began importing wine remains unclear). Certainly, in the early-to-mid-1990s, the diversity and volume of imported wine offerings in Mainland China were minuscule and much is owed, therefore, to Montrose, ASC, Aussino and also Torres China (the importation and distribution business created by the Torres dynasty in 1997) for the foundation of a viable market for imported wine. Clearly, taking the whole market into account at that point – i.e. to include domestically produced wines – the percentage contribution of imported wine was negligible.

By China's Olympic year in 2008, however, imports were said to account for 10% of the market by volume with the other 90% obviously being represented by domestic products; with a significant percentage of that latter market share accounted for by the three major Chinese domestic wine players: Great Wall (COFCO), Changyu and Dynasty. Though the market share of imported wines was small, it garnered considerable value relative to its size; and imported wines also, unsurprisingly, captured much of the burgeoning on-trade by value. Admittedly, the on-trade was, and still is, skewed in Mainland China by the fact that most Chinese restaurants do not operate wine lists to international standards and their sale of wine relative to beer and the domestic white spirit (*baijiu*) is comparatively small – such that restaurants serving "Western food" understandably are biased towards imported wine. Thus, some caution needs to be exercised in distinguishing between "the Chinese on-trade" – i.e., restaurants serving Chinese cuisines predominantly owned and run by Chinese nationals – and the "on-trade in China," which may include a wide variety of international cuisines and may employ foreign nationals (these latter establishments often handling imported wine and/or other imported alcoholic drinks).

The current share of the market for wine imports is now estimated to be closer to 15–17% relative to domestic wine and the picture in the on-trade has changed slightly also in that high-end Chinese restaurants – such as the Da Dong Roast Duck chain in Beijing – do operate increasingly diverse wine lists to approximately international standards. The off-trade, by contrast, has seen domination in volume by domestic players such as the aforementioned Great Wall, Changyu and Dynasty (alongside some cheaper imports). Purchase of imported wines in specialist retail outfits is, however, generally speaking, quite limited and relatively uncommon in Mainland China. Plenty of chains of "wine shops" abound in 1st, 2nd and even 3rd-tier cities, but these are often fronts for distribution businesses (or sometimes individual wineries) with little actual retail of wine occurring, whether domestic or imported. Indeed, much of China's "off-trade" is not conducted through store-front or supermarket purchases but through face-to-face sales meetings or phone or Internet orders (this latter form having a degree of impersonality that suits some Chinese consumers, especially those whose knowledge of wine may be limited, which is, potentially, socially embarrassing and might result in "loss of face," culturally speaking).

With the understandable buzz – and hype – created by the 2008 Beijing Olympics, much was written at that time, especially in the international wine press, as to the growth potential and actual percentage growth of the imported wine market in China (a practice that continues, to some extent, at the time of writing). Although accurate statistics are notoriously hard to acquire with respect to Mainland China, the growth in the market since the heyday of the Olympics provided many international

The Rise of Wine Education in Mainland China: A First-hand Account

wine producers with the hope that the PRC might shortly become an oasis for selling imported wine. However, the figures in volume terms underscore how comparatively small the Mainland Chinese market is, despite its initially rapid rise. Of the 16 million 9 liter-cases imported in 2010, around 26 million 9 liter-cases passed through China Customs in 2011. Although this represented an encouraging percentage increase, it must be borne in mind that this still made Mainland China a fairly small market for imported wine compared with mature, significantly more developed markets such as those of Germany, the UK or US (Germany being the top importer globally in 2012 with around 160 million cases, the UK being the largest importer by value of EU wines and the second largest importer globally in 2012 with around 148 million cases; and the US being the largest importer by volume of EU wines, the third largest importer globally in 2012 and the largest consumer overall).[2]

Nor was the Olympics, in fact, the game-changer that some outside of China were led to believe. Many importers experienced having shipments delayed in Customs, not least because 2008 also saw a Chinese government inquiry into alleged under-declaration of value on wines coming into China (with several leading importers being investigated at that time). With slower processing of visas for international visitors occurring in the last few months before the Olympics, the Chinese hotel business also encountered less occupancy than expected during the 2008 Games, resulting in fewer on-trade sales in 5-star and other hotels. In other words, unsold inventory was building up in China in the summer of 2008; and, though institutions and importers began to run through the back-log in the two year period after the Olympics – thereby creating the demand for new orders which helped assist the percentage growth of the market in 2010–2011 – only the more established importers could cope flexibly with this changing environment. This would represent important preparation for the next period of over-supply (in 2012) when, again, the more experienced operators adapted to a more saturated environment in terms of stock build-up compared with those trading companies, inexperienced with wine, who entered the market caught up in the buzz of China's "potential" in precisely that 2010–2011 period of "heady" growth.

---

[2]Cf. Morgan Stanley Research *Global Wine Industry* report (22nd October 2013) and USDA Foreign Agricultural Service *Wine Annual Report and Statistics* (25th February 2013), this latter for the EU-27 countries.

274 Strategic Winery Tourism and Management

But what of 2012 going into 2013? As far as is known, Mainland China only imported approximately 29 million 9 liter-cases in 2012, a mere 3 million more cases than in 2011. This decidedly modest growth was mostly attributable to the large quantities of unsold sock that had accrued in China in 2011. But the problem was exacerbated by the new regime instituted in the wake of President Xi Jinping's arrival in office. President Xi's initiative to rein in official spending on entertaining – and scrutinize the overall spending of officials in a bid to tackle extravagance and corruption, not least in the area of banqueting – put paid to many wine-distributing and wine-importing businesses' growths, especially those mostly dependent on courting government patronage and, in particular, those with pre-existing commercial relationships with government. Importers and distributors alike all recorded decreases in sales relative to previous years in the all-important gift-giving periods of Mid-Autumn Festival and Chinese New Year (which themselves account for much of the overall wine business conducted in China annually). Thus, 2012's Mid-Autumn Festival and the 2013 Chinese New Year saw significant shrinkage which has extended into 2013: Pernod Ricard, for example, recently announced that its sales had fallen by 1% to €2.013 billion ($2.776 billion USD) for the July-Sept 2013 period, noting a double-digits shipment decline to China and attributing this shrinkage precisely to the "anti-extravagance measures" initiated in Mainland China in 2013 and late 2012.[3]

Indeed, it is hard to overemphasize just how significant this change in consumption behavior – instituted at the highest government level – has been. Businesses which had flourished in selling super-premium wines, such as Bordeaux's Grands Crus Classés, to the Chinese political elite have had little room to manoeuvre in such an environment without wider portfolios and offerings at a wider and more competitive range of prices. Of course, gifting and consumption must be carefully differentiated: in that, wine may be gifted one or several times without in actual fact being consumed. But conspicuous consumption among China's officials, not least following a spate of social media-disseminated scandals (made possible by the likes of social media platforms such as Weibo), has been, at least publicly, curtailed: certainly, in the sense that overt consumption of

---

[3]"Pernod's Sales Decline By 1% In Q1, As Chinese Clampdown Hits Bottom Line" *Shanken News Daily* (24th October 2013).

The Rise of Wine Education in Mainland China: A First-hand Account   275

an important segment of fine wine (predominantly high-end Bordeaux) has diminished.

When one looks at the first nine months of 2013, the latest imports data are especially revealing. The total wine imports, including in bottle and bulk, amounted to 290,000 hl (29 million liters) at a value of 1.159 billion USD, representing an increase in value of only 1.62% compared with the equivalent period for 2012. Of those 290,000 hl (29 million liters), 216,800 hl (21.68 million liters) were bottled imports, to the value of 1.07 billion USD. This represented an increase of 9.39% in volume and 4.87% in value, making abundantly clear that bottled imports have recently been on the rise both by volume and value. More striking still is the decline in bulk imports: only 73,000 hl (7.3 million liters) of bulk wine passed Chinese Customs in Jan-Sept 2013, a decrease of 29.93% from the previous year, worth 90.48 million USD (a decrease in value of 25.6%). In terms of country-of-origin, the top twelve exporters to China remained unchanged, however, accounting for 97.79% of the value of the import market (but the speed of their growths is decreasing). Indeed, France and New Zealand actually experienced negative growth. In the case of France, the import market leader, China imported 101,900 hl (10.19 million liters) of French wine representing 6.43% growth in volume, worth 512 million USD; but this was a 7.64% decrease in value. France's market share of bottled imports has decreased to 47.9%. The average growth of the top 12 exporting countries is 4.87% and the average price of bottled wine imported has decreased to 4.93 USD per liter (a decrease of 4.0% in value from the previous year). Finally, it is noteworthy, that, looking at the segmentation of importers, some 7 companies imported over 10 million USD worth of wine between them, with a further 13 companies accounting for imports at the value range of 5–10 million USD.[4]

What does this suggest? The decline in bulk imports is attributable to a wide range of factors, including the strength of the RMB, a shorter supply of bulk wine coming out of Europe, increasing volumes of domestically produced wine and perhaps increased demand for better quality wine in bottle (as suggested by the rise in volume and value of bottled imports). The real importing muscle in terms of value is flexed by around 20 companies;

---

[4]All data released by the China Association of Importers & Exporters of Wine & Spirits (7th November 2013).

which underscores the fact that the number of serious wine importers in China is relatively small. When one reviews the 2008–2013 period, it becomes quickly apparent that, despite its advances in importation in 2010–2011, China was not especially well-equipped to deal with the over-exaggerated hopes for heady growth in the import sector much touted in the international wine press. Of course, international wineries can be forgiven for supposing Mainland China really was on a significant rise during 2010–2011 because of the orders importers and trading companies with import licenses were placing during the period (in the case of the latter, such companies subsequently found that they could not rely on their personal connections to sell as much wine as they had anticipated and that they also lacked experience and education in the handling of wine).

The 2012–2013 period thus shows rationalization and consolidation with the more professional importers reviewing their portfolios carefully and attempting to deplete current stock accordingly. Portfolio balancing should not be an especial challenge with respect to country selection, however; because the market shares by country-of-origin have not shifted much over the last five years. As mentioned, France still accounts for around 47% of the imported sector, followed by Australia (around 20%) with Spain, Chile, Italy and US representing 6–8% shares. Compared with the early 1990s, however, although ASC, Aussino, Torres China, Pernod Ricard China and Summergate are still significant forces in the import market, they have been joined by similarly professional outfits like East Meets West, The Wine Republic, China Wine & Spirits and smaller specialist operations such as Ruby Red, Globus, Altavis and others. The larger players are now also competing with Chinese drinks companies who likewise began expanding into wine importation in the 2010–2011 spike, such as VATS and C&D (these, along with COFCO, having considerable distribution muscle and very strong local connections nationally). As competition in the imported market has moved increasingly out of the more saturated 1st-tier city environments of Shanghai, Beijing, Guangzhou and Shenzhen, the battle for competitive ground and market development for imported wine is now fought predominantly in 2nd tier cities (among them provincial capitals) and even in some 3rd tier cities in the hope of attracting new consumers with some degree of disposable income. Here there is reason to be optimistic that growth will continue; as consumption of wine, though small by per capita compared with other countries – around

The Rise of Wine Education in Mainland China: A First-hand Account 277

1.6 liters per head in Mainland China (compare 25.9 liters per head in the UK) – is undeniably on the rise in China.[5]

One area of activity that has neither contracted nor seen slower than expected growth, however, is wine education; and the thirst for such education, generally speaking, goes hand-in-hand with precisely that increase in consumption, certainly where imported wine in bottle is expanding. Indeed, the demand for wine education – though this was palpable before the 2008 Olympics – has risen significantly in the last five years and especially in the last two-three year period. The China trade, as it has become more professionalized, and as it has realized the necessity of understanding one's products and empowering those selling them by sponsoring wine education for employees (not that this is, unfortunately, universal by any means), has undoubtedly embraced education. This has coincided with a significant rise in consumer education as China develops a new generation of wine lovers, many of whom have had opportunities to travel and/or study abroad in wine-making countries – in Europe, Australasia and the Americas – and who aspire either to become more regular and more informed consumers of wine or at least desire contact with an idea of a sophisticated and healthier lifestyle associated with wine consumption (this latter aspirational element is encountered most clearly on social media platforms such as Weibo and Renren).

But what paths are open to those seeking wine education and what are their motivations for doing so?

15.3 PATHS TO WINE EDUCATION IN MAINLAND CHINA

15.3.1 THE RISE OF THE WSET, SOCIAL AND PRINT MEDIA, WINE CHALLENGES AND TRADE BODY INVOLVEMENT

The most recognized provider of formal wine education in Mainland China is the UK-based *Wine & Spirit Education Trust* (WSET). The impetus for the adoption of the WSET as the most desirable organization with which to study for certification in wine in China clearly derives from the position the organization holds internationally in terms of its recognition

---

[5]Cf. aforementioned Morgan Stanley Research *Global Wine Industry* report and *WSTA UK Wine and Spirits: Market Overview 2013* (September 2013).

as an industry-standard and global provider of formal wine education. Other wine education bodies, whether geared towards consumers or trade or both, such as the Society of Wine Educators (SWE), International Sommelier Guild (ISG) and Court of Master Sommeliers (CMS) have not, by contrast, gained the traction in Mainland China which the WSET has enjoyed in recent years; again, because, rightly or wrongly, the latter organizations are not viewed as offering as international in scope a programme – or as internationally recognized and tiered an approach to wine education – as the WSET. It is important to stress also the Chinese reverence for international certification especially in the period since Deng Xiaoping's reforms, which clearly initiated China's economic and social opening up to the outside world. Under such conditions, the kudos of an internationally recognized qualification in wine is clearly of social, cultural and often professional significance.

The WSET has consolidated its position in recent years also by the translation into Mandarin of its Level 1 Awards in Wine, Spirits and Wine Service as well as the Level 2 Award in Wines & Spirits, both in terms of study materials and also exam offerings; with WSET Level 3 – both the Advanced Certificate and International Higher Certificate (IHC) options for this level – also undergoing translation at the time of writing (with prospected availability in 2014). This has had a significant impact on the Trust's penetration of the Mainland Chinese market. In the 2010–2011 academic year, some 655 candidates took examinations in Mandarin Chinese relative to 902 candidates taking equivalent WSET qualifications in English in the Chinese mainland. However, by 2011–2012, 1,727 candidates took exams in Mandarin Chinese relative to 1,462 candidates selecting to take their exams in English in China. The latest figures for the academic year 2012–2013 paint an even greater increase in uptake of WSET qualifications in Mandarin Chinese with 3,048 candidates being examined in Mandarin relative to only 1,602 opting to take their exams in English in the Chinese mainland.

To take the examining of WSET Level 2 in China as an illustration: in the 2010–2011 academic year, when the Mandarin course and exam were first introduced, only 71 candidates took their Level 2 qualification in their native language. However, for 2011–2012, the figure increased to 628 candidates; and the latest figures for 2012–2013 indicate that some 1,579 individuals took their Level 2 examinations in Mandarin Chinese.

To put the overall figures for Mandarin Chinese uptake of WSET qualifications in context, in the academic year 2012–2013 some 48,434 candidates took WSET qualifications globally. Of these, 12,577 candidates took WSET exams in languages other than English (in 17 different languages). Of those being examined in languages other than English, Mainland China accounted for 4,850 of the global candidates examined. During the same period, examinations were conducted by 117 WSET Approved Programme Providers (APPs) internationally. It is notable that 41 of those APPs are based in Mainland China, where there is a considerable rise not only in students studying for WSET qualifications but in wine trainers preparing to become WSET Certified Educators, often with a view to establishing their own APPs.[6]

The latter version of WSET Level 3, the International Higher Certificate, is also potentially an important offering for Mainland China in that it is open to students whose first language is not English and does not involve the written component of the Advanced Certificate. Although the WSET has occasionally faced a challenge in convincing Chinese candidates that the IHC option is the same level of difficulty, at least with respect to wine knowledge, as the Advanced Certificate, this feature has also given the Trust flexibility in attracting new candidates for its Level 3 qualification in a country where clearly English is not the mother-tongue and where there is more stigma attached to failure than in some "Western" countries (thus making the IHC, theoretically at least, an attractive option). That said, if IHC candidates wish to study for the Trust's flagship trade qualification, the Level 4 Diploma, then they must currently sit a Diploma Entry exam which tests their English language capabilities and powers of analysis in order to be prepared to sit the WSET Level 4 Award in Wines & Spirits (which is not currently available in Mandarin Chinese, but will doubtless be translated in time).

It is, therefore, hard to over-emphasize the very real and rapid pace with which some students have progressed through the WSET's levels of study (as represented by the latest figures detailed above). Though

---

[6]All data from *The Wine & Spirit Education Trust*. The WSET does distinguish carefully between Mainland China – as per the figures above – and 'Greater China' (including Mainland China, Hong Kong, Macau and Taiwan). It is notable that the 2012–2013 figures for 'Greater China' place the region at around 11,000 candidates, not far behind the UK which saw a little over 12,000 students study for WSET qualifications during the same period.

these students may lack regular tasting experience, they have grown up in a culture, which venerates study and academic success. The pace in accumulation of WSET qualifications (Level 1–3) has, more recently, stimulated early demand for the WSET Level 4 Diploma. The first WSET Level 4 Diploma courses to be offered in China (in 2012) were run by the wholly independent Dragon Phoenix Wine Consulting, based in Beijing – of which the present author was co-founder – and ASC Fine Wines (which was the first WSET programme provider in China), both in conjunction with the WSET's London school. These programmes registered Chinese students with WSET London as distance learners – with an online support component – but enabled candidates to take their examinations in Mainland China. In 2014, Dragon Phoenix will also be the first WSET provider in Mainland China to provide an entirely taught WSET Level 4 Diploma course.

This is significant in a number of respects. That some students, effectively only 6 years after the WSET became active in China, were willing to take on what is at least a two-year commitment of study with examination in English attests to the very real desire for specialist wine education (among largely trade individuals, admittedly). There are now also some six candidates for the Master of Wine based in Mainland China, four of these Chinese nationals, with Fongyee Walker of Dragon Phoenix having passed her Master of Wine Theory and Tasting exams, making her Mainland China's most qualified wine educator. These are all graduates of the WSET Diploma, a number of them also WSET Certified Educators; and their enrolment on the Master of Wine programme has also indirectly raised the profile of the WSET in the mainland. Again, such a rapid pace of change, as with so many other aspects of life in contemporary China, is truly staggering.

It is important to distinguish, however, between general wine education and the taking of courses such as those offered by the WSET and some other organizations. General wine education can encompass overall "wine information," notwithstanding the problems with misinformation that may arise from poor translation, poor understanding and unadulterated misinformation itself. Chinese social media are having a massive influence on communication concerning wine, with Weibo and Renren both playing their parts (especially Weibo) and apps such as Weixin

(WeChat) supplementing the forms of communication favored in micro-blogs or via influential Chinese websites relating to wine. It is not uncommon, for example, for wine students to form Weixin groups to discuss ideas and tasting opportunities. Where prominent "key influencers" are also invited on regional tours of wine producing countries, they often disseminate information via Weibo as to their experiences: posts which may be followed by hundreds of thousands of fans, making such individuals prominent, if exclusive, "wine tourists" in their own rights.

The wine print media has also become much more significant since 2008 with *Wine in China Magazine, Food & Wine Magazine China, Wine Press* and the *La Revue du Vin de la France* (the Chinese edition of the French RVF) all testing the water for professional wine journalism – these publications also capitalizing on the roles social media and the Internet play in creating awareness of their activities, authors and publications. Added to this, are the contributions that come from visiting wine trade bodies and the rise of some influential wine challenges, not least where such organizations make a point of offering education to consumers and/or the trade. The most prominent wine challenges in the mainland to date have been the *Shanghai International Wine Challenge,* the *Yantai International Wine Challenge,* the *China Wine Challenge* – promoted by *The Hurun Report* of China's wealthiest – and *Wine 100. Wine 100* has been especially effective in stimulating wine education for consumers and trade alike by attracting international judges who are often Masters of Wine (most notably, Andrew Caillard MW, Lisa Perotti-Brown MW, Jane Skilton MW and Ned Goodwin MW) who give master classes attached to the show, combined with consumer tastings based on the results of the judging. The penetration by this particular wine show of Chinese social media is also striking.

The most active trade bodies and organizations representing either national entities or smaller wine-producing regions have included: Sopexa and UbiFrance (representing France in general), the Bordeaux Wine School, the Union des Grands Crus of Bordeaux, the China Burgundy Wine Tour (BIVB-backed), Wines of Spain – including Wines of Rioja – Wine Australia (especially its A+ Marketing and Wine School initiatives), New Zealand Winegrowers, the Napa Valley Vintners, the California Wine Institute, the Vintage Port Academy, Vini Portugal and Wines of South

Africa, among other organizations. Such trade body visits have become gradually more "specialist" on a country-by-country and/or region-by-region basis: for example, in addition to Wine Australia's activities, the Australian First Families of Wine as well as the Victorian state government and even the Australian Wine Research Institute (AWRI) have all given specialist seminars in China's leading "wine hubs" in 2013.

Clearly, education and the promotion of regions go hand-in-hand here, which also spills over into wine tourism. For example, New Zealand Winegrowers and New Zealand Trade & Enterprise offered a Weibo competition in 2012, in conjunction with Air New Zealand, which asked Chinese competitors to describe an experience with New Zealand wine, with the winners then receiving airline tickets to visit New Zealand. An illustration of the thirst for wine education, especially with regard to a famous region of production, was also clear in 2013 when the Napa Valley Vintners (NVV) conducted a regional tour of 4 Chinese cities, offering over 20 different events in a mere 9–10 days (Dragon Phoenix was at that time contractor to the Napa Valley Vintners and instrumental in arranging this wine tour). During that trip, the Napa Valley Vintners Mandarin Chinese website actually crashed because of the sheer numbers of mainland Chinese users attempting to download the NVV's Mandarin version of its "Napa Rocks" educational presentation: proof, if any were needed, that there was genuine interest in learning more about – or at least acquiring further information on – the Napa Valley and its wines.

15.4 WHO IS STUDYING? MOTIVATIONS FOR WINE EDUCATION (TRADE AND THE NEW CONSUMERS)

Based on our experience of operating a WSET APP since 2008 and also on our involvement in organizing seminars and trade events for a wide range of international wine trade bodies, it is clear that 25–40 year-old, male and, more often than not, female Chinese nationals are most likely to study wine formally, compared with other groups. This relatively young demographic spans not only the 1st-tier cities of Beijing, Shanghai, Guangzhou and Shenzhen, but attracts individuals from 2nd-tier cities – from Shijiazhuang to Zhengzhou to Xian to Chengdu – and further afield.

The Rise of Wine Education in Mainland China: A First-hand Account

It is important to appreciate that this group comprises both those working in the trade and a large body of private consumers, some of whom will also be able to travel internationally and visit wine-producing regions (and have already been doing so, especially over the last 2–3 years as they have embraced and have begun learning about wine). In a Dragon Phoenix survey of recent WSET students (2012–2013), it was revealed that most students had studied for the WSET Level 2 qualification and that, among all students polled, the overriding motivations for study were "personal interest" and also "career development" under the initiative of the students themselves (rather than by being sponsored by their employers, in the case of Chinese trade). This demonstrates that there is a considerable personal impetus among younger Chinese consumers who have disposable income – and can, therefore, afford to study for a WSET qualification – to learn about wine and that this personal drive also accords with a wider desire to enhance professional standing (either in Chinese or international contexts) through the acquisition of wine knowledge. As we shall see, this has a knock-on effect for the levels of wine education among Chinese wine tourists visiting international regions of production.

As to the Chinese wine trade, it is also clear that acquisition of WSET qualifications has become an industry standard; especially in the absence of any commensurate Chinese qualification for wine professionalism recognized by the Chinese state or some other official body. In the case of Dragon Phoenix, the majority of WSET students are drawn from the China trade, incorporating students from the food-and-beverage sector, wine media and the importation and distribution sides of the business. The majority of these students also fall within the 25–40 year-old sector with an increasing representation of female students.

15.5 CHALLENGES ENCOUNTERED IN WINE EDUCATION

It is often suggested that it is hard to bring some aspects of "international wine education" to a culture such as that of Mainland China in which wine is a fairly unusual and far from everyday product for most people. Wine is, however, not entirely alien to Chinese minds as references to grape wine can be found in poetry going back to the Tang Dynasty. True enough, the expansion of China's vineyards only really occurred in the 1980s; and the real influence of the aforementioned "big three" domestic producers (Changyu, Great Wall and Dynasty) stems from this relatively recent period. When one considers that a basic bottle of Chinese wine is still 5–6 times the price of an acceptable quality Chinese beer, then it is not surprising that wine remains relatively unknown to most Chinese consumers (basic Beijing beer is 4–6RMB for a 600 ml bottle compared with basic Chinese wine coming in around 25–35RMB per 750 ml bottle).

Certainly, linguistic habits can also mask the basic reality of even elementary factors such as the colors of wine. In Mainland China, wine is casually referred to as *hong jiu* (red alcohol). So there is an expectation that wine is red rather than being any other kind of color. Because the standard "white alcohol" or *bai jiu* is a heady spirit of around 50–60% abv., this also masks somewhat the existence of white wine (and pink or rosé wines are even less recognized by most consumers). However, these are hardly insurmountable problems when wine is referred to in Mandarin correctly by substituting the term *putao* (grape): *hong putao jiu* (red grape alcohol), *bai putao jiu* (white grape alcohol) and *taohong putao jiu* (pink grape alcohol). Education itself plays a corrective role in this respect, especially when fermentation to produce wine rather than distillation is explained.

The international wine press occasionally queries whether Chinese or other Asian consumers can readily pick up also, in a tasting context, on fruits used to describe wine aromas and flavors in international terms. For example, it is sometimes suggested that because blackberries and blackcurrants are uncommon in China, that it may be hard for Chinese consumers to understand what more international wine tasters mean when they describe such fruits with reference to grapes like Cabernet Sauvignon or Cabernet Franc. This, however, is something of a myth or at least a far from insurmountable "problem." China does have mulberries as a point of reference – and "Western" and other international fruits are available in high-end supermarkets in at least 1st-tier cities. Moreover, in our experience as educators, it is common for Chinese tasters to learn both a so-called "international vocabulary" for describing wine – in part promulgated by the WSET – along with reference to their own more immediate, cultural products, drawn from China's diverse food cultures. It might be added that the notion of an "international vocabulary" for describing wine is itself somewhat spurious; or at least, that in many cultural contexts, tasters adjust to and calibrate their palates all the time with respect to different ways of describing wine aromas, flavors and textures. Certainly, Chinese students of wine are quite adept at adopting unfamiliar terms – provided they are taught correctly – and combining these with descriptors in Mandarin Chinese, which are numerous and highly relevant to describing wine.

There are, though, undeniable challenges, which do arise from problems in translation. Two examples will suffice: one is the translation of the rather ambiguous English word "spicy." This is often taken to indicate "chili-hot" by Chinese readers of English – rather than conveying a general term that could incorporate spices that are traceable, for example, to the use of new oak in winemaking (such as the detection of clove or vanilla as aromas/flavors during tasting). This has led to some confusion where wine labels are translated into Mandarin indicating a wine either smells like chilies or will have a similar reaction to capsaicin on the palate. Another victim of translation, for more understandable reasons, is the use of the English word "cream" for the admittedly small category of Cream Sherry in Mainland China. Where this is translated literally – rather than as a descriptor for style/sweetness level – this had led to the understandable misunderstanding that such a fortified wine has had cream added to it at some point in its production.

Though there are other challenges, again often of a linguistic nature – for example, translations of grape varieties and wine regions are not standardized in Mandarin Chinese – it has to be said that Chinese tasters are relatively easy to coach and are very quick to respond to the sensations of wine. In other words, they are especially sensitive to the mouth-feel of wines and are able to distinguish relatively easily between different levels of sweetness, acidity, alcohol, tannin and bitterness, with some practice and exposure. The term "mouth-feel" – more usually used by English speakers involved in some way with either the food-and-beverage industry or wine and food production – is also an everyday word or expression in Mandarin (*kou gan*). Thus, there are aspects of the Chinese language that may aid rather than hinder uptake of and understanding of wine.

15.6 IMPACTS ON WINE TOURISM

As should be clear from the preceding discussion, there are some obvious impacts on wine tourism that arise from the overall increase in wine education among certain groups in Mainland China (I refer to an international context because winery tourism within Mainland China itself is limited and rarely akin to what can be experienced internationally). Where Chinese individuals are wealthy enough to travel outside of China and can acquire the visas to do so – and, especially, where such individuals have a pre-existing interest in wine – then it is clear that international wineries will experience increased visits from mainland Chinese wine tourists both currently and, foreseeably, in the future. Indeed, the period analyzed in this chapter (2008–2013) has already seen a significant number of Chinese visitors on the increase in wine regions internationally, especially those regions close to major cities. Thus, in the case of Australia, Chinese visitors to wineries are on the increase in regions like the Hunter Valley, the Yarra Valley and the Barossa Valley or McLaren Vale because of these regions' proximities to, respectively, Sydney, Melbourne and Adelaide. Likewise, the Napa Valley benefits here from its prestige and relative proximity to San Francisco. Even British Columbia's Okanagan Valley – some four hours' drive from Vancouver – has noticed an increased influx of mainland Chinese visitors in recent years, spurred by the development of Vancouver's sizeable and influential "Chinese community" (which incorporates not only those of the Cantonese diaspora, but increasing numbers of Mandarin-speaking mainland Chinese).

Some wineries have already adjusted to these new mainland Chinese wine tourists by having Mandarin language materials available for visitors and even Mandarin-speaking staff on hand in cellar door facilities and/ or wineries with restaurants. Famous Old World-producing countries like France, Italy and Spain have been typically less well-equipped to accommodate such visitors as, apart from some notable exceptions, many of its regions are less well culturally adapted to receiving wine tourists. Having said that, there is a cultural love affair of sorts between France and China, with a number of young Chinese having studied wine in French regions (most notably Bordeaux, Burgundy and the Rhône). China's increasing trade with some European Union partners has meant that those involved in

The Rise of Wine Education in Mainland China: A First-hand Account   287

business in Europe also often become "wine tourists" of sorts as they pick up on local customs and often may even subsequently import gastronomic products, including wine, into China on the back of personal interest or other trade connections.

One immediate consequence of the rise of Chinese social media has been the extent to which more savvy international wineries have also sought a presence on Weibo in particular. Indeed, there are several companies now operating in China that offer services to international wineries enabling these producers to have a presence on Weibo that is updated regularly and designed to stimulate interest among Chinese consumers. This can assist wineries who expect visits from Chinese tourists, whether or not they actually have a distribution presence in Mainland China.

15.7 CONCLUSION: THE PRESENT AND FUTURE OF WINE EDUCATION IN MAINLAND CHINA

As is clear from the picture painted above of the development of the Chinese wine markets over the 2008–2013 period, it seems likely that wine education will conceivably continue to rise in Mainland China as both trade and consumers alike desire to learn more about this manifold subject. Provided the imported wine sector is not reduced or limited perhaps by protectionist measures on the part of the Chinese government, then it is plausible that wine education will focus predominantly on international wines rather than Chinese products (notwithstanding the growing interest both within China and internationally as to the development of some Chinese wine regions in the province of Ningxia and elsewhere). Because both trade and consumers alike require and desire wine education at a variety of levels, it seems likely that the WSET will continue to be dominant as the major provider of wine education in the PRC (barring any mishaps in branding or challenges relating to reputation and quality control). With increasing numbers of mainland Chinese individuals being able to travel and study internationally, it is clear that winery tourism will have to engage with the growing numbers of mainland Chinese visitors keen to visit a wide range of regions of production. It is expected that Chinese social media will also continue to play a powerful role in the dissemination of imagery, discussion and experiences relating to wine in all its facets or production, marketing and consumption. If the imported wine sector can grow sustainably, however modest its current growth, then it is anticipated that trade body and producer visits to China will also supplement overall wine education and experiences with wine in this challenging, but profoundly inspiring market.

KEYWORDS

- **anti-extravagance measures**
- **challenges**
- **impacts on wine tourism**
- **motivations**
- **wine culture**
- **wine education**

APPENDIX

FIGURE A1

FIGURE A2

FIGURE A3

INDEX

A

Added value strategies, 59
Affective tourist reaction, 172, 174–178
Anti-extravagance measures, 274, 288
Artificial neural networks (ANNs), 167–170, 182, 183
    model building, 170
Australia's Barossa Valley, 4, 90
Australian Wine Research Institute, 282
Autumn Creek Vineyards, 78
AVA regional appellation, 76
Awards, excellence, 116
    Best of Wine Tourism Awards of Excellence, 116
    Decanter Award, 122

B

Baden, 19, 21, 38
Baden Wuerttemberg, 19, 21
Bai jiu, 128, 130, 284
Bai putao jiu, 284
Baijiu, 272
Balanced scorecard methodology, 5
Bandwaggoning effect, 55
Bavaria, 38
Berlin, 38
Besenwirtschaft, 37
Beychevelle, 96
Biltmore Estates, 79
    Biltmore House, 79
Bordeaux, 37, 69, 89–95, 97, 99–103, 105–113, 116, 122, 136, 137, 139, 164, 274, 275, 281, 286
Bordeaux City Hall, 96
Bordeaux wines, 93, 95, 102, 111, 113
Bordeaux's traditions, 93, 113
Broaden horizon, 175, 176, 178–181

Brown-Forman, 249, 253, 257, 258, 265–267
Burgundian varietals, 4
Burgundy, 37, 72, 93, 136, 281, 286
Business model, 5, 6, 7, 34, 75, 91, 162, 200
Business and growth of, wine industry, 1, 2
    see, wine industry
    see, wine making tradition

C

Cabernet Franc, 137, 284
Cabernet Sauvignon, 137, 284
Campaigns, 10, 13, 15–17, 45, 94
    wine tourism, 10
Casual visitors, 158, 159
Cellar door, 72, 87, 91, 122, 208, 214, 215, 231, 232, 236, 238, 242, 244, 286
    sales, 153
Challenges, 10, 17, 18, 24, 34, 48, 50, 55, 90, 112, 124, 146, 153, 191, 193, 194, 196, 200, 210, 215, 222, 270, 271, 281, 285, 287, 288
Challenges in wine education, 283
Champions, 19, 20, 23, 25
Changyu, 129, 132, 133–137, 271, 272, 284
    Changyu Wine Company, 135, 136
Characteristics of, German wine production and supply, 35
Chardonnay, 5, 6, 135, 137, 162, 163
Chateau Changyu Custer, 135
Chateau Helan Winery, 122
Chateau Junding, 136
Chateau Yuanshi, 138
Châteaux, 90, 92–97, 101, 110, 111
Chenin Blanc, 137
Child orientation, 174

Childress, 79, 87
Chinese alcohol beverages, 127, 142
Chinese domestic wine brands, 132
  Changyu, 132
  Dynasty, 132
  Great Wall, 132
  Weilong, 132
Chinese domestic wine production
  growth, 132
Chinese rice wine, 128
Chinese vineyards, 121
Chinese wine industry, 127, 142
Chinese winery tourism, 128, 142
CIRET database, 116, 125
Cluster theory, 42, 45, 47
Clusters and identity formation, 71
COFOC's Great Wall Wine Company,
  137
Collective reputation, 43
Commitment, 73, 74, 80, 103, 208, 220,
  226–230, 280
Constellation, 247–251, 253–257, 259,
  261, 263–265
  brands, 247, 248, 265, 252, 263–266
    Constellation Wines Australia,
    248
    Constellation Wines New
    Zealand, 250
    Constellation Wines North
    America, 248
    Crown Imports, 250
Constellation's common stock, 248, 250,
  256, 264
Constellation's financial ratios, 248
Continuous quality improvement, 205,
  219, 223, 232
Cultural sustainability, 25
Customer equity, 145, 154
Customer lifetime value, 143–150,
  152–154
  benefits, 148
  concept, 144
  estimations, 144
  long-term customer relationship, 152
  see, marketing

short-term customer relationship, 149
  techniques and practice, 146
Customer loyalty, 37, 92, 145, 153, 154,
  158–160, 165, 188, 227, 228–230, 243
  barrel tastings, 160
  behind-the-scenes visits, 160
  casual visitors, 159
  educational experiences, 160
  marketing events, 160
  wine clubs, 160
  wine collectors, 159
  wine country aficionados plan, 159
  wine library, 159
  winery tourists, 159
Customer relationship management, 115,
  117–119, 121, 201
Customer tacking system, 6
Cuvaison estate wines, 161, 162, 165

D

Data mining techniques, 169, 183
Daycations, 212
Deliberate (planned) strategy, 21
Deliberate and emergent concept, 10, 13
Deliberate and emergent strategic processes, 13, 15
Deliberate strategy, 10, 13–15, 18, 19,
  26, 27
Deliberate/emergent equation, 27
Destination-marketing organizations,
  120
Diageo, 247–249, 251, 253–255, 257,
  258, 266
Diageo plc, 251, 265
Direct customers, 39, 45, 62
Direct-to-consumer, 5–7, 122, 158, 162,
  165, 187, 195, 199
  customer tacking system, 6
  direct to consumer model, 7
  lower prices, 6
  sales incentives, 6
  sales, 122, 162, 165, 187
  see, chardonnay
  see, pinot noir
  stock keeping units, 6

Index 293

Disconfirmation paradigm, 224, 225
Discount customers, 39, 62
Dividend growth model, 248, 257, 258,
 264, 265
Double-edge sword, 111
Dragon Phoenix, 269, 280, 282, 283
Duplin, 79
Dynamics of, Mainland Chinese market,
 270

E

Earnings model, 116, 207, 248, 257,
 262, 263, 264, 265
Eastern Helan, 137
Eco-tourism, 121
Efficiency ratios, 265
Elkin Creek Vineyard, 77
Emergent approaches, 14, 19, 25
Emergent strategy, 10, 14, 21, 24–26
Emerging issues, 115, 116, 117–123,
 125
 advanced measurement tools, 123
 changing consumer motivations and
 CRM, 118, 119
 environmental impact, 117, 118
 GPS/mobile technology, 117, 120
 increased saturation and competition,
 122, 123
 innovative partnerships, 120, 121
 rise of, Asian wine tourism, 121, 122
 social media growth, 117, 119
Emotional attachment, 168–170, 173,
 175–180
Environmental impact, 117, 125
Explorative clusters, 57

F

Facebook, 119, 120
Fenjiu, 131
Financial ratio, 247, 251–257, 265
 efficiency ratios, 254
 long-term solvency (debt) ratios, 254
 market value ratios, 256, 257
 profitability ratios, 255
 EBITDA margin, 255

gross profit margin, 255
 net profit margin, 255
 return on equity, 256
 short-term solvency ratios, 251–253
Food retailer customers, 39, 62
Framework, 10
 conceptual components, 10
 deliberate strategy, 10
 emergent strategy, 10
 intended strategy, 10
 realized strategy, 10
 unrealized strategy, 10
 strategic process, 10
 strategy making, 10
Franken region, 44, 45, 47
Free cash flow model, 248, 257, 259,
 260, 264, 265
Free-riders, 57, 58
French Champagne-Ardenne region, 90
Future behavioral intentions, 214, 221,
 227, 231

G

Gary Farrell Vineyards and Winery, 187,
 189
German brewery landscape, 52
German wine market, 33–37, 51
 context, 34
German wineries, 32–34, 36, 37, 39, 44,
 48–50, 54, 58–61
 production, 35, 49
German winery landscape, 53
Gift cards, 243
Global tourism, 210
Global warming, 118
Gourmet tourism, 209, 213, 232
Grassy Creek Vineyards and Winery, 77
Great Wine Capitals, 103, 106, 110, 162
Green Certified Hotels, 117
Gross domestic product, 210, 232
Guo jiu, 128, 129, 142

H

Haut-Bage, 96

Haw River AVA, 81, 82
Heckenwirtschaft, 37
Hedonic consumption experience, 72, 73
Heirloom, 6
Heredity theory, 244
Highly cross-linked epoxy-amine polymers, 244
Hong putao jiu, 284
Human factor, 170, 173–175, 178–181

I

Identifying touristic assets, 20
Impacts on wine tourism, 286, 288
Indications for transition, 55
Infrastructure, 6, 18, 19, 23, 25, 112, 117, 122, 123, 211
  Bordeaux infrastructure, 113
Innovation management, 46, 61, 62
Innovative behaviors, 25
Instagram, 119
Intended strategy, 10, 16, 17, 25
Intentions realized, 13
International Wine Marketing and Wine Tourism Database, 116
Inter- and intra-region perspectives, 19
Italy, 2, 37, 95, 101, 103, 120–122, 131, 136, 139, 276, 286

J

Jacobi matrix, 172–174
  spider web diagram, 174
Jiaodong Peninsula, 137
Jiu, 128–130, 141, 142, 284

K

Kou gan, 285
Kulturland Rheingau, 45

L

La Place de Bordeaux, 93
Le Marathon du Médoc, 96
Leadership issues, 24
Learning by doing, 75
Learning school, 10, 18

Leisure activity, 11, 176, 177, 181
Leisure travelers, 11
Likert scale, 170, 178, 179, 181, 225
Literature review, 10, 40, 168
Long-term solvency, 251, 254, 265
Loyalty, 36, 37, 54, 55, 58, 59, 61, 70, 98, 124, 144–147, 150, 152–154, 160, 162, 168–170, 173–178, 180–183, 207, 208, 214, 216, 226–232, 238–241
Loyalty profit chain, 231
Lynmar Estate, 1, 5, 7, 162, 163, 165

M

Mainland China, 269–274, 276–280, 283–287
Maisons de Négoce, 93
Managerial implications, 110, 111, 265
Maotai wine, 132
Marketing, 12, 32, 35, 41, 43, 45–47, 56, 58, 70, 72, 84–86, 97, 109–111, 116, 119, 120, 144–146, 150, 153, 154, 160, 164, 182, 188, 190–193, 196, 197, 200, 203, 207, 216, 227, 228, 250, 270, 288
Marketing research, 17
Marketing tools, 109, 144
  GWC Wineries tools, 109
Measurement tools, 24, 123, 125
Medaloni Cellars, 84
Medoc area, 90
Merlot, 137
Middle-up-down, 14, 22, 23, 25
Modeling, 169, 244
Motivations, 98–101, 111, 112, 118, 189, 270, 277, 283, 288
Multiplier effect, 210, 232
Munich, 44, 96
  Oktoberfest, 44

N

Napa Valley, 72, 90, 117, 121, 122, 140, 281, 286
Napa Valley Vintners, 117, 282
Naysayers, 17

Index 295

NC Department of Agriculture and Consumer Affairs, 75, 76
NC Department of Commerce, 75, 76
NC Wine and Grape Growers Association, 86
Ningxia, 122, 133, 136, 137, 287
Ningxia Hong Wine Company, 139
Noir, 3, 6, 162, 163
North Carolina, 69, 71, 73, 74, 76, 81, 82, 84, 85
North-Rhine Westphalia, 38

O

Office of Travel and Tourism Industries, 211
Open form model, 183
Overhead costs, 3

P

Paraduxx winery, 163, 165
Penglai City, 133
Perceptions of visitors, 105–107
  Bordeaux wineries, 105, 106
  GWC wineries, 107
Piedmont, 76–84
Pinot noir, 5
Pinterest, 119
Place de Bordeaux, 94
Planning approaches to strategy, 15
Planning school, 15, 16, 27
Pleasure, 98, 168–170, 173, 175–179, 183
Problem solving, 203
Profitability ratios, 248, 255, 265
Putao, 128, 284

Q

Qingming festival, 129
Quail Hill, 5
Qualitative methods, 12
Quality assurance requirements, 12
Quantitative measurement, 224
Quick ratios, 253

R

Raffaldini, 79, 87
Raylen, 79
Realized strategy, 10, 18, 21, 26, 27
Region promotion, 24
Relationship-building proclivity, 197, 198, 203
Relative value, 248, 257, 263, 265
Return on assets, 252, 253, 256, 267
Return on equity, 256, 263
Revenue management, 238, 241, 242, 244
Rhone-Alps, 21–23
Ridge regression, 183
Rock of Ages Winery, 78
Russian River Valley, 5, 189

S

Saint-Emilion, 90, 93
Sales incentives, 6
Sales leadership, 199, 201, 203
Satisfaction, 5, 22, 25, 40, 42, 83, 124, 168–178, 181, 183, 207–210, 214, 215, 218–232, 241
Sebastopol's agrarian setting, 163
Secondary data methods, 12
Selective offer extensionists, 57, 59
Service quality, 54, 99, 138, 169, 207, 213, 215, 216, 218, 219, 221, 222, 224–226, 228, 232, 239, 240, 241, 244
Servicescape, 218, 219, 232
SERVPERF perception model, 226
SERVQUAL scale, 224
Share of mouth, 37
Shede, 131
Shelton, 79
Short-term solvency, 251, 265
Social media, 5, 58, 119, 120, 270, 274, 277, 280, 281, 287
Sonoma County, 6, 116, 121, 122
Sonoma County Pinot, 6
Spending, 44, 117, 144, 147, 148, 168–177, 181, 182, 207, 211, 214, 242, 257, 274
Stakeholders, 12, 13, 15, 17–19, 23–25

food service, 12
local crafts industry, 12
lodging, 12
regional government, 12
tour operators, 12
wineries, 12
Standardized service system, 242
Start-up, 3, 84
Staycations, 211
Stewardship, 6
Stock keeping units, 6
Strategic landscape of, German wineries and performance impact, 51
Strategic management, 10, 12, 27, 48
Strategic positioning of, German wineries, 48
Strategic winery management perspective, 41, 42, 60
Strategies beyond product centrism, 31
Strategy implementation, 22, 23
  middle-up-down implications, 22
Strategy-making process, 10, 13, 14, 16, 22, 24, 26
Straubwirtschaft, 37
Stuck in the middle, 59
Supermarket customers, 39, 62
Surry Community College, 78
SWOT market analysis, 17

T

Tang Dynasty, 128, 130, 283
Taohong putao jiu, 284
Tasting room, 5, 6, 70, 74, 76, 78, 80, 81, 84, 119, 144, 145, 153, 160–164, 166, 187–203, 208, 230, 238, 240–244
Tasting room management, 190, 192, 200
  importance, 188
  manager qualities, 196
    problem solving, 198
    relationship-building proclivity, 198
    sales leadership, 199
    team development, 198
    time management, 197

measuring tasting room effectiveness, 199
  strategic operations, 190
Tasting room manager, 188, 190, 192, 193, 196, 197, 200–203
Team development, 198, 203
Technology, 170, 183, 243, 244
Terroir, 6, 75, 87, 93, 99, 100, 118, 240
Time management, 203
Times interest earned, 252–254, 266, 267
Total Quality Management, 205, 219, 220
Tourism organizations, 9, 47, 230
Tourism sectors, 212, 213, 232
  archeological tourism, 212
  cultural tourism, 213
  disaster tourism, 213
  ecotourism, 213
  gourmet tourism, 213
  health and wellness tourism, 212
  heritage tourism, 213
  literary tourism, 213
  medical tourism, 212
  music tourism, 213
  poverty tourism (or poorism), 213
  religious tourism, 213
  rural tourism, 212
  sex tourism, 213
  space tourism, 212
  wine tourism, 213
Tourism strategy, 10, 11, 13
Tourism trends, 211, 232
Tourist experience, 10, 14, 215
Touristic terroir, 11, 19, 20, 27
Tourists' perceptions and expectations, 99
  Bordeaux wineries, 99
Traditional three-tier wine distribution system, 238, 244
TripAdvisor, 90, 119, 189, 191
Trust, 21, 75, 178, 180, 181, 208, 209, 225–227, 229
Trust and commitment, 226, 227
Twitter, 119

Index

297

Typical trajectory of, wine business entrepreneurs, 2–7
 wine as an experience, 5, 6
  Lynmar Estate, 5
  wine industry profitability, 5
  winemaking style, 6
 wine as product, 2, 3
  grape prices, 3
  overhead costs, 3
  start-up, 3
 winery as a system, 4, 5
  balanced scorecard methodology, 5
  Burgundian varietals, 4
  cost of goods, 4
  customer satisfaction, 5
  financial performance, 5
  internal performance, 5
  retention, 5
  return on investment, 5
  see, business model

U

UNESCO World heritage village, 90
Unrealized strategy, 10, 18
Uwharrie Vineyards, 77, 78

V

Valuation methods, 257–264
 dividend growth model, 257–259
 earnings model, 263
 free cash flow model, 259–261
 intrinsic prices average model, 264
 relative value (multiples) model, 262
Value buy segment, 36
Value creation potential, 41
Value of, wine tourism, 32
Value-added offerings, 31, 32, 53
Variety seekers, 39, 62
Vimeo, 119
Vineyard, 3, 5, 6, 70, 74, 75, 116, 121, 136, 137, 141, 157, 162, 163, 239, 243
Vintners quality assurance, 21
Visitor experiences, 158

Vitis vea database, 47

W

Weddings as wine tourism, 83
Weibo, 270, 274, 277, 280–282, 287
Weighted Average Cost of Capital, 261
Wein Kultur Land Model, 45
Weinreich Rheinland-Pfalz, 45
Weixin, 280, 281
Wikipedia, 212
Wine and Spirit Education Trust (WSET), 270, 277–280, 282–284, 287
 WSET approved programme providers, 279
Wine and tourism, in Germany, 44
Wine business education, 2
Wine business entrepreneurs, 2, 3
Wine centric shopping, 36
Wine club, 5–7, 78, 81, 124, 145, 163, 164, 188, 191, 192, 194–196, 200–203
Wine club conversion, 203
Wine CLV techniques and practice, 146
Wine consumption, in Germany, 37
Wine culture, 141, 270, 288
Wine education, 59, 145, 270, 277–283, 286–288
Wine festivals, 37, 44, 97, 138, 141, 145, 146, 240
Wine industry, 1, 2, 5, 7, 41, 43, 46, 47, 60, 62, 74, 85, 122, 131, 133, 139–142, 146, 147, 154, 158, 189, 202, 208, 209, 213, 215, 221, 244, 250, 256
Wine Institute, 1, 2, 116, 281
Wine making, 1, 7, 71, 73–75, 80, 81, 85, 96, 104, 128, 137, 164
 tradition, 1, 7
Wine producers' perception on wine tourists, 103
Wine store customers, 39, 62
Wine tourism, 9–27, 32–35, 38, 39, 44–46, 54, 57, 61–76, 82–87, 90–92, 96–103, 110–125, 144, 145, 153, 154, 164, 170, 175, 183, 207–209, 213–215, 218, 230–232, 271, 282, 286, 288
 development, 10

literature, 25
North Carolina, 73
products, 12
research, 10
see, Bordeaux
strategic planning, 10
strategy making, 9
strategy, 9, 10, 14, 17, 22, 26
Wine tourists, 11, 77, 90, 92, 97–101,
105, 109, 111, 116, 118, 120, 121,
124, 138, 139, 170, 173, 215, 281,
283, 286, 287
perceptions and expectations, 99
Wine trails, 71, 72, 76, 81, 82, 84, 86
Wine versus weddings, 69
Winery as a system, 4
Winery clusters towards tourism, 56
Winery product, 7
Winery system, 7
Winery tourism, 77, 128, 133, 139, 141,
142, 157, 165, 187, 188, 203, 213,
270, 286, 287
Winery tourists, 159

Winescape, 218
World Tourism Organization, 116, 209
World Travel and Tourism Council, 210
Württemberg, 19, 38

X

Xia Dynasty, 128

Y

Yadkin Valley, 82, 84
Yadkin Valley Wine Tours, 82
Yanghe, 131
Yelp, 119, 189, 191, 193
Yield management, 242, 244
fractal analysis of, macromolecules,
244
YouTube, 119
Yuan Dynasty, 128

Z

Zones of tolerance, 221, 222